COMMON CORE

ELA EXEMPLAR RESOURCE

Instruction with Performance Assessment

Grades 6–8

Printed in the U.S.A.

ISBN 978-0-544-02650-6

8 9 10 0928 21 20 19 18 17 16

4500588973 A B C D E F G

Table of Contents

About the Common Core ELA Exemplar Resource

6–8 TEXT EXEMPLARS

Stories

Drama

Poetry

Informational Texts: English Language Arts

Informational Texts: History/Social Studies

Informational Texts: Science, Mathematics, and Technical Subjects

Student Selection Copy Masters

Academic Vocabulary

Performance Task Student Checklists

Bibliography

Internet Resources

Overview

The *Common Core ELA Exemplar Resource* was developed to provide instruction for the Grades 6–8 text exemplars listed in Appendix B of the *Common Core State Standards for English Language Arts*.

Use this guide to complement the reading instruction of exemplars within your main reading program, or use it separately to provide students with questions and activities that deepen their comprehension of text exemplars selected for independent reading or group discussion.

Text Exemplars

The list of text exemplars provided in Appendix B of the *Common Core State Standards for English Language Arts* was compiled based on the texts' quantitative and qualitative complexity, quality, and range.

The text exemplars are presented in a band for three levels for grades 6–8 and are meant to suggest "the breadth of texts that students should encounter in the text types required by the Standards." The works listed were never intended to serve as a partial or complete reading list but rather as a guide to the types of reading materials that will help students successfully meet the Standards.

Organization of This Guide

This guide is organized into three parts.

CONTENTS WITH SUGGESTED PACING
The table of contents lists all the exemplars in the order given in Appendix B, along with the page references for where to find each exemplar in this resource. You will need to select and obtain the texts separately. This section also includes suggested pacing for reading each exemplar and teaching its lesson.

EXEMPLAR LESSONS Most lessons for stories and informational texts are four pages, while most lessons for poetry are two pages. See **Lesson Setup** on p. vii for more information.

ENDMATTER RESOURCES

- **Copying Masters** In the back of this guide, you will find copying masters for several public-domain text exemplars, provided for your convenience.

- **Student Performance Checklists** These checklists will help students assess their writing and speaking and listening.

- **Academic Vocabulary** This compilation lists all the academic vocabulary, or Tier 2 words, introduced and defined in each lesson.

- **Bibliography and Exemplar Websites** These sections include the bibliographic information for each exemplar included in this guide, as well as a list of useful websites that offer additional information for teaching the exemplars and implementing the Standards.

Lesson Setup

Here is the basic setup of a four-page lesson.

PAGE 1 The first part of each lesson provides background information about the text and guidance for introducing the lesson to the class. The following features are included:

- Objectives
- Suggested Instructional Segments
- Options for Reading
- Summary
- About the Author
- Discuss Genre and Set Purpose
- Text Complexity Rubric
- Common Core State Standards met

PAGES 2–4 Each lesson includes two sets of questions that correspond to a "First Read" and a "Second Read" of the text.

- **First-Read Questions** Use these questions during and after an initial reading of the text to help students think through the text and learn to cite text evidence in their responses.

- **Second-Read Questions** Use these questions to guide students through a deeper analysis of the text. These questions give students opportunities for close reading and ask them to make deeper connections between ideas. Here, too, students must cite text evidence to support their ideas.

PERFORMANCE TASK Each lesson culminates in a performance task in which students are asked to demonstrate understanding of the exemplar text. Within each task, students are expected to complete a short writing assignment as well as engage in a speaking and listening activity. Where applicable, the performance task matches the performance-task suggestion provided in Appendix B.

Additional Lesson Features

TEXT COMPLEXITY RUBRIC To help you assess text complexity at a glance, a rubric is provided in every lesson. It identifies the overall complexity as Accessible, Complex, or More Complex. The rubric also includes quantitative measures for the Lexile and the Guided Reading Level and shows qualitative measures on a four-point continuum with text-specific rationales.

DOMAIN SPECIFIC VOCABULARY These content-area Tier 3 words are included only for texts with heavy discipline-specific content. Students are likely to use these words only within a specific discipline, such as *osmosis* in science.

INDEPENDENT/SELF-SELECTED READING This feature, included on the last page of every lesson, suggests two on-level developmentally and age appropriate books students might use for independent reading and additional application of the Standards addressed in the lesson.

RESPOND TO SEGMENT—Classroom Collaboration These activities are aimed to help students wrap up each segment of text. Students summarize what they've already learned and address any questions they have before moving on.

Tips for Getting Started

- **Review the list of text exemplars for your grade span.** The exemplars include a variety of classic and contemporary complex texts. Many of the texts will likely relate to cross-curricular topics already present in your current curriculum and can be used as supplementary material to further discuss a given topic.

- **Consider the needs and the reading levels of the students in your classroom.** Each list of exemplars covers a two-grade span, so some titles may not be at the right level for your class at a given point in the year. Use the text complexity rubric to help you select the exemplars that best suit your students' reading or listening comprehension abilities throughout the school year.

- **Work with your school librarian.** Your librarian can help you find copies of the exemplar texts, online magazine articles, and any poems and stories that are in the public domain.

- **Preview the exemplars.** As you prepare for a lesson, make notes to help you consider additional connections that students can make to the text and how you might best prepare them for reading and discussion.

Literature Discussion Groups

The *Common Core ELA Exemplar Instructional Resource* can be effectively implemented with literature discussion groups. You can support students in collaborative discussion to further explore the text exemplars in ways that can foster higher-level thinking and the use of comprehension strategies, vocabulary acquisition, and speaking and listening skills—all essential for meeting the Common Core State Standards for English Language Arts. Use the following tips.

Before Reading

Divide students into small, mixed-proficiency groups, and schedule a time for the groups to meet each day. Assign roles to students, or allow them to choose their own. Possible roles include the following:

- **Discussion Director** moderates the discussion by asking questions provided by the teacher or by creating original questions to pose to the group.

- **Passage Finder** chooses passages that are particularly interesting, revealing, or challenging for the group to focus on.

- **Vocabulary Detective** identifies and records unknown words for the group to look up and discuss.

- **Connector** makes connections between the text and other texts and aspects of real life, either in general terms or in relation to the students' experiences.

- **Summarizer** summarizes the segment of text read by the group or the teacher prior to the group's discussion and describes major characters, settings, and events or main ideas and details.

Discuss Genre and Set Purpose As groups begin to discuss the text, encourage them to

- identify elements of the text's genre and name other texts in that genre.

- consider the author's purpose in writing.

- review their purpose for reading.

First Read

Have groups read a segment of the text.

- Ask students to take notes or flag sections of the text to later discuss and cite as text evidence.

- Have each group's Summarizer offer a summary of what was read. Others can add missing information as needed.

- Provide Discussion Directors with questions from the lesson, or have them make up their own questions.

- Guide students to use the context of the text to understand academic vocabulary.

- Monitor discussions to ensure groups stay focused and cite text evidence to support responses.

Second Read

Have each group reread portions of the text to further analyze ideas and concepts.

- Guide groups to connect a segment to previous segments. Ensure they understand how the segments and ideas build throughout the text.

- Help groups focus on figurative language and literary elements, such as theme.

- Have groups support their responses with evidence from the text.

- Wrap up the discussion by having students summarize what they've learned.

OBJECTIVES

- Determine a theme or central idea of a text
- Describe how characters respond or change
- Analyze text using text evidence

Little Women is broken into three instructional segments.

SEGMENTS

SEGMENT 1 . . . . pp. 7–171
SEGMENT 2 . . . . . . pp. 172–352
SEGMENT 3 . . . . . . pp. 353–500

Options for Reading

Independent Students read the book independently or with a partner and then answer questions posed by the teacher.

Supported Students read a segment and answer questions with teacher support.

 Common Core Connection

Grade 6: RL 2 determine a theme or central idea of a text/provide a summary; **RL 3** describe how a story's or drama's plot unfolds and how characters respond or change

Grade 7: RL 3 analyze how particular elements of a story or drama interact

Grade 8: RL 3 analyze how dialogue or incidents in a story or drama propel action, reveal a character, or provoke a decision

Grades 7–8: RL 2 determine a theme or central idea of text/analyze development/ provide a summary

Grades 6–8: RI 1 cite textual evidence to support analysis of what the text says explicitly as well as inferences drawn

Little Women
by Louisa May Alcott

SUMMARY This book, set in the 15 years during and after the Civil War, describes the lives of four sisters: Meg, Jo, Beth, and Amy March. They live with their mother in New England while their father is serving as a chaplain to the Union Army. The girls face many challenges as they grow up.

ABOUT THE AUTHOR Louisa May Alcott was a famous novelist during the late 1800s. She wrote poems, plays, and short stories Her novels for young adults are based on her own life. Many of her books, including *Little Women, Little Men,* and *Jo's Boys* are still popular.

Discuss Genre and Set Purpose

FICTION Discuss that a work of fiction include characters, setting, and a plot. Explain that, although fiction is made up, some of the characters, setting, and events in *Little Women* are loosely based upon the author's real family and home in Massachusetts. Point out that *Little Women* was written more than 140 years ago so it shows a way of life and use of language that may be somewhat unfamiliar to students.

SET PURPOSE Help students set a purpose for reading, such as to find out what happens to the four sisters in the story or to understand the book's themes.

▲ TEXT COMPLEXITY RUBRIC

Overall Text Complexity		*Little Women* STORY
		MORE COMPLEX
Quantitative Measures	Lexile	1240
	Guided Reading Level	Z
Qualitative Measures	Text Structure	somewhat complex story concepts
	Language Conventionality and Clarity	archaic, unfamiliar language
	Knowledge Demands	many references or allusions to other texts
	Purpose/Levels of Meaning	multiple levels of meaning

SEGMENT 1 pp. 7–171

Academic Vocabulary

Read each word with students and discuss its meaning.

impertinent (p. 8) • rude; impolite

mortification (p. 49) • embarrassment; humiliation

voraciously (p. 65) • eagerly

calamity (p. 81) • disaster; distress

skirmishes (p. 130) • brief fights between two people or groups

consoler (p. 170) • comforter

Domain Specific Vocabulary

Pilgrim's Progress (p. 15) • a Christian-based allegory written in 1677

blancmange (p. 54) • a cold, milk-based dessert

Apollyon (p. 15) • a Greek and Biblical term for the destroyer, or Satan

saleratus (p. 118) • baking powder

abroad (p. 127) • away from one's own country

millinery (p. 406) • women's hats

FIRST READ ## Think Through the Text

Have students cite text evidence and draw inferences to answer questions.

pp. 7–17 • *Describe the setting and the main characters.* The setting is the March family's home during the Civil War. The main characters are Meg, Jo, Beth, and Amy March, and their mother, Marmee. Their father is away fighting in the Civil War. Meg is sixteen and ladylike. Jo is fifteen and a tomboy. Beth is thirteen and shy. Amy is twelve and the baby of the family. **RL 1**

pp. 40–47 • *What is the current family financial situation and how does each girl deal with it?* Mr. March lost his property when helping a friend, so the family is poor. Meg and Jo work outside the home. Meg is a governess for four children. Jo takes care of their Aunt March. Beth and Amy take care of household chores. Amy wears her cousin's used clothes. **RL 3**

pp. 114–124 • *Marmee allows the girls to experiment with being idle for a week. What is the result of this experiment?* At first they enjoy it, but by the end of the week, they are glad to get back to work. **RL 1**

SECOND READ ## Analyze the Text

• Have students reread pages 19–22 to answer the questions: *What do the girls do with their Christmas breakfast?* They give their breakfast to a poor family. *Which story themes does this action show?* This action shows the story themes of selflessness, generosity, and moral behavior. **RL 2**

• Guide students to reread pages 78–88. Say: *Summarize the events that take place between Jo and Amy.* Jo refuses to take Amy with her to watch a play with Laurie. In retaliation Amy burns Jo's only copy of her manuscript. Jo refuses to accept her apology. When they go ice skating, Jo ignores Amy, who falls through the ice. Laurie rescues Amy. Later Jo talks to Marmee about her temper. *Which story themes do these events show?* These events show the importance of family as well as love and forgiveness. **RL 2**

 ENGLISH LANGUAGE LEARNERS

Use Gestures

Use gestures and simplified language to help students describe some of the events and the March sisters' actions. Have students complete sentence frames such as, *On Christmas, the girls _____ to a poor family.* gave their breakfast

RESPOND TO SEGMENT 1

Classroom Collaboration

Have partners work together to create and present a summary, as well as raise questions that might be answered in the next segment.

ENGLISH LANGUAGE LEARNERS

Use Peer Learning

Organize students into groups. Have each group choose one of the March sisters and draw a web with her name in the center. Tell students to pass around the web and add an adjective that describes that character. Ask groups to share their webs.

RESPOND TO SEGMENT 2

 Classroom Collaboration

Have small groups work together to summarize what they have learned. Have them ask questions about what they don't understand.

 Common Core Connection

Grade 6: RL 2 determine a theme or central idea of a text/provide a summary; **RL 3** describe how a story's or drama's plot unfolds and how characters respond or change; **SL 4** present claims and findings, sequence ideas, and use details to accentuate main ideas or themes

Grade 7: RL 3 analyze how particular elements of a story or drama interact

Grade 8: RL 3 analyze how dialogue or incidents in a story or drama propel action, reveal a character, or provoke a decision

Grades 7–8: RL 2 determine a theme or central idea of a text/analyze development/provide a summary; **SL 4** present claims and findings, emphasizing points in a focused, coherent manner

Grades 6–8: RL 1 cite textual evidence to support analysis of what the text says explicitly as well as inferences drawn; **RL 10** read and comprehend literature; **W 2** write informative/explanatory texts; **W 5** develop and strengthen writing by planning, revising, editing, rewriting, or trying a new approach

Academic Vocabulary

Read each word with students and discuss its meaning.

remorseful (p. 182) • guilty; regretful

meddle (p. 209) • interfere

tranquilly (p. 248) • calmly, free from emotion

vortex (p. 272) • something overwhelming

constitution (p. 307) • health

apprehensively (p. 330) • nervously

FIRST READ # Think Through the Text

Have students cite text evidence and draw inferences to answer questions.

pp. 208–210 • *Marmee and Jo discuss love, marriage, and wealth. What is Marmee's opinion on these topics?* *Marmee recognizes the importance and necessity of having money, but she thinks love is more important. She would rather have her girls marry for love than for money. She is especially thinking of Meg and John here.* ▬ RL 1

pp. 227–229 • *How have the girls changed since the previous Christmas?* *They recognize that even though there had been some hardships, the year had been good overall. They have been brave and have worked hard. They have cared for each other as a family.* ▬ RL 3

pp. 341–352 • *Summarize Jo's adventures in New York.* *She takes a room in a rooming house, where she is a governess. She becomes interested in Professor Bhaer and begins to learn German. She is enjoying her time there.* ▬ RL 2

SECOND READ # Analyze the Text

• Ask students to reread pages 172–179. Ask: *What themes are highlighted in the letters the girls write to their mother?* *Sample answer: Meg's letter discusses the themes of family and the importance of meaningful work. Jo's letter covers the themes of gratitude and correct behavior. Beth's letter discusses the importance of work and responsibility, as well as sharing. Amy's letter reveals her desire to behave and to learn.* ▬ RL 2

• Have students reread pages 329–340. *What do Jo's actions reveal about her character?* *She values her own independence. She is also willing to sacrifice her own happiness for the good of her sister.* ▬ RL 3

Academic Vocabulary

Read each word with students and discuss its meaning.

ballast (p. 355) • something that gives stability

inconsolable (p. 366) • heartbroken

detriment (p. 406) • disadvantage; loss

prudence (p. 414) • carefulness

relish (p. 434) • enjoyment; delight

gravity (p. 465) • seriousness

FIRST READ ## Think Through the Text

Have students cite text evidence and draw inferences to answer questions.

pp. 385–395 • *Where are Amy and Laurie?* They are in Nice, France. **What do they discover about themselves and about each other?** *Laurie is getting over his heartbreak with Jo. He notices that Amy is not as shy as she used to be, and he likes this. Amy enjoys her popularity at the dance and also the attention from Laurie.* ▬ **RL 3**

pp. 422–427 • *Summarize the events that lead up to Beth's death.* The family members create a special room for Beth and fill it with her favorite things. They spend a lot of time with her. Jo writes a poem describing her feelings for Beth. Beth says she does not fear death. The family is with her when she dies. ▬ **RL 2**

p. 470 • *How is Demi a true Yankee?* He asks many questions and wants exact answers. ▬ **RL 1**

SECOND READ ## Analyze the Text

- Review pages 489-494. Ask: *How does Aunt March's death benefit Jo?* *Aunt March leaves her house to Jo. Jo decides to open a school for boys. She and Professor Bhaer marry, and the school is a success.* ▬ **RL 3**

- Guide students to review pages 496–498. Ask: *Which of the story's themes is shown in this final scene?* *The theme of the importance of marriage and the family is shown.* ▬ **RL 2**

Independent/Self-Selected Reading

If students have demonstrated comprehension of *Little Women*, have them read other stories to practice skills. Suggested titles:

- *Eight Cousins* by Louisa May Alcott

- *Little Men* by Louisa May Alcott ▬ **RL 10**

WRITE & PRESENT

1. Have small groups refer to the text to discuss ways the author presents and elaborates on the main themes in the story. Encourage students to take notes. ▬ **RL 2**

2. Have individual students select one theme they discussed and create a detailed chart that shows how the author presents information about that theme. Then students use their chart to write a summary. ▬ **W 2**

3. Students reconvene in their groups to share their summaries and edit their writing. ▬ **W 5**

4. Students present their final summaries to classmates. ▬ **SL 4**

5. Individual students turn in their final summaries to the teacher.

See Copying Masters, pp. 164–171.

STUDENT CHECKLIST

Writing

☑ Write about how the author presents a main theme in the story.

☑ Include ways in which the author elaborates on the theme.

☑ Use correct language conventions.

Speaking & Listening

☑ Engage effectively in collaborative conversations.

☑ Logically present claims and findings.

☑ Cite text evidence demonstrating the main themes in the story.

▶ OBJECTIVES

- Determine a theme or central idea of a text
- Describe how a plot unfolds and how characters respond or change
- Analyze text using text evidence

Tom Sawyer is broken into three instructional segments.

SEGMENTS

SEGMENT 1 . . . . pp. 1–83
SEGMENT 2 . . . . . . .pp. 84–165
SEGMENT 3 . . . . . .pp. 166–225

Options for Reading

Independent Students read the book independently or with a partner and then answer questions posed by the teacher.

Supported Students read a segment and answer questions with teacher support.

 Common Core Connection

Grade 6: RL 2 Determine a theme or central idea of a text/provide a summary; **RL 3** determine how a story's or drama's plot unfolds and how characters respond or change; **RL 4** determine the meaning of words and phrases, including figurative and connotative meanings/analyze impact of word choice

Grade 7: RL 3 analyze how particular elements of a story or drama interact ; **RL 4** determine the meaning of words and phrases as they are used in a text/analyze impact of rhymes and other repetitions of sound

Grade 8: RL 3 analyze how dialogue or incidents in a story or drama propel action, reveal a character, or provoke a decision; **RL 4** determine the meaning of words and phrases as they are used in a text/analyze impact of word choices

Grades 7–8: RL 2 determine a theme or central idea of a text/analyze development/provide a summary

Grades 6–8: RL 1 cite textual evidence to support analysis of what the text says explicitly as well as inferences drawn

The Adventures of Tom Sawyer

by Mark Twain

SUMMARY This book describes the adventures of a boy named Tom Sawyer who lives in Missouri sometime in the 1800s. Tom's adventures begin with innocent fun, but soon take a serious turn as he is required to make several moral choices.

ABOUT THE AUTHOR Mark Twain is the pen name of Samuel Langhorne Clemens (1835–1910). He grew up in Hannibal, Missouri, and then spent most of his adult life on the East Coast and in Europe. He was called "The People's Author." *The Adventures of Tom Sawyer* and *The Adventures of Huckleberry Finn* are his best-known works.

Discuss Genre and Set Purpose

FICTION Help students recall the elements of fiction, including characters, setting, and plot. Point out that *The Adventures of Tom Sawyer* was written more than 100 years ago, so today's readers may find the novel's perspective and many elements of the setting old-fashioned or unfamiliar.

SET PURPOSE Help students set a purpose for reading, such as to find out about the themes of the book and how Tom develops and changes over the course of the plot.

▲ TEXT COMPLEXITY RUBRIC

Overall Text Complexity		The Adventures of Tom Sawyer STORY
		MORE COMPLEX
Quantitative Measures	Lexile	960
	Guided Reading Level	Z
Qualitative Measures	Text Structure	complex, unfamiliar story concepts
	Language Conventionality and Clarity	increased unfamiliar or academic words
	Knowledge Demands	distinctly unfamiliar situation
	Purpose/Levels of Meaning	multiple levels of complex meaning

Academic Vocabulary

Read each word with students and discuss its meaning.

circumstantial (p. 13) • based on inference

diligence (p. 15) • persistent effort

derision (p. 17) • mocking scorn

alacrity (p. 23) • eager readiness

pariah (p. 50) • outcast

cogitating (p. 66) • thinking carefully

Domain Specific Vocabulary

conflagration (p. 117) • destructive fire

temperance (p. 147) • not drinking alcohol

sepulchral (p. 162) • having to do with a funeral

rifts (p. 182) • shallow water

chasms (p. 182) • deep holes in the earth

FIRST READ ## Think Through the Text

Have students cite text evidence and draw inferences to answer questions.

pp. 12–13 • *According to Aunt Polly, what does Tom hate the most? He hates work more than anything else. Why does she feel she must make him do the thing he hates so much? She does not want to be responsible for his ruination.* ▬ RL 1

pp. 20–24 • *How does Tom get out of whitewashing the whole fence? He pretends that he is having a good time. Soon his friends all want to take turns, and Tom gladly trades them the opportunity for various goods.*
▬ RL 3

pp. 50–57 • *Why does Tom like to play with Huckleberry Finn? Huckleberry is an outcast, and Tom envies his freedom. Also, Tom is not supposed to play with Huck, so he wants to do it even more. What happens to Tom at school when he admits that he is late because he stopped to talk to Huck? The schoolmaster whips Tom's arms.* ▬ RL 1

SECOND READ ## Analyze the Text

- Reread page 12. Ask: *What is the meaning of the phrase "get my dander up"? get angry Who is Old Scratch? the devil* Point out the words *middling, warm,* and *powerful warm* on page 13. Ask: *What is the impact of the author's use of figurative language and regional dialect? The use of figurative language and regional dialect give the reader a better sense of the setting and the characters.* ▬ RL 4

- Guide students to review pages 1–75 to answer the question: *How do Tom's activities change from the beginning of the story through the event in the graveyard? At first his activities are innocent, childish pranks. The event in the graveyard changes to more serious issues.* ▬ RL 3

- Reread Tom's comments at the top of page 80. Ask: *What do Tom's comments show about his sense of morality? Tom is beginning to see the consequences of his actions and to regret some of his more foolish ones.* ▬ RL 2

 **ENGLISH LANGUAGE LEARNERS**

Use Gestures

Use gestures and simplified language to help students articulate Tom's various activities. Have students complete sentence frames such as, *When Tom whitewashed the fence, he _____ it. painted*

 RESPOND TO SEGMENT 1

Classroom Collaboration

Have partners work together to create and present a summary, as well as raise questions that might be answered in the next segment.

ENGLISH LANGUAGE LEARNERS

Use Peer Learning
Have small groups draw a web with the words *Tom Sawyer* in the center. Have them take turns adding an adjective to the web that describes Tom. Call on groups to share their webs.

RESPOND TO SEGMENT 2

Classroom Collaboration

Have small groups work together to summarize what they have learned. Have them ask questions about what they don't understand.

Common Core Connection

Grade 6: RL 2 Determine a theme or central idea of a text/provide a summary; **RL 3** determine how a story's or drama's plot unfolds and how characters respond or change; **RL 4** determine the meaning of words and phrases, including figurative and connotative meanings/analyze impact of word choice; **SL 4** present claims and findings, sequence ideas, and use details to accentuate main ideas or themes

Grade 7: RL 3 analyze how particular elements of a story or drama interact; **RL 4** determine the meaning of words and phrases as they are used in a text/analyze impact of rhymes and other repetitions of sound

Grade 8: RL 3 analyze how dialogue or incidents in a story or drama propel action, reveal a character, or provoke a decision; **RL 4** determine the meaning of words and phrases as they are used in a text/analyze impact of word choices

Grades 7–8: RL 2 determine a theme or central idea of a text/analyze development/provide a summary; **SL 4** present claims and findings, emphasizing points in a focused, coherent manner

Grades 6–8: RL 1 cite textual evidence to support analysis of what the text says explicitly as well as inferences drawn; **RL 10** read and comprehend literature; **W 2** write informative/explanatory texts; **W 5** develop and strengthen writing by planning, revising, editing, rewriting, or trying a new approach

Academic Vocabulary
Read each word with students and discuss its meaning.

inveterate (p. 88) • having a particular habit; unlikely to change
consternation (p. 89) • shocked dismay
plausibilities (p. 99) • things that can be believed
conjectured (p. 108) • guessed
industry (p. 162) • hard work

FIRST READ ## Think Through the Text
Have students cite text evidence and draw inferences to answer questions.

pp. 94–96 • *What have Tom's feelings of being forsaken and friendless led him to conclude?* He is going to lead a life of crime and become a pirate. *How does he act on this plan and with whom?* He, along with Joe and Huck, take a raft to Jackson's Island in the river. *What interferes with their plan?* Their consciences intrude, and they are concerned that they should not have run away. **RL 1, RL 3**

pp. 122–123 • *When do the boys return home? Where do they go? How are they received?* They return home and go to the church during their funeral. The mourners all sing a hymn in thanks for their return. Aunt Polly welcomes Tom and Huck. She gives Tom a combination of cuffs and kisses. **RL 1**

pp. 154–157 • *What unexpected event occurs during Muff Potter's trial? What is the result of this event?* Tom is called to testify, and he tells the truth. Injun Joe escapes, but Potter is pronounced innocent. Tom receives praise as a hero. **RL 1, RL 3**

SECOND READ ## Analyze the Text

• Have students reread pages 132–134. Say: *Aunt Polly confronts Tom about his secret visit to the house. What does Tom's response to Aunt Polly show about his moral development?* He recognizes the effects of his actions. He feels remorse for scaring his aunt. When Aunt Polly later checks his jacket pocket, she realizes he had told her the truth about his secret visit. **RL 2**

• Guide students to reread pages 135–139. Say: *Summarize the ways that Tom's actions in this chapter show his moral development.* Sample answer: *First Tom apologizes to Becky. Next he takes the punishment for spilling ink in the book and thinks he may actually be responsible for it. Last he covers up for Becky when she tears the picture. These actions all show Tom's new willingness to think about others before he thinks about himself.* **RL 2**

Academic Vocabulary

Read each word with students and discuss its meaning.

inclination (p. 181) • feeling

ransacked (p. 194) • thoroughly searched

quiver (p. 212) • shudder; tremble

prodigious (p. 220) • enormous

FIRST READ ## Think Through the Text

Have students cite text evidence and draw inferences to answer questions.

p. 172 • *What does Tom realize about Injun Joe's comment regarding revenge?* Tom realizes that Injun Joe may want to take revenge on him and Huck. ▬RL 1

p. 210 • *What is the meaning of "been on my pins"?* Huck is able to walk again. ▬RL 4

pp. 218–221 • *What happens to the money that Huck and Tom found?* They are able to keep it and split it. Judge Thatcher and the Widow Douglas invest it for them and give the boys a generous allowance. ▬RL 1

SECOND READ ## Analyze the Text

• Reread page 197 aloud to students. Ask: *What is the impact of the words the author uses to describe the cave?* Words such as bewitching and clammy hand *make the cave seem like a person.* ▬RL 4

• Have students reread pages 199–206. Say: *Summarize the main events that occurred while Tom and Becky were lost in the cave. How did Tom show his accountability in this situation?* Tom kept his wits and searched until he found an exit. He took good care of Becky. ▬RL 2

• Say: *Think about the ways that Tom Sawyer behaved at the beginning of the story. How did his behavior change? How did it stay the same?* Sample answer: Tom developed a clearer sense of accountability and morality. He began to think about the consequences of his actions, and he was more aware of helping others. He still kept much of his childish behavior in wanting to be a pirate or a robber and having fun adventures with his friends. ▬RL 2

Independent/Self-Selected Reading

If students have demonstrated comprehension of *The Adventures of Tom Sawyer*, have them read other stories to practice skills. Suggested titles:

• *From Alice to Zen and Everyone in Between* by Elizabeth Atkinson

• *Maniac Magee* by Jerry Spinelli ▬RL 10

Performance Task

WRITE & PRESENT

1. Have small groups refer to the text to summarize the development of the morality of Tom Sawyer and analyze its connection to themes of accountability and authenticity by noting how it is conveyed through characters, setting, and plot. ▬RL 2

2. Have students work with a partner to create a three-column chart labeled *Characters, Setting,* and *Plot* that shows how the author presents information. Then have individual students use their chart to write a summary. ▬W 2

3. Small groups reconvene to share their summaries with other groups and edit their writing. ▬W 5

4. Students present their final summaries to classmates. ▬SL 4

5. Individual students turn in their final summaries to the teacher.

See Copying Masters, pp. 164–171.

STUDENT CHECKLIST

Writing

☑ Write a summary of the book.

☑ Describe how the author conveys the development of Tom Sawyer's morality through characters, setting, and plot.

☑ Use correct language conventions.

Speaking & Listening

☑ Engage effectively in collaborative conversations.

☑ Logically present claims and findings.

☑ Cite text evidence.

OBJECTIVES

- Describe how a character changes
- Determine the theme
- Analyze text using text evidence

A Wrinkle in Time is broken into three instructional segments.

SEGMENTS

SEGMENT 1 . . . . pp. 5–71
SEGMENT 2 . . . . . . pp. 72–137
SEGMENT 3 . . . . . pp. 138–202

Options for Reading

Independent Students read the selection independently or with a partner and then answer questions posed by the teacher.

Supported Students read a segment and answer questions with teacher support.

 Common Core Connection

Grade 6: RL 2 determine a theme or central idea of a text/provide a summary; **RL 3** describe how a story's or drama's plot unfolds and how characters respond or change; **RL 5** analyze how a sentence, chapter, scene, or stanza fits in the overall structure

Grade 7: RL 2 determine two or more central ideas in a text/analyze their development/ provide a summary; **RL 3** analyze how particular elements of a story or drama interact

Grade 8: RL 2 determine a theme or central idea of a text/analyze development/provide a summary; **RL 3** analyze how dialogue or incidents in a story or drama propel action, reveal a character, or provoke a decision

Grades 6–8: RL 1 cite textual evidence to support analysis of what the text says explicitly as well as inferences drawn

A Wrinkle in Time
by Madeleine L'Engle

SUMMARY High-school misfit Meg Murry journeys through time and space with her younger brother, Charles Wallace, and her popular classmate Calvin O'Keefe to save her father from an evil force that has imprisoned him on another planet.

ABOUT THE AUTHOR Madeleine L'Engle was born in 1918. She grew up in New York City, Switzerland, South Carolina, and Massachusetts. After she got married, she turned to writing full time. *A Wrinkle in Time* won the Newbery Medal in 1963.

Discuss Genre and Set Purpose

SCIENCE FICTION Have students read the title and table of contents. Discuss with students how they can tell this story is fiction. Then help them recall that science fiction is a genre of fiction that has a futuristic setting and includes science and technologies that may be possible in the future.

SET PURPOSE Help students set a purpose for reading, such as to find out if Meg's journey is successful and determine the book's theme.

TEXT COMPLEXITY RUBRIC

Overall Text Complexity		A Wrinkle in Time STORY
		COMPLEX
Quantitative Measures	Lexile	710
	Guided Reading Level	W
Qualitative Measures	Text Structure	several shifts in chronology; use of flashback
	Language Conventionality and Clarity	increased, clearly-assigned dialogue
	Knowledge Demands	situation includes unfamiliar aspects
	Purpose/Levels of Meaning	multiple levels of meaning

SEGMENT 1 pp. 5–71

Academic Vocabulary

Read each word with students and discuss its meaning.

delinquent (p. 6) • a person who is often in trouble with the law or the authorities

prodigious (p. 12) • amazing

dignity (p. 21) • a calm, serious manner that makes someone worthy of respect

tractable (p. 28) • easy to deal with

dilapidated (p. 36) • falling apart

apprehension (p. 62) • nervousness; worry

FIRST READ ## Think Through the Text

Have students cite text evidence and draw inferences to answer questions.

pp. 13–14 • *What problems is Meg having at school? Cite details from the text.* She feels like she is an oddball and not pretty. She tries to pretend she is like everyone else, but it doesn't help. *What does Meg's mother wish she would learn?* moderation; a happy medium ⬤ **RL 1, RL 3**

pp. 53–60 • *Where does Charles Wallace think he, Meg, and Calvin are going?* He thinks they are going to find his father. *Which characters help them begin their journey?* Mrs. Whatsit, Mrs. Who, and Mrs. Which *How are they able to travel through space?* They wrinkle. ⬤ **RL 3**

pp. 70–71 • *What does Mrs. Whatsit show Meg, Charles, and Calvin?* She shows them a dark, black shadow. *What does the shadow represent?* The shadow represents evil. *What does Meg realize about the dark Thing?* She realizes that it might be what her father is fighting. ⬤ **RL 3**

SECOND READ ## Analyze the Text

• Reread pages 22–23. Say: *Foreshadowing is when the author provides hints about characters or future events. How does the author foreshadow that Mrs. Whatsit is not an ordinary tramp?* Mrs. Whatsit tells Mrs. Murry about the tesseract. Mrs. Murry turns white and wonders how she could have known. This shows that Mrs. Whatsit is not an ordinary character. ⬤ **Grade 6 RL 5**

• Reread pages 30–47. Ask: *How are Charles Wallace and Calvin alike?* They are both able to do things that they don't understand. Charles Wallace can tell what is happening with Meg and his mother without being told. Calvin gets a compulsion to do certain things, and he always obeys it. *What does Mrs. Murry want Meg to understand about people?* People are more than just the way they look. ⬤ **RL 3**

• Reread page 61. Ask: *What is a lesson that Meg must learn? Why?* She must learn patience. She needs it to help find her father. ⬤ **RL 2**

 ENGLISH LANGUAGE LEARNERS

Use Sentence Frames
Guide students to generate words that could describe Meg, such as *different*, *angry*, and *protective*. Then have them orally complete sentence frames, such as *Meg is ____ because ____*.

RESPOND TO SEGMENT 1
 Classroom Collaboration

Have small groups summarize what they have read. Have them ask questions about what they don't understand.

ENGLISH LANGUAGE LEARNERS

Use Peer Supported Learning

After each chapter, have students of differing abilities work together to generate gist statements about the chapter content. Provide sentence frames such as *In this chapter, Meg and Charles _____*.

RESPOND TO SEGMENT 2

 Classroom Collaboration

Have partners work together to create and present a summary of what has happened so far, as well as make predictions about what might happen in the next segment.

 Common Core Connection

Grade 6: RL 2 determine a theme or central idea of a text/provide a summary; **RL 3** describe how a story's or drama's plot unfolds and how characters respond or change; **RL 4** determine the meaning of words and phrases, including figurative and connotative meanings/analyze impact of word choice; **SL 4** present claims and findings, sequence ideas, and use details to accentuate main ideas or themes/use appropriate eye contact, volume, and pronunciation

Grade 7: RL 3 analyze how particular elements of a story or drama interact

Grade 8: RL 3 analyze how dialogue or incidents in a story or drama propel action, reveal a character, or provoke a decision;

Grades 7–8: RL 2 determine a theme or central idea of a text/analyze development/provide a summary; **SL 4** present claims and findings, emphasizing points in a focused, coherent manner

Grades 6–8: RL 1 cite textual evidence to support analysis of what the text says explicitly as well as inferences drawn; **RL 10** read and comprehend literature; **W 2** write informative/explanatory texts; **W 5** develop and strengthen writing by planning, revising, editing, rewriting, or trying a new approach

---

Academic Vocabulary

Read each word with students and discuss its meaning.

serenely (p. 74) • calmly; peacefully

dwindled (p. 86) • became smaller and smaller

malignant (p. 94) • growing out of control

furtive (p. 100) • sneaky; sly

ominous (p. 133) • threatening

FIRST READ **Think Through the Text**

Have students cite text evidence and draw inferences to answer questions.

pp. 74–75 • *What is a tesseract?* *A tesseract is the fifth dimension. When you add it to the other dimensions, it's a way to travel through time.* ⬤ RL 1

pp. 98–101 • *What is unusual about the planet of Camazotz?* *Everything is identical. Everyone does things at exactly the same time and in the same way.* ⬤ RL 1

pp. 132–133 • *Who is in control on Camazotz? What does he do?* *IT is in control. He controls everyone's thoughts so that they think the same thing.* ⬤ RL 1

SECOND READ **Analyze the Text**

• Reread page 98. Ask: *What does Mrs. Whatsit caution Charles Wallace about?* *She tells him not to go off on his own and to beware of his pride and arrogance.* *What happens on page 126 that proves her warning correct?* *Charles Wallace goes into IT and is replaced by a boy who isn't really Charles Wallace.* ⬤ RL 3

• Reread page 134. Say: *Charles Wallace, speaking as IT, tells Meg that differences create problems. How does Meg respond?* *She says that she may not like being different, but she wouldn't want to be the same as everyone else.* *How does this show that Meg is starting to change?* *At the beginning of the story, she could not see the positive side of being different. Now she is beginning to value her uniqueness.* ⬤ RL 3

Academic Vocabulary

Read each word with students and discuss its meaning.

omnipotent (p. 151) • having unlimited power

permeating (p. 197) • spreading throughout

tangible (p. 202) • able to be touched

FIRST READ Think Through the Text

Have students cite text evidence and draw inferences to answer questions.

pp. 142–143 • *How does Meg finally reach her father? She puts on Mrs. Who's glasses and runs through the column. Her father is on the other side.* ⬤ RL 1, Grade 6 RL 3

p. 151 • *Why does Meg feel some disappointment after finding her father? She thought that finding him would make everything better. Instead it has become more complicated.* ⬤ RL 3

p. 153 • *How do Meg's faults help her fight IT? Her faults are anger, impatience, and stubbornness. She uses them to resist IT and avoid falling into its pulsing rhythm.* ⬤ RL 1, Grade 6 RL 3

p. 198 •*What does Meg realize that she has that IT does not? How does she use it? She realizes that she has love and IT does not. She uses it to save Charles Wallace and free him from IT.* ⬤ RL 3

SECOND READ Analyze the Text

• Reread page 153 with students. Ask: *Why is it ironic that Meg chooses to recite the Declaration of Independence to fight IT? There is no independence on Camazotz. Everyone is controlled by IT. Why do you think the author makes a distinction between the words like and equal? She wants to point out that being alike is not the same thing as being equal. Equality still allows for individual differences.* ⬤ RL 2

• Reread page 190. Ask: *How is life like a sonnet? It has a strict form, but there is freedom within it to live the way you want to.* ⬤ Grade 6 R 4

• *Meg is able to get Charles Wallace back with her love for him. What do you think one of the themes of this story is? Love has the power to help good conquer evil.* ⬤ RL 2

Independent/Self-Selected Reading

If students have already demonstrated comprehension of *A Wrinkle in Time*, have them read other stories to practice skills. Suggested titles:

• *A Wind in the Door* by Madeleine L'Engle

• *A Swiftly Tilting Planet* by Madeleine L'Engle ⬤ RL 10

WRITE & PRESENT

1. Have small groups refer to the text to discuss one or more themes in the story, such as the value of the individual or good vs. evil. ⬤ RL 2

2. Individual students write an explanatory text describing one of the themes and how it is developed with details. ⬤ W 2

3. Have groups reconvene to share and edit their writing. ⬤ W 5

4. Students present their final explanations to their classmates. ⬤ SL 4

5. Individual students turn in their final drafts to the teacher.

See Copying Masters, pp. 164–171.

STUDENT CHECKLIST

Writing

☑ Write an explanatory text describing one of the themes of the book.

☑ Give specific details that develop the theme.

☑ Use correct language conventions.

Speaking & Listening

☑ Participate effectively in a collaborative discussion.

☑ Provide reasons and details to support points.

☑ Speak clearly at an understandable pace.

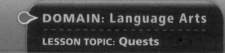
OBJECTIVES

- Describe how a story's plot unfolds as series of episodes
- Determine the theme
- Explain how chapters and scenes fit together
- Analyze text using text evidence

The Dark Is Rising is broken into three instructional segments.

SEGMENTS

SEGMENT 1 . . . . pp. 3–74
SEGMENT 2 . . . . . . pp. 75–162
SEGMENT 3 . . . . . pp. 163–244

Options for Reading

Independent Students read the selection independently or with a partner and then answer questions posed by the teacher.

Supported Students read a segment and answer questions with teacher support.

 Common Core Connection

Grade 6: RL 3 describe how a story or drama's plot unfolds and how characters respond or change

Grade 7: RL 3 analyze how particular elements of a story or drama interact

Grade 8: RL 3 analyze how dialogue or incidents in a story or drama propel action, reveal a character, or provoke a decision

Grades 6–8: RL 1 cite textual evidence to support analysis of what the text says explicitly as well as inferences drawn

The Dark Is Rising
by Susan Cooper

SUMMARY On his eleventh birthday, Will Stanton learns that he is the last of the Old Ones, who are dedicated to fighting evil. He must find the six Signs of Light to help keep the world from being dominated by the forces of evil, the Dark.

ABOUT THE AUTHOR Susan Cooper was born in Buckinghamshire, England in 1935. Growing up during World War II helped shape Cooper's writing by giving her a strong sense of good and evil. *The Grey King*, which is part of *The Dark Is Rising* series, won the Newbery Medal in 1976.

Discuss Genre and Set Purpose

FANTASY Have students read the title and table of contents. Discuss with students how they can tell this story is fiction and is about made-up characters and events. Then help students recall that a fantasy is a story that includes elements that are not realistic, such as magic and imaginary creatures.

SET PURPOSE Help students set a purpose for reading, such as to identify the elements of fantasy in this book or to find out if Will is successful in finding all six Signs of Light.

TEXT COMPLEXITY RUBRIC

Overall Text Complexity		*The Dark Is Rising* STORY
		MORE COMPLEX
Quantitative Measures	Lexile	910
	Guided Reading Level	X
Qualitative Measures	Text Structure	somewhat complex story concepts
	Language Conventionality and Clarity	some unfamiliar or academic words
	Knowledge Demands	distinctly unfamiliar situation
	Purpose/Levels of Meaning	multiple levels of meaning

Academic Vocabulary

Read each word with students and discuss its meaning.

amiably (p. 11) • in a friendly way

contemplating (p. 13) • in a thoughtful way

auspicious (p. 24) • promising success; fortunate

derisively (p. 25) • scornfully

disconcerted (p. 40) • disturbed one's composure; ruffled

vanquishing (p. 43) • conquering; defeating

FIRST READ ## Think Through the Text

Have students cite text evidence and draw inferences to answer questions.

p. 8 • *What does Mr. Dawson give Will?* He gives him a black iron ornament. *What evidence shows that the gift is something special?* Mr. Dawson tells him to keep it with him at all times and to keep it safe. He says not to talk about it. **RL 1**

p. 43 • *What does Merriman tell Will that he is?* He says that Will is one of the Old Ones. Will is bound to devote himself to the conflict between light and dark. *What problem does Merriman give Will to solve?* Will must find and guard the six great signs of the Light. **RL 3**

pp. 64–66 • *Who gives Will the second sign?* the Walker *Who tries to take the sign from him?* Maggie Barnes, the dairy girl from Dawson's farm *Is Maggie on the side of the Dark or the Light? How do you know?* the Dark; she does not want Will to have the sign **RL 1**

SECOND READ ## Analyze the Text

• Reread pages 4–7. Say: *Foreshadowing is when the author provides hints about things that are about to happen. How does the author foreshadow the unusual events that are about to occur?* The animals act strangely. The clouds grow darker and take on a yellow tinge. The wind rises. **RL 3**

• Reread page 43. Ask: *What does Merriman mean when he says that any great gift or power or talent is a burden?* He means that gifts come with responsibilities and it is people's responsibility to use their gifts whether they want to or not. *What role will Merriman play for Will?* He will be his teacher and protector. **RL 3**

• Reread page 71. Ask: *How does the author move Will back and forth between the fantasy world and the real world? Give details from the text.* Will had been walking with Merriman and then he sees Max. When he looks back at the snow, he sees only his own footprints and Merriman has disappeared. Things that happen in the fantasy world aren't necessarily happening in Will's real world. **RL 3**

 ENGLISH LANGUAGE LEARNERS

Use Sentence Frames
Guide students to generate words that could describe Will, such as *brave, determined, strong,* and *wise.* Then have them use the words to orally complete sentence frames, such as *Will is _____ because _____.*

RESPOND TO SEGMENT 1

Classroom Collaboration

Have small groups summarize what they have read. Have them ask questions about what they don't understand.

ENGLISH LANGUAGE LEARNERS

Use Peer Supported Learning

After each chapter, have small groups work together to generate gist statements about the chapter content. Provide sentence frames such as *In this chapter, Will _____.*

RESPOND TO SEGMENT 2

 Classroom Collaboration

Have partners work together to create and present a summary of what has happened so far, as well as make predictions about what might happen in the next segment.

 Common Core Connection

Grade 6: RL 2 determine a theme or central idea of a text/provide a summary; **RL 3** describe how a story's or drama's plot unfolds and how characters respond or change; **SL 4** present claims and findings, sequence ideas, and use details to accentuate main ideas or themes

Grade 7: RL 2 determine a theme or central idea of a text/analyze its development/provide a summary; **RL 3** analyze how particular elements of a story or drama interact

Grade 8: RL 2 determine a theme or central idea of a text/analyze its development/provide a summary; **RL 3** analyze how dialogue or incidents in a story or drama propel action, reveal a character, or provoke a decision;

Grades 7–8: SL 4 present claims and findings, emphasizing points in a focused, coherent manner

Grades 6–8: RL 1 cite textual evidence to support analysis of what the text says explicitly as well as inferences drawn; **RL 10** read and comprehend literature; **W 2** write informative/explanatory texts; **W 5** develop and strengthen writing by planning, revising, editing, rewriting, or trying a new approach

---

Academic Vocabulary

Read each word with students and discuss its meaning.

begrudgingly (p. 83) • to give in a reluctant way

hindrances (p. 92) • obstacles

apprehension (p. 101) • the feeling that something bad will happen

inexorably (p. 107) • relentlessly; endlessly

grotesque (p. 131) • very strange or ugly

FIRST READ **Think Through the Text**

Have students cite text evidence and draw inferences to answer questions.

pp. 86–90 • *Why is Will surprised when he goes caroling at the Manor?* Merriman, not the butler, opens the door. *Where does Merriman take Will?* to a different time and a different Christmas ◼ RL 1

pp. 91–92 • *How does Will know that he has gone back in time again?* Miss Greythorne appears younger. *What does Will get at the party? How does this help move the plot of the story along?* He gets the Sign of Wood. Will must get all six signs, so readers know he will begin looking for the next one. ◼ RL 3

p. 101 • *Why must Will read* The Book of Gramarye? It will teach him about his place as an Old One. It has all the knowledge he needs. ◼ RL 1

pp. 146–147 • *How does Will find the fourth sign?* He puts his signs together into a half circle and uses them to push away the Dark. The signs begin to glow. The fourth sign begins to glow, too, and Will removes it from the wall. ◼ RL 3

SECOND READ **Analyze the Text**

• Ask: *How does Will feel after he finishes reading* The Book of Gramarye? *Cite evidence from page 108.* He feels sad and weighted down. He feels worried about all that has been and all that is to come. *How does this connect to Merriman's earlier words about the burden of gifts?* Will is realizing that knowledge is power, but it can also be a burden because it comes with great responsibility. ◼ RL 3

• Review page 112. Ask: *What mistake does Merriman realize he has made with Hawkin?* Merriman realizes he has expected Hawkin to risk his life for nothing in return. *What point about humans and their love is the author making?* Sample answer: Most humans require proof that their love is returned in order for them to be loyal. ◼ RL 2

• Reread page 149. Ask: *How does Will speak to the rector?* as an Old One, wise beyond his years *What problem does this create?* Will realizes that his brother is afraid of him. *What new challenge does Will face?* He must keep his two worlds separate. ◼ RL 3

Academic Vocabulary

Read each word with students and discuss its meaning.

lugubriously (p. 167) • sadly

stoical (p. 196) • uncomplaining; bearing difficulties calmly

writhing (p. 226) • twisting and wriggling in pain

FIRST READ ## Think Through the Text

Have students cite text evidence and draw inferences to answer questions.

p. 176 • *What does the Lady tell Will he must do to release the country from the hold of the Dark?* He must find the sign of fire. *What does Will need to find?* He needs to find the nine enchanted candles. ▬RL 3

p. 199 • *What does Will's family think has happened to Mary?* They think she has been kidnapped. *What does Will realize?* The Dark has her. ▬RL 3

pp. 216–235 • *How does Will get the final sign?* With Merriman's permission, he takes it from the hands of the dead king. *How are the signs joined together?* The blacksmith links them together into a beautiful chain. *What does the Lady tell him about the signs?* They will be used in the future when the Dark rises again. ▬RL 3

SECOND READ ## Analyze the Text

• Reread page 233 with students. Say: *Will thinks, "Every one of us is linked, for the greatest purpose in the world." What is the purpose?* To fight the darkness. *What do the Old Ones symbolize?* They symbolize the power of good in the world. ▬RL 2

• Help students recall the Lady's words on page 235. Ask: *What do the Lady's words say about the Dark?* It will come back again and make a more dreadful attempt. *What does this say about the battle between good and evil?* Even when one test is passed, there will always be others. The battle between good and evil always goes on. ▬RL 2

• *How does the joining of the signs bring the plot to its resolution?* When the signs are joined, Will has completed the challenge that was set for him at the beginning of the story. Each sigh that he found brought the story closer to its resolution. ▬RL 3

Independent/Self-Selected Reading

If students have already demonstrated comprehension of *The Dark Is Rising*, have them read other stories to practice skills. Suggested titles:

• *Silver on the Tree* by Susan Cooper

• *The Grey King* by Susan Cooper ▬RL 10

Performance Task

WRITE & PRESENT

1. Have small groups refer to the text to discuss how the story's plot unfolds and how Will responds to change as the plot moves toward its conclusion. ▬RL 3

2. Individual students write an explanatory text describing how Will's quest for the six signs moves the story to its resolution. ▬W 2

3. Have groups reconvene to share and edit their writing. ▬W 5

4. Students present their final explanations to their classmates. ▬SL 4

5. Individual students turn in their final work to the teacher.

See Copying Masters, pp. 164–171.

STUDENT CHECKLIST

Writing

☑ Write an explanatory text describing how Will's quest for the six signs moves the story to its resolution.

☑ Give specific details about how the events work together to bring the plot to its resolution.

☑ Use correct language conventions.

Speaking & Listening

☑ Participate effectively in a collaborative discussion.

☑ Provide reasons and details to support points.

☑ Speak clearly at an understandable pace.

▶ OBJECTIVES

- Compare and contrast fictional and historical accounts
- Draw conclusions
- Analyze point of view
- Analyze text using text evidence

Dragonwings is broken into three instructional segments.

SEGMENTS

SEGMENT 1 . . . . pp. 1–94
SEGMENT 2 . . . . . . pp. 95–174
SEGMENT 3 . . . . . pp. 175–248

Options for Reading

Independent Students read the book independently or with a partner and then answer questions posed by the teacher.

Supported Students read a segment and answer questions with teacher support.

Common Core Connection

Grade 6: RL 4 determine the meaning of words and phrases, including figurative and connotative meanings/analyze the impact of word choice; **RL 6** explain how an author develops the point of view of the narrator or speaker

Grade 7: RL 4 determine the meaning of words and phrases as they are used in a text/ analyze impact of rhymes and other repetitions of sound; **RL 9** compare and contrast a fictional portrayal of a time, place, or character and a historical account of the same period

Grade 8: RL 4 determine the meaning of words and phrases as they are used in a text/ analyze impact of word choices

Grades 6–8: RL 1 cite textual evidence to support analysis of what the text says explicitly as well as inferences drawn

Dragonwings
by Laurence Yep

SUMMARY This book describes events in the life of Chinese immigrant Moon Shadow Lee, who comes to live with his father, Windrider, in San Francisco in 1903. The father and son build a functional airplane that they name *Dragonwings*. Windrider becomes a partner in the laundromat where he works and is able to bring his wife to America.

ABOUT THE AUTHOR Laurence Yep was born and raised in San Francisco, California, and still lives in California. Many of his books deal with the theme of being an outsider. *Dragonwings* was a Newbery Honor book. It also received the Boston Globe Book/Horn Book Award and the International Reading Association's 1976 Children's Book Award.

Discuss Genre and Set Purpose

HISTORICAL FICTION Tell students that they will be reading a book of historical fiction. Help them recall that works of historical fiction are made-up stories that are set in the past. The setting is real and drawn from history and usually includes details that are historically accurate.

SET PURPOSE Help students set a purpose for reading, such as to think about details in the setting and how they show historical facts about real events.

▲ TEXT COMPLEXITY RUBRIC

Overall Text Complexity		*Dragonwings* STORIES
		MORE COMPLEX
Quantitative Measures	Lexile	860
	Guided Reading Level	W
Qualitative Measures	Text Structure	few, if any, shifts in point of view
	Language Conventionality and Clarity	some unassigned dialogue
	Knowledge Demands	unfamiliar perspective
	Purpose/Levels of Meaning	multiple levels of meaning

Academic Vocabulary

Read each word with students and discuss its meaning.

unperturbed (p. 8) • not troubled

immigrants (p. 12) • people who move to another country to settle there

dictate (p. 59) • speak aloud words to be written down by another

contraption (p. 61) • machine

confrontation (p. 68) • fight

prudent (p. 94) • practical; sensible

FIRST READ # Think Through the Text

Have students cite text evidence and draw inferences to answer questions.

pp. 1–14 • *Where does Moon Shadow live at the beginning of the story, and with whom?* He lives in China with his mother and grandmother. *How does his living situation change by the end of the chapter?* He goes to live with his father in San Francisco. ●RL 1

p. 17 • *What do Father and Lefty's comments about Hand Clap mean?* Hand Clap exaggerates. ●RL 4

pp. 61–64 • *What important historical events does Moon Shadow learn about?* The Wright Brothers have flown their first airplane. A man named Baldwin made and flew a dirigible. *How do Father, Uncle, and Moon Shadow feel about these events?* Father wants to fly the same way as the Wright Brothers. Uncle does not believe the event really happened. Moon Shadow does not understand why Uncle is so skeptical. ●RL 1

SECOND READ # Analyze the Text

• Remind students that *Dragonwings* is a fictional story that includes real events and details. Ask: *What details about Chinese immigrants in San Francisco does this fictional account provide?* It provides dialogue that describes the characters' interactions and descriptions of their daily lives. It describes their relationships with their relatives in China. *What details about Chinese immigrants in San Francisco would you expect a nonfiction account to provide?* You might expect a nonfiction account to have names, ages, occupations, and addresses. ●RL 1, Grade 7 RL 9

• Review pages 1–10 with students. Ask: *Who is the narrator of the story?* Moon Shadow, the young boy, is the narrator. *What does his narration so far reveal about him?* Sample answer: He is a dutiful son. He is also curious about his father. He is brave enough to make the move from China to San Francisco. ●RL 1, Grade 6 RL 6

Domain Specific Vocabulary

demons (p. 1) • Chinese term for the white people

Middle Kingdom (p. 1) • the Chinese name for their country, based on the belief that the country was in the middle of the world

Tang (p. 3) • a dynasty that ruled China from 618–907 AD

queue (p. 27) • a man's pigtail

opium (p. 52) • an addictive drug

glider (p. 122) • an aircraft without an engine

ELL ENGLISH LANGUAGE LEARNERS

Use Cognates

Point out the English/Spanish cognates to aid comprehension: *mountain/montaña; vegetable/vegetal; patience/paciencia; marvelous/maravilloso; stomach/estómago*. Have students use the words in sentences related to the text.

RESPOND TO SEGMENT 1
 Classroom Collaboration

Have partners work together to create and present a summary, as well as raise questions that might be answered in the next segment.

ENGLISH LANGUAGE LEARNERS

Use Peer Learning
Have small groups each draw a web with the words *Moon Shadow* and *Windrider* in the center. Tell group members to pass the web around and add a verb that describes something the father and son did. Call on groups to share their webs.

RESPOND TO SEGMENT 2
 Classroom Collaboration

Have small groups work together to summarize what they have learned. Have them ask questions about what they don't understand.

 Common Core Connection

Grade 6: RL 4 determine the meaning of words and phrases, including figurative and connotative meanings/analyze the impact of word choice; **RL 6** explain how an author develops the point of view of the narrator or speaker; **SL 4** present claims and findings, sequence ideas, and use details to accentuate main ideas or themes

Grade 7: RL 4 determine the meaning of words and phrases as they are used in a text/ analyze impact of rhymes and other repetitions of sound; **RL 6** analyze how an author develops and contrasts points of view of different characters or narrators; **RL 9** compare and contrast a fictional portrayal of a time, place, or character and a historical account of the same period

Grade 8: RL 4 determine the meaning of words and phrases as they are used in a text/ analyze impact of word choices

Grades 7–8: SL 4 present claims and findings, emphasizing points in a focused, coherent manner

Grades 6–8: RL1 cite textual evidence to support analysis of what the text says explicitly as well as inferences drawn; **RL 10** read and comprehend literary nonfiction; **W 2** write informative/explanatory texts; **W 5** develop and strengthen writing by planning, revising, editing, rewriting, or trying a new approach

Academic Vocabulary

Read each word with students and discuss its meaning.

tenement (p. 96) • apartment building, usually in a city

exasperation (p. 104) • frustration; irritation

reluctantly (p. 121) • unwillingly

typical (p. 140) • usual; normal

pagan (p. 149) • religions that believe in many gods

boycott (p. 151) • stay away from; refuse to buy

FIRST READ # Think Through the Text

Have students cite text evidence and draw inferences to answer questions.

pp. 100–104 • *What does Moon Shadow learn about the white demons from his first meeting with Miss Whitlaw?* He learns that his ideas about the white demons are not all correct. Miss Whitlaw looks like a regular person, and she is kind to him. He also discovers that he likes gingerbread. **RL 1**

pp. 123–124 • *What does the dialogue between Windrider and Robin show?* Robin's comment is a figure of speech, but Windrider and Moon Shadow don't know enough English to understand the connotation. Robin does not realize this, and she thinks Windrider is being rude, when he is just taking the literal meaning of her words. **RL 4**

SECOND READ # Analyze the Text

• Review the segment with students. Ask: *What kinds of details about the Wright Brothers does this fictional account provide?* It provides details about their correspondence with Moon Shadow and Windrider. *What details about the Wright Brothers would you expect a nonfiction account to provide?* A nonfiction account would tell when and where their flight took place and how they worked. *What kinds of details about the earthquake does this fictional account provide?* It provides details about what Moon Shadow and Windrider experienced and how they coped afterwards. *What details about the earthquake would you expect a nonfiction account to provide?* It would include details about the number and kinds of buildings that fell, how people coped, and the magnitude of the earthquake. **RL 1, Grade 7 RL 9**

• Have students reread pages 154–162. Ask. *What does the narrator's description of the earthquake show?* He compares and contrasts the responses of his father and Miss Whitlaw with other people who refuse to help. *How does he feel about the people who don't help?* He recognizes that they are frightened and probably not thinking clearly. **RL 1, Grades 6–7 RL 6**

Academic Vocabulary

Read each word with students and discuss its meaning.

rubble (p. 177) • fragments of broken buildings

sprightlier (p. 182) • more active and energetic

ethnic (p. 190) • of a particular culture or origin

contemptuously (p. 192) • in a scornful or sneering manner

groping (p. 222) • feeling the way

FIRST READ ## Think Through the Text

Have students cite text evidence and draw inferences to answer questions.

pp. 190–195 • *Why were some of the Tang people able to rebuild in the same place instead of moving?* Uncle used the laws to his advantage. The Tang people owned part of the land, so they were entitled to rebuild there. He also recognized that the white residents needed the services of the Tang residents. ⬤RL 1

pp. 196–200 • *What activity do Windrider and Moon Shadow agree to pursue? Why?* They want to build an airplane. Windrider feels he should follow his dream. Moon Shadow wants to stay with his father. ⬤RL 1

pp. 238–243 • *What decision does Windrider make after his flight with Dragonwings?* He realizes his family is more important than flying. He agrees to be a partner in the Company and goes to China for his wife. ⬤RL 1

SECOND READ ## Analyze the Text

• Review pages 175–248 with students. Ask: *What kinds of details about the aftermath of the earthquake does this fictional account provide?* It tells what the members of the Company and Miss Whitlaw did to rebuild and how they felt after the earthquake. *What details about the aftermath of the earthquake would you expect a nonfiction account to provide?* A nonfiction account might tell how many buildings were destroyed or how many people were killed or wounded. It would also describe efforts to rebuild. ⬤RL 1, Grade 7 RL 9

• Review pages 242–243. Ask: *What does the dialogue between Windrider and Uncle show about them?* It shows they are willing to change their minds and look at a situation differently. ⬤RL 1, Grades 6–7 RL 6

Independent/Self-Selected Reading

If students have already demonstrated comprehension of *Dragonwings*, have them read other stories to practice skills. Suggested titles:

• *By the Great Horn Spoon!* by Sid Fleischman

• *Weedflower* by Cynthia Kadohata ⬤RL 10

Performance Task

WRITE & PRESENT

1. Have partners compare and contrast the fictional portrayal of Chinese immigrants in *Dragonwings* to historical accounts of the same period to gain a deeper understanding of how authors use or alter historical sources to create a sense of time and place as well as make fictional characters lifelike and real. ⬤RL 1, Grade 7 RL 9

2. Have partners record their observations on a Venn diagram. Then they use their diagram to write about how Yep used or altered historical sources to create a sense of time and place as well as make the fictional characters in *Dragonwings* realistic. ⬤W 2

3. Partners share their paragraphs with other sets of partners and edit their writing. ⬤W 5

4. Partners present their final paragraphs to classmates. ⬤SL 4

See Copying Masters, pp. 164–171.

STUDENT CHECKLIST

Writing

☑ Write an explanatory text.

☑ Describe how the author uses or alters historical sources to create a sense of time and place as well as make the fictional characters in *Dragonwings* lifelike and real.

☑ Use correct language conventions.

Speaking & Listening

☑ Engage effectively in collaborative conversations.

☑ Logically present claims and findings.

☑ Cite text evidence to compare and contrast.

OBJECTIVES

- Describe how story elements interact
- Analyze how the author develops the narrator's point of view
- Analyze text using text evidence

Roll of Thunder, Hear My Cry is **broken into three instructional segments.**

SEGMENTS

SEGMENT 1 . . . . pp. 3–101
SEGMENT 2 . . . . . . pp. 102–194
SEGMENT 3 . . . . . . pp. 195–276

Options for Reading

Independent Students read the selection independently or with a partner and then answer questions posed by the teacher.

Supported Students read a segment and answer questions with teacher support.

 Common Core Connection

Grade 6: RL 3 describe how a story's or drama's plot unfolds and how characters respond or change

Grade 7: RL 3 analyze how particular elements of a story or drama interact

Grade 8: RL 3 analyze how dialogue or incidents in a story or drama propel action, reveal a character, or provoke a decision

Grades 6–8: RL 1 cite textual evidence to support analysis of what the text says explicitly as well as inferences drawn

Roll of Thunder, Hear My Cry

by Mildred D. Taylor

SUMMARY Set in the South in the 1930s, *Roll of Thunder, Hear My Cry* tells the story of an African-American family struggling to endure the racial injustices of the time.

ABOUT THE AUTHOR **Mildred D. Taylor** was born in Jackson, Mississippi, in 1943. She grew up listening to her parents' stories about surviving in a society that gave them few rights. These family stories formed the basis of many of her stories. She has won many awards, including a Newbery Medal and four Coretta Scott King awards.

Discuss Genre and Set Purpose

HISTORICAL FICTION Have students read the title and discuss the cover illustration. Discuss how they can tell this story is fiction. Then help students recall that historical fiction is set in a different time period. Ask students what they think the setting might be, based on the cover illustration.

SET PURPOSE Help students set a purpose for reading, such as to find out how the Logan family stays together and how the setting affects the characters and plot.

▲ TEXT COMPLEXITY RUBRIC

Overall Text Complexity		*Roll of Thunder, Hear My Cry* STORY
		COMPLEX
Quantitative Measures	Lexile	860
	Guided Reading Level	W
Qualitative Measures	Text Structure	conventional story structure
	Language Conventionality and Clarity	increased unfamiliar language
	Knowledge Demands	somewhat unfamiliar experience
	Purpose/Levels of Meaning	multiple themes

Academic Vocabulary

Read each word with students and discuss its meaning.

meticulously (p. 3) • carefully and with attention to detail

undaunted (p. 8) • not discouraged

tarpaulin (p. 21) • a waterproof canvas covering

indignation (p. 29) • anger caused by something that seems unfair

maverick (p. 30) • a person who does not follow the rules

interest (p. 100) • a fee paid for borrowing money

ELL ENGLISH LANGUAGE LEARNERS

Use Sentence Frames

Guide students to generate words that could describe Cassie, such as *proud, protective,* and *independent.* Then have them orally complete sentence frames, such as *Cassie is _____ because _____.*

FIRST READ ## Think Through the Text

Have students cite text evidence and draw inferences to answer questions.

pp. 3–7 • *Who is the narrator of the story?* Cassie, a school-aged African-American girl *Where and when does the story take place?* It takes place in the South in the 1930s. RL 1

pp. 21–26 • *How does Cassie feel about the books she gets at school? Cite evidence from the text.* At first, she is excited about getting books. Then she sees that the books are worn and dirty, and her excitement turns to disappointment. She is angry when she sees the word nigra stamped inside the book. RL 3

p. 40 • *What happens to John Henry Berry?* He dies after being burned by white men. *How did the white men justify the burning?* They said he was flirting with a white woman. RL 3

SECOND READ ## Analyze the Text

• Review page 7. Ask: *Why do you think land is so important to Cassie's papa? Cite evidence from the text.* Land is important because Papa wants Cassie to always have land that she can call her own. He grew up in a time when African Americans did not have land of their own, so he values owning his own land and wants his family to do the same. RL 1

• Reread page 27. Ask: *How does Cassie's refusal to accept the book develop her point of view as a narrator?* The reader learns that Cassie is a narrator with strong opinions. We know that she will stand up for what she thinks is right and does not just accept things. Point out that Cassie's actions are an example of civil disobedience, which is a nonviolent way of rebelling against rules that are unfair. RL 3

• Reread pages 39–40. Ask: *How does the setting of this story shape the problems the characters face?* This story is set in the South during the 1930s when African Americans were not treated equally. The characters are worried about lynching, which is seen as a way of "keeping them in line." RL 3

RESPOND TO SEGMENT 1

Classroom Collaboration

Have small groups summarize what they have read. Have them ask questions about what they don't understand.

ENGLISH LANGUAGE LEARNERS

Use Comprehensible Input

Students may be unfamiliar with the dialogue between the characters. Model putting the dialogue in more familiar words. For example, restate "What you and him got to talk 'bout?" as "What do you and he have to talk about?" Have peers work together to read and interpret lines of dialogue.

RESPOND TO SEGMENT 2

Classroom Collaboration

Have partners work together to create and present a summary of what has happened so far, as well as make predictions about what might happen in the next segment.

Common Core Connection

Grade 6: RL 2 determine a theme or central idea of a text/provide a summary; **RL 3** describe how a story's or drama's plot unfolds and how characters respond or change; **RL 5** analyze how a sentence, chapter, scene or stanza fits in the overall structure; **SL 4** present claims and findings, sequence ideas, and use details to accentuate main ideas or themes

Grade 7: RL 3 analyze how particular elements of a story or drama interact

Grade 8: RL 3 analyze how dialogue or incidents in a story or drama propel action, reveal a character, or provoke a decision

Grades 7–8: RL 2 determine a theme or central idea of a text/analyze its development/provide a summary; **SL 4** present claims and findings, emphasizing points in a focused, coherent manner

Grades 6–8: RL 1 cite textual evidence to support analysis of what the text says explicitly as well as inferences drawn; **RL 10** read and comprehend literature; **W 2** write informative/explanatory texts; **W 5** develop and strengthen writing by planning, revising, editing, rewriting, or trying a new approach

---

Academic Vocabulary

Read each word with students and discuss its meaning.

malevolently (p. 112) • harmfully
admonished (p. 141) • scolded
flaunting (p. 144) • showing off
shunned (p. 192) • avoided or ignored

FIRST READ ## Think Through the Text

Have students cite text evidence and draw inferences to answer questions.

p. 111 • *What happens when Mr. Barnett refuses to wait on T.J.?* Cassie stands up to him and asks him why he isn't helping them even though they were waiting first. **RL 3**

p. 140 • *How does Uncle Hammer trick the Wallaces? What does Mama think about his trick?* Uncle Hammer has the same kind of car as Mr. Granger. The Wallaces let him pass because they think he is Mr. Granger. They tip their hats respectfully and are shocked when they discover who is driving. Mama says they will have to pay. **RL 3**

p. 161 • *What does Mr. Jamison offer to do? Why is this significant?* He offers to help with the boycott of the Wallaces' store by backing the credit of the sharecroppers. This means that the Logans won't have to back the credit with their land. **RL 3**

SECOND READ ## Analyze the Text

- Reread page 118. Ask: *What is the difference between Stacey and Cassie's reaction to Big Ma's making Cassie apologize? What does this tell you about each character?* Cassie is angry at Big Ma and thinks she shouldn't have had to apologize. Stacey is sympathetic to Big Ma. He tells Cassie that there are things she doesn't understand. Stacey is older than Cassie and perhaps knows more about the struggles and racism Big Ma has endured. **RL 3**

- Reread page 157 and 158. Ask: *What does Papa tell Stacey about his friendship with Jeremy? What role does the setting play in his words?* Papa tells Stacey that he doesn't think he should be friends with Jeremy because he's white and their friendship isn't based on equality. Papa's advice is influenced by the setting because at the time the story takes place, African Americans aren't treated equally. Papa is mistrustful based on his experiences. **RL 3**

Academic Vocabulary

Read each word with students and discuss its meaning.

persnickety (p. 197) • particular; fussy

despondently (p. 223) • hopelessly

lethargically (p. 227) • sluggishly; without energy

condescending (p. 240) • in a way that shows you think you are better than someone else

crescendo (p. 254) • gradually becoming louder

FIRST READ Think Through the Text

Have students cite text evidence and draw inferences to answer questions.

pp. 200–206 • *How do the Wallaces and Mr. Granger attempt to end the boycott of the Wallaces' store? Mr. Granger threatens to kick the boycotters off his land. The Wallaces threaten to make anyone who can't pay their debts work on a chain gang.* RL 3

pp. 231–235 • *How does Mr. Granger try to get Papa to stop resisting? He tells him that the mortgage on his land has to be paid. How does Uncle Hammer help? Uncle Hammer sells his car and some other things.* RL 3

pp. 257–273 • *Ask: How does everyone think the fire started? They think lightning started the fire and burned the cotton field. How did the fire really start? Papa started it to distract the men and stop them from hanging T.J.* RL 1, Grade 6 RL 3

SECOND READ Analyze the Text

• Reread page 263 with students. Say: *Cassie is the narrator, so readers only know what Cassie knows. Why do you think the author chooses to have Cassie sleep through the fire? It adds an element of surprise when the reader learns that Papa set the fire. At the time Cassie fell asleep, she thought lightning had started it.* Grade 6RL 5

• Reread page 273. Say: *Throughout the story, the land has been the most important thing to Papa. What might the author be trying to say when she has Papa set fire to the land to save T.J.? She might be trying to say that as important as land is, life and commitment to friends and family are even more important.* RL 2

Independent/Self-Selected Reading

If students have demonstrated comprehension of *Roll of Thunder, Hear My Cry*, have them read other stories to practice skills. Suggested titles:

• *Let the Circle Be Unbroken* by Mildred D. Taylor

• *Bud, Not Buddy* by Christopher Paul Curtis RL 10

Performance Task

WRITE & PRESENT

1. Have small groups refer to the text to discuss how the setting affects the plot events in the story. RL 3

2. Individual students write an explanatory text describing the impact of the setting on the plot. They should include specific details and examples from the text. W 2

3. Have students reconvene in small groups to share and edit their writing. W 5

4. Students present their final explanations to their classmates. SL 4

5. Individual students turn in their final drafts to the teacher.

See Copying Masters, pp. 164–171.

STUDENT CHECKLIST

Writing

☑ Write an explanatory text describing the impact of the setting on the plot.

☑ Give specific details and examples that develop the relationship between the setting and the plot.

☑ Use correct language conventions.

Speaking & Listening

☑ Participate effectively in a collaborative discussion.

☑ Provide reasons and details to support points.

☑ Speak clearly at an understandable pace.

▶ OBJECTIVES

- Describe characters and events
- Determine the theme
- Analyze the use of figurative language
- Analyze text using text evidence

"The People Could Fly" is broken into three instructional segments.

SEGMENTS

Options for Reading

Independent Students read the selection independently or with a partner and then answer questions posed by the teacher.

Supported Students read a segment and answer questions with teacher support.

Common Core Connection

Grade 6; RL 2 determine a theme or central idea of a text/provide a summary; **RL 4** determine the meaning of words and phrases, including figurative and connotative meanings/analyze impact of word choice

Grade 7; RL 3 analyze how particular elements of a story or drama interact; **RL 4** determine the meaning of words and phrases as they are used in a text/analyze impact of rhymes and other repetitions of sound

Grade 8; RL 4 determine the meaning of words and phrases as they are used in a text/ analyze impact of word choices

Grades 7-8; RL 2 determine a theme or central idea of a text/analyze its development/ provide a summary

Grades 6–8; RL 1 cite textual evidence to support analysis of what the text says explicitly as well as inferences drawn

"The People Could Fly"

by Virginia Hamilton

SUMMARY In this traditional African-American folktale, a group of people from Africa lost their wings when they were forced into slavery. They worked alongside other slaves who didn't have their magic power. One day, Toby brings back the magic and some of the slaves soar to freedom. The slaves who are left behind tell the story to their children.

ABOUT THE AUTHOR Virginia Hamilton was born in 1934 in Ohio, in the house that had been her family's home since the late 1850s, when her grandfather came there as a baby on the Underground Railroad. During her lifetime Hamilton wrote 41 books and won every major award in children's literature.

Discuss Genre and Set Purpose

FOLKTALE Display the story, and read the title with students. Discuss characteristics of folktales: they are usually set in the past, include magical creatures, and teach a lesson.

SET PURPOSE Help students set a purpose for reading, such as to determine the theme of the story and find out the magical elements in this folktale.

▲ TEXT COMPLEXITY RUBRIC

Overall Text Complexity		"The People Could Fly" STORY
		COMPLEX
Quantitative Measures	Lexile	570
	Guided Reading Level	W
Qualitative Measures	Text Structure	some unconventional story structure elements
	Language Conventionality and Clarity	some unfamiliar language
	Knowledge Demands	situation includes unfamiliar aspects
	Purpose/Levels of Meaning	multiple levels of meaning

SEGMENT 1 pp. 166–169

Academic Vocabulary

Read each word with students and discuss its meaning.

misery (p. 166) • great suffering caused by pain or sorrow

soothe (p. 167) • to calm someone who is upset

FIRST READ ## Think Through the Text

Have students cite text evidence and draw inferences to answer questions.

p. 166 • *What happened to the people who could fly when they were captured for slavery? Why?* They had to shed their wings. They couldn't take their wings on the slave ship because it was too crowded. ◗ RL 1

p. 167 • *How were the people who could fly the same as the other slaves?* They had their same dark skin. *How were they different?* They kept their magical powers even though they didn't keep their wings. ◗ RL 1

p. 169 • *What text details show that Sarah is tired?* Sarah can't stand anymore. She sits down in the row. *How does Toby help Sarah?* He says some magic words and Sarah flies away. ◗ RL 1

SECOND READ ## Analyze the Text

• Reread page 166. Ask: *What do you notice about the language that the author uses? Is it formal language or does it sound like spoken language?* It sounds like spoken language. *Why does the author choose to write the story this way?* The author uses this language to write the story to help readers experience what the tale would have sounded like when it was told by slaves to their children. ◗ Grade 7 RL 3

• Say: *The story says that the master was a hard lump of clay, a hard, glinty coal. What kind of figurative language is this?* It is a metaphor. *It says the master is these things, not that he is like them. What is the meaning of these sentences?* The master shows no kindness or sympathy to the slaves. ◗ RL 4

• Review that characters' words and actions help reveal the theme. Ask: *What is Sarah like as she flies away?* She is like a bird. *What are birds often a symbol of?* freedom *So what is a possible theme of this story?* Freedom from slavery might be a theme of this story. ◗ RL 2

 ENGLISH LANGUAGE LEARNERS

Use Sentence Frames

Guide students to generate words that could describe Toby, such as *old, wise, kind,* and *magical.* Then have them orally complete sentence frames, such as *Toby is _____ because _____.* *magical; he helps Sarah fly*

RESPOND TO SEGMENT 1

Classroom Collaboration

Have partners summarize what they have read so far. Tell them to ask questions about anything they don't understand.

ENGLISH LANGUAGE LEARNERS

Use Visuals

Point to the illustration on page 170. Say: *Toby reached out his arms.* Have students repeat and reach out their arms.

 RESPOND TO SEGMENT 2

Classroom Collaboration

Have small groups work together to summarize what they have read so far. Have them ask questions about what they don't understand.

 Common Core Connection

Grade 6: RL 2 determine a theme or central idea of a text/provide a summary; **RL 3** describe how a story's or drama's plot unfolds and how characters respond or change; **RL 4** determine the meaning of words and phrases, including figurative and connotative meanings/analyze impact of word choice; **SL 4** present claims and findings, sequence ideas, and use details to accentuate main ideas or themes/use appropriate eye contact, volume, and pronunciation

Grade 7: RL 3 analyze how particular elements of a story or drama interact; **RL 4** determine the meaning of words and phrases as they are used in a text/analyze impact of rhymes and other repetitions of sound

Grade 8: RL 3 analyze how dialogue or incidents in a story or drama propel action, reveal a character, or provoke a decision; **RL 4** determine the meaning of words and phrases as they are used in a text/analyze impact of word choices

Grades 7–8: RL 2 determine a theme or central idea of a text/analyze its development/provide a summary; **SL 4** present claims and findings, emphasizing points in a focused, coherent manner

Grades 6–8: RL 1 cite textual evidence to support analysis of what the text says explicitly as well as inferences drawn; **RL 10** read and comprehend literature; **W 2** write informative/explanatory texts; **W 5** develop and strengthen writing by planning, revising, editing, rewriting, or trying a new approach

FIRST READ **Think Through the Text**

Have students cite text evidence and draw inferences to answer questions.

p. 170 • *Why are the slaves falling over?* They are falling over because it is so hot. *How does Toby help them?* He says the magic words and helps them fly. ●RL 1

p. 171 • *What happens when Toby says the magic words?* All the slaves who can fly join hands and rise into the air. *Who was left behind? Why?* The people who could not fly were left behind. Toby did not have time to teach them to fly. ●RL 3

SECOND READ **Analyze the Text**

• Reread page 170. Ask: *To what does the author compare the people who were flying?* She compares them to sticks. *What kind of figurative language is this an example of?* metaphor *What does it help you picture about the slaves?* It shows that they are flying so high that they look like sticks instead of people. ●RL 4

• Reread page 171. Ask: *Where does the author say the people who could fly are flying to?* She says they are flying to freedom. *How does this help reveal the theme?* It reinforces the idea of freedom and how the slaves longed to be free from the Overseer, the Master, and the Driver. ●RL 2

• Reread the second-to-last paragraph on page 171. *How does the author express the struggle of those slaves who remain?* Their looks say "Take us with you" but they are too afraid to say the words. ●RL 1

Performance Task

FIRST READ Think Through the Text

Have students cite text evidence and draw inferences to answer questions.

p. 172 • *When did the slaves who could not fly tell their children about the people who could fly?* when they were free *Why is the story still being told? Those children told their children and now the author is sharing the story with readers.* ⬛ RL 1

p. 173 • *Who does the author say this story is a testament to?* It is a testament to the millions of slaves who could not "fly" away. ⬛ RL 1

SECOND READ Analyze the Text

• Reread the author's explanation on page 173. Say: *How was this story connected to real slave escapes? It might have been told to explain how slaves got away. "Come fly away" might have been code for escaping.*
⬛ RL 1

• *Why would flying away be an example of wish fulfillment for slaves? Life as a slave was so terrible that slaves might have wished they could fly away. They told the story to give voice to their dreams of freedom.*
⬛ RL 1

• *What statement is the author making about the power of imagination? No matter how difficult your life is, you can always be free in your mind.*
⬛ RL 2

Independent/Self-Selected Reading

If students have demonstrated comprehension of "The People Could Fly," have them read other folktales to practice skills. Suggested titles:

• *Many Thousand Gone: African Americans from Slavery to Freedom* by Virginia Hamilton

• *Her Stories: African American Folktales, Fairy Tales, and True Tales* by Virginia Hamilton ⬛ RL 10

WRITE & PRESENT

1. Have small groups refer to the text to discuss ways the author uses story details and figurative language to reveal the theme. ⬛ RL 2

2. Individual students write an expository text that explains how the author uses details and figurative language to reveal the theme. ⬛ W 2

3. Have students reconvene to share and edit their writing. ⬛ W 5

4. Students present their final explanations to the class. ⬛ SL 4

See Copying Masters, pp. 164–171.

STUDENT CHECKLIST

Writing

☑ Write a text explaining how the author reveals the theme.

☑ Give specific details and examples that show how the author reveals the theme.

☑ Use correct language conventions.

Speaking & Listening

☑ Participate effectively in a collaborative discussion.

☑ Provide reasons and details to support points.

☑ Use appropriate eye contact and volume.

OBJECTIVES

- Identify and explain cause-and-effect relationships
- Determine a theme in a text
- Draw inferences
- Analyze text using text evidence

The Tale of the Mandarin Ducks is broken into three instructional segments.

SEGMENTS

SEGMENT 1. . . . . .pp. 6–15
SEGMENT 2. . . . . . . .pp. 16–25
SEGMENT 3. . . . . . . .pp. 26–37

Options for Reading

Independent Students read the book independently or with a partner and then answer questions posed by the teacher.

Supported Students read a segment and answer questions with teacher support.

COMMON CORE — Common Core Connection

Grade 6: RL 2 determine a theme or central idea of a text/provide a summary

Grades 7–8: RL 2 determine a theme or central idea of a text/analyze its development/provide a summary

Grades 6–8: RL 1 cite textual evidence to support analysis of what the text says explicitly as well as inferences drawn

The Tale of the Mandarin Ducks
by Katherine Paterson

SUMMARY This book is a retelling of a Japanese folktale. A vain, greedy lord captures a mandarin drake, separating it from its mate. A kitchen maid and the lord's steward set the drake free, but are discovered and sentenced to drown. The ducks take human form and rescue the maid and the steward.

ABOUT THE AUTHOR Katherine Paterson has written more than forty books, including both fiction and nonfiction. Paterson has won the Newbery Award twice, as well as many other awards.

Discuss Genre and Set Purpose

FOLK TALE Tell students they will be reading a retelling of a Japanese folktale. Discuss characteristics of folktales: they are usually set in the past, include magical creatures, and teach a lesson. Page through the book, and ask students to comment on the illustrations. Discuss what they can learn about the setting through the illustrations.

SET PURPOSE Help students set a purpose for reading, such as to find out the events in the plot and the story's theme or lesson.

▲ TEXT COMPLEXITY RUBRIC

Overall Text Complexity		*The Tale of the Mandarin Ducks* STORY
		SIMPLE
Quantitative Measures	Lexile	950
	Guided Reading Level	P
Qualitative Measures	Text Structure	simple, linear chronology
	Language Conventionality and Clarity	clear, direct language
	Knowledge Demands	moderately complex theme
	Purpose/Levels of Meaning	multiple levels of meaning

Academic Vocabulary

Read each word with students and discuss its meaning.

drake (p. 7) • a male duck

plumage (p. 7) • feathers of a bird

luster (p. 12) • shine

Domain Specific Vocabulary

steward (p. 8) • an estate manager

samurai (p. 8) • a Japanese warrior

retainers (p. 7) • servants

FIRST READ **Think Through the Text**

Have students cite text evidence and draw inferences to answer questions.

pp. 8–9 • *Why did the drake get caught?* *He wanted the acorns, so he forgot to be cautious.* RL 1

pp. 12–13 • *What happened to the drake while he was in the cage? Why?* *He lost his luster and became silent because he was grieving for his mate.* ◼ RL 1

pp. 14–15 • *Why didn't the lord listen to Shozo's suggestion?* *He did not like having his servant tell him what to do.* ◼ RL 1

SECOND READ **Analyze the Text**

- Guide students to look back over pages 6–15 to answer the question: *How would you describe the lord?* *He is stubborn, proud, vain, and greedy.* ◼ RL 1

- *On page 8 the text says that the lord secretly despises Shozo. Why is this?* *Shozo is no longer handsome because he was wounded in battle, and the lord likes only things that are beautiful and bring him honor.* ◼ RL 1

- Guide students to look back over pages 6–15 to answer the question: *How would you summarize the text?* Sample answer: *The greedy lord captures a beautiful drake, but someone releases it.* ◼ RL 2

ELL **ENGLISH LANGUAGE LEARNERS**

Use Visuals and Sentence Frames

Use the illustrations to have students compare and contrast the drake's appearance before and after his captivity. Then help them complete sentence frames such as, *When he was free, the drake looked _____. magnificent After he was captured, the drake looked _____. sad, droopy*

RESPOND TO SEGMENT 1

Classroom Collaboration

Have partners work together to create and present a summary, as well as raise questions that might be answered in the next segment.

ENGLISH LANGUAGE LEARNERS

Use Peer Supported Learning

Organize students into mixed-proficiency small groups. Have each group draw a web with the words *Tale of the Mandarin Ducks* in the center. Tell students to pass the web from student to student, and have each student add a word or phrase related to the story. Call on groups to share their completed webs with other groups. Suggest that groups add information from other groups to their own webs.

RESPOND TO SEGMENT 2

 Classroom Collaboration

Have small groups work together to summarize what they have learned. Have them ask questions about what they don't understand.

 Common Core Connection

Grade 6: RL 2 determine a central idea of a text/provide a summary; **RL 3** describe how a story's or drama's plot unfolds and how characters respond or change; **SL 4** present claims and findings, sequence ideas, and use details to accentuate main ideas or themes

Grade 7: RL 3 analyze how particular elements of a story or drama interact

Grade 8: RL 3 analyze how dialogue or incidents in a story or drama propel action, reveal a character, or provoke a decision

Grades 7–8: RL 2 determine a theme or central idea of a text/analyze its development/provide a summary; **SL 4** present claims and findings, emphasizing points in a focused, coherent manner

Grades 6–8: RL 1 cite textual evidence to support analysis of what the text says explicitly as well as inferences drawn; **RL 10** read and comprehend literature; **W 2** write informative/ explanatory texts; **W 5** develop and strengthen writing by planning, revising, editing, rewriting, or trying a new approach; **W 9** draw evidence from literary or informational texts to support analysis, reflection, and research

---

Academic Vocabulary

Read each word with students and discuss its meaning.

defense (p. 19) • reasons offered

mischief (p. 19) • trouble, disruption

oppose (p. 24) • be against something; resist

abolish (p. 24) • do away with

capital punishment (p. 24) • the death penalty

FIRST READ **Think Through the Text**

Have students cite text evidence and draw inferences to answer questions.

pp. 17–18 • *What does Yasuko do with the drake?* *She takes him to the edge of the woods to set him free.* ◖RL 1

pp. 22–23 • *Why does the lord sentence Yasuko and Shozo to death?* *He thinks they conspired to release the duck, and he wants to make an example of them.* ◖RL 1

pp. 24–25 • *What news do the messengers bring?* *The emperor has abolished capital punishment, and Yasuko and Shozo are to be taken to the Imperial Court.* ◖RL 1

SECOND READ **Analyze the Text**

• Review the illustration and the text on pages 20–21. Ask: *What does Shozo's response to Yasuko reveal about him?* Sample answer: *He is a kind person with a sense of fairness. He seems comfortable with his decision.* ◖RL 3

• Review the illustration and reread the text on pages 24–25. Ask: *Why is the lord angry when he hears the messengers' news?* *He has to obey the emperor, so he can no longer kill Yasuko and Shozo.* *What clue to the ending of the story do you see in the illustration?* Sample answer: *The messengers have their faces covered, so they may be hiding a secret that will help the couple.* ◖RL 3

FIRST READ **Think Through the Text**

Have students cite text evidence and draw inferences to answer questions.

pp. 26–27 • *What is the real reason the retainers yell at the couple? The retainers are afraid of the dark woods.* ◼ RL 1

pp. 28–30 • *What happens to Yasuko and Shozo? The Imperial Messengers lead them out of the woods and to a safe hut.* ◼ RL 1

pp. 34–35 • *What do Yasuko and Shozo discover when they wake up the next morning? The Imperial Messengers are gone, but there is food cooking. When they look outside, they see the two Mandarin ducks.* ◼ RL 1

SECOND READ **Analyze the Text**

- Guide students to compare the illustrations on pages 30–31 and 34–35. Ask: *What inference can you draw about the messengers?* Sample answer: *The messengers are the ducks in disguise.* ◼ RL 1

- Guide students to review the text. Ask: *What is the theme of the folktale? Why do you think so?* Sample answer: *It's better to be kind. The greedy, vain lord is left with nothing, but the kind, generous couple is rewarded.* ◼ RL 2

Independent/Self-Selected Reading

If students have demonstrated comprehension of *The Tale of the Mandarin Ducks,* have them read other texts to practice skills. Suggested titles:

- *Tales Our Abuelitas Told* by Alma Flor Ada and F. Isabel Campoy

- *All Our Relatives* by Paul Goble ◼ RL 10

Performance Task

WRITE & PRESENT

1. Have small groups cite text evidence and draw inferences about the drake and the duck to discuss and support an analysis of the perils of vanity. Encourage students to take notes. ◼ RL 1

2. Have individual students use their notes from their discussion of the story to write a paragraph that analyzes the perils of vanity. ◼ W 2, W 9

3. Students work with partners to share and edit their work. ◼ W 5

4. Have students present their work to the class. ◼ SL 4

5. Individual students turn in their final paragraphs to the teacher.

See Copying Masters, pp. 164–171.

STUDENT CHECKLIST

Writing

☑ Cite text evidence and draw inferences about the drake and the duck to support an analysis of the perils of vanity.

☑ Write a paragraph that analyzes the perils of vanity as presented in the story.

☑ Use correct language conventions.

Speaking & Listening

☑ Engage effectively in collaborative conversations.

☑ Logically present claims and findings.

☑ Cite text evidence and draw inferences to support an analysis.

OBJECTIVES

- Describe characters and events
- Determine how the author develops the speaker's point of view
- Analyze text using text evidence

"Eleven" is broken into three instructional segments.

SEGMENTS

SEGMENT 1 . . . . pp. 6–7
SEGMENT 2 . . . . p. 8
SEGMENT 3 . . . . p. 9

Options for Reading

Independent Students read the selection independently or with a partner and then answer questions posed by the teacher.

Supported Students read a segment and answer questions with teacher support.

Common Core Connection

Grade 6 RL 4 determine the meaning of words and phrases, including figurative and connotative meanings/analyze impact of word choice; **RL 6** explain how an author develops the point of view of the narrator or speaker

Grade 7 RL 4 determine the meaning of words and phrases as they are used in a text/analyze impact of rhymes and other repetitions of sound

Grade 8 RL 4 determine the meaning of words and phrases as they are used in a text/analyze impact of word choices

Grades 6–8: RL 1 cite textual evidence to support analysis of what the text says explicitly as well as inferences drawn

"Eleven"
by Sandra Cisneros

SUMMARY In this short story, Rachel knows she should feel happy because it is her eleventh birthday, but a misunderstanding with her teacher spoils her special day.

ABOUT THE AUTHOR Writer and poet **Sandra Cisneros** was born in 1954 in Chicago, Illinois. Her works focus on the experience of being a Latina woman in the United States. She is best known for her novel *The House on Mango Street*, a coming-of-age story set in Chicago. It has sold over two million copies.

Discuss Genre and Set Purpose

REALISTIC FICTION Display the book, and read the title of the short story together. Have students skim the text and discuss how they can tell that this story is realistic fiction.

SET PURPOSE Help students set a purpose for reading, such as to determine how the main character feels about turning eleven.

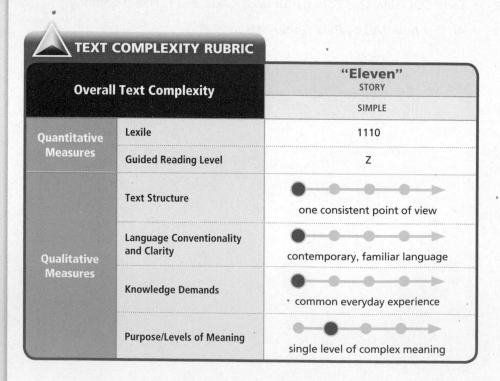

TEXT COMPLEXITY RUBRIC

Overall Text Complexity		"Eleven" STORY
		SIMPLE
Quantitative Measures	Lexile	1110
	Guided Reading Level	Z
Qualitative Measures	Text Structure	one consistent point of view
	Language Conventionality and Clarity	contemporary, familiar language
	Knowledge Demands	common everyday experience
	Purpose/Levels of Meaning	single level of complex meaning

Academic Vocabulary

Read each word with students and discuss its meaning.

raggedy (p. 7) • torn; frayed

nonsense (p. 8) • foolish talk or behavior

FIRST READ ## Think Through the Text

Have students cite text evidence and draw inferences to answer questions.

p. 6 • *What does Rachel say that they never tell you about birthdays?* She says that they never tell you that when you're eleven, you're also ten, and nine, and eight, and seven, and six, and five, and four, and three, and two, and one. *Who do you think she means by "they"?* She means grownups. RL 1

p. 7 • *Why does Rachel wish she was one hundred and two?* She wishes she was one hundred and two because then she would have known what to say when Mrs. Price put the red sweater on her desk. *What text details show how Rachel feels about the sweater?* She calls it ugly and says it's all stretched out like a jump rope. She says that even if it was hers, she wouldn't say so. RL 1, Grade 6 RL 6

SECOND READ ## Analyze the Text

• Review that authors can develop their characters' point of view through the characters' words. Ask: *How does Rachel feel about her eleventh birthday?* She says she doesn't feel eleven at all. She says that everything is just like yesterday. RL 4, Grade 6 RL 6

• *Explain how Sandra Cisneros's comparison of birthdays to an onion or the rings of a tree, or the wooden dolls develops Rachel's point of view.* Rachel thinks that's how birthdays are. Each year fits inside the other ones so that when you're eleven, you are also all the other years that came before it. RL 4, Grade 6 RL 6

ELL ENGLISH LANGUAGE LEARNERS

Use Sentence Frames

Guide students to use sentence frames to talk about the story. Have students complete frames such as *Rachel is ___ years old. Rachel does not like_____. eleven; the red sweater* Have students read their completed frames aloud with a partner to talk about the story.

RESPOND TO SEGMENT 1

 Classroom Collaboration

Have partners summarize what they have read so far. Tell them to ask questions about anything they don't understand.

Use Demonstrations

Use demonstration to illustrate Rachel's actions, such as squeezing your eyes shut tight and biting down on your teeth really hard. Guide students to generate words that describe how Rachel is feeling, such as *sad, angry,* or *frustrated.* Have them say the words or use them in complete sentences.

RESPOND TO SEGMENT 2

 Classroom Collaboration

Have small groups work together to summarize what they have read so far. Have them ask questions about what they don't understand.

 Common Core Connection

Grade 6 RL 3 describe how a story's or drama's plot unfolds and how characters respond or change; **RL 4** determine the meaning of words and phrases, including figurative and connotative meanings/analyze impact of word choice; **RL 6** explain how an author develops the point of view of the narrator or speaker; **SL 4** present claims and findings, sequence ideas, and use details to accentuate main ideas or themes

Grade 7 RL 3 analyze how particular elements of a story or drama interact; **RL 4** determine the meaning of words and phrases as they are used in a text/analyze impact of rhymes and other repetitions of sound

Grade 8: RL 3 analyze how dialogue or incidents in a story or drama propel action, reveal a character, or provoke a decision; **RL 4** determine the meaning of words and phrases as they are used in a text/analyze impact of word choices

Grades 7–8: SL 4 present claims and findings, emphasizing points in a focused, coherent manner

Grades 6–8: RL 1 cite textual evidence to support analysis of what the text says explicitly as well as inferences drawn; **RL 10** read and comprehend literature; **W 2** write informative/explanatory texts; **W 5** develop and strengthen writing by planning, revising, editing, rewriting, or trying a new approach

---

FIRST READ · **Think Through the Text**

Have students cite text evidence and draw inferences to answer questions.

- *What does Rachel think about to make herself feel better?* She thinks about Mama making her a cake and Papa coming home and everybody singing happy birthday. **RL 1**

- *Why does Mrs. Price get upset with Rachel?* She sees that Rachel has shoved the sweater to the corner of her desk and now it's hanging over the side. *What does she make her do?* She makes her put on the sweater. **RL 3**

SECOND READ · **Analyze the Text**

- Reread the first paragraph on page 8. Say: *How does Rachel feel during math class? Explain how Sandra Cisneros's word choice develops Rachel's point of view.* Rachel says that she feels sick and like the part of her that's three wants to come out of her eyes. This develops how upset Rachel feels and also reiterates Rachel's belief that you are every age you've ever been. **RL 4, Grade 6 RL 6**

- Explain how Cisneros's words develop Rachel's point of view about being forced to wear the sweater. *Rachel describes the sweater as smelling like cottage cheese and describes standing with her arms apart like the sweater is hurting her. She says it is itchy and full of germs that aren't hers. These words all show how upset Rachel is and how disgusting she thinks the sweater is.* **RL 4, Grade 6 RL 6**

FIRST READ ## Think Through the Text

Have students cite text evidence and draw inferences to answer questions.

- *What happens after Rachel puts the sweater on?* *She starts crying.* ▬RL 1

- *Who does the sweater really belong to?* *It belongs to Phyllis Lopez.* ▬RL 1

- *Is Rachel still excited for her birthday? How do you know?* *No, Rachel imagines the cake and the candles and the presents and singing, but then she says "only it's too late." She means that her excitement about her birthday has been spoiled and nothing can fix it.* ▬RL 1

SECOND READ ## Analyze the Text

- *How does Rachel feel once she starts crying? Explain how the words Sandra Cisneros uses help develop Rachel's point of view.* *Rachel says, "I wish I was invisible, but I'm not. I'm eleven and it's my birthday and I'm crying like I'm three in front of everybody." The words Cisneros chooses help us picture the conflict Rachel is feeling. She wants to be happy because she's eleven and instead she's sad and feels like she's three. It further develops Rachel's point of view that you are other ages underneath the age you really are.* ▬RL 4, Grade 6 RL 6

- *Why does Rachel say she wants to be far away like a runaway balloon?* *She wants to disappear and get away from all the things that have gone wrong today. Her words help the reader picture how small and free she wants to feel.* ▬RL 3, Grade 6 RL 6

Independent/Self-Selected Reading

If students have demonstrated comprehension of "Eleven," have them read other texts to practice skills. Suggested titles:

- *Baseball in April and Other Stories* by Gary Soto

- *Becoming Naomi León* by Pam Muñoz Ryan ▬RL 10

Performance Task

WRITE & PRESENT

1. Have small groups refer to the text to discuss how the words Sandra Cisneros chooses develop Rachel's point of view. ▬RL 4, Grade 6 RL 6

2. Individual students write an expository text that explains how the author's word choice develops the speaker's point of view. ▬W 2

3. Have small groups reconvene to share and edit their writing. ▬W 5

4. Students present their final explanations to the class. ▬SL 4

See Copying Masters, pp. 164–171.

STUDENT CHECKLIST

Writing

☑ Write a text explaining how the author's word choice develops the speaker's point of view.

☑ Give specific examples of word choices that develop the speaker's point of view.

☑ Use correct language conventions.

Speaking & Listening

☑ Participate effectively in a collaborative discussion.

☑ Provide claims and findings to support important points.

☑ Adapt speech to contexts and tasks.

OBJECTIVES

- Describe how a story's plot unfolds in a series of episodes
- Analyze how characters respond to change as the plot unfolds
- Analyze text using text evidence

Black Ships Before Troy is broken into three instructional segments.

Options for Reading

Independent Students read the selection independently or with a partner and then answer questions posed by the teacher.

Supported Students read a segment and answer questions with teacher support.

COMMON CORE Common Core Connection

Grade 6: RL 3 describe how a story's or drama's plot unfolds and how characters respond or change

Grade 7: RL 3 analyze how particular elements of a story or drama interact

Grade 8: RL 3 analyze how dialogue or incidents in a story or drama propel action, reveal a character, or provoke a decision

Grades 6–8: RL 1 cite textual evidence to support analysis of what the text says explicitly as well as inferences drawn

Black Ships Before Troy
The Story of the Iliad
by Rosemary Sutcliff

SUMMARY Rosemary Sutcliff retells Homer's epic poem *The Iliad*. When King Menelaus's queen, Helen, leaves with Paris, the Prince of Troy, it sparks a ten–year conflict between the Greeks and the city of Troy.

ABOUT THE AUTHOR Rosemary Sutcliff was born in England in 1920. Though she did not learn to read until she was nine years old, she went on to write 50 novels, primarily for young people.

Discuss Genre and Set Purpose

MYTH Explain that *Black Ships Before Troy* is a retelling of an ancient Greek poem. Then have students recall any Greek myths they know. Help them recall that a myth is an old story that has been handed down to retell historical events or to explain phenomena in nature. Greek myths often tell tales of humans who interact with gods and goddesses.

SET PURPOSE Help students set a purpose for reading, such as to find out the story of the Trojan War and the series of events that unfolded.

▲ TEXT COMPLEXITY RUBRIC

Overall Text Complexity		Black Ships Before Troy STORY
		MORE COMPLEX
Quantitative Measures	Lexile	1260
	Guided Reading Level	N/A
Qualitative Measures	Text Structure	somewhat complex story concepts
	Language Conventionality and Clarity	archaic, unfamiliar language
	Knowledge Demands	cultural and literary knowledge useful
	Purpose/Levels of Meaning	multiple levels of meaning

Academic Vocabulary

Read each word with students and discuss its meaning.

mortal (p. 6) • human; not able to live forever

discord (p. 6) • disagreement

siege (p. 21) • the surrounding of a place, such as a city or a fortress, in order to capture it

vengeance (p. 31) • action taken to pay back for hurt done to you or someone you support

summons (p. 51) • orders to do something or be somewhere

FIRST READ ## Think Through the Text

Have students cite text evidence and draw inferences to answer questions.

pp. 10–14 • *Who is Helen?* She is the wife of King Menelaus and the most beautiful of the mortal women. *What happens as a result of Paris sailing off with Helen?* It starts all the sorrows that came after. ◗RL 3

p. 15 • *What details does the author use to show how Menelaus feels when he finds his queen has left with the Trojan prince?* She says that a black grief and a red rage came upon him. *How does Menelaus respond to his discovery?* He organizes a fleet of black ships to sail to Troy. ◗RL 3

p. 34 • *Helen says she will go back to Menelaus. Why does Aphrodite cast a spell on her so that she will stay with Paris?* Aphrodite knows that the war will be over if Helen goes back to Menelaus and she knows Hera and Athena will mock her, so she wants Helen to stay with Paris. ◗RL 1

SECOND READ ## Analyze the Text

• Reread page 18. Ask: *When Achilles's mother tells him he must choose between a long life or long fame, which does he choose?* fame *What does this tell you about what the ancient Greeks valued?* It shows that they valued courage and heroism over caution and a long life. ◗RL 1

• Reread page 35. Ask: *How do gods and goddesses affect the outcome of events? Cite evidence from the text.* The gods interfere with events to meet their own desires. The war may have ended, but Athene was on the side of the Greeks and broke the truce. She convinced Pandarus to try to shoot down Menelaus, and the truce was broken. ◗RL 3

• Reread page 49. Ask: *What is the author's point of view about Ajax's words to Achilles?* She thinks Ajax should not have added his own words to the argument. *How do you know?* In parentheses, it says that maybe it would have been better if he had not. Tell students that this is an aside. It is something the author says directly to the readers that is separate from story events. ◗RL 1

ELL **ENGLISH LANGUAGE LEARNERS**

Use Comprehensible Input

Restate quoted text in simpler language and more familiar sentence structures. For example, restate the words *very splendid are the promises of the High King* as "The High King makes nice promises." Have students repeat. Then confirm understanding by asking yes/no or short response questions, such as, *Will Achilles fight for the High King?* no *Achilles does not _____ the High King.* trust

---

RESPOND TO SEGMENT 1

 Classroom Collaboration

Have small groups summarize what they have read. Have them ask questions about what they don't understand.

ENGLISH LANGUAGE LEARNERS

Use Comprehensible Input
Pause after each main event to summarize the action of the story in one or two simple sentences. Invite students to pose questions they have about the content or have students complete simple sentence frames with action verbs. *The Greeks and Trojans _____.*

RESPOND TO SEGMENT 2

Classroom Collaboration

Have partners work together to create and present a summary of what has happened so far, as well as make predictions about what might happen in the next segment.

Common Core Connection

Grade 6: RL 3 describe how a story's or drama's plot unfolds and how characters respond or change; **SL 4** present claims and findings, sequence ideas, and use details to accentuate main ideas or themes

Grade 7: RL 3 analyze how particular elements of a story or drama interact

Grade 8: RL 3 analyze how dialogue or incidents in a story or drama propel action, reveal a character, or provoke a decision; **RL 9** analyze how a modern work of fiction draws on themes, patterns of events, or character types from myths, traditional stories, or religious works

Grades 7–8: SL 4 present claims and findings, emphasizing points in a focused, coherent manner

Grades 6–8: RL 1 cite textual evidence to support analysis of what the text says explicitly as well as inferences drawn; **RL 10** read and comprehend literature; **W 2** write informative/explanatory texts; **W 5** develop and strengthen writing by planning, revising, editing, rewriting, or trying a new approach

---

Academic Vocabulary

Read each word with students and discuss its meaning.

torrent (p. 63) • a flood of water or other liquid

tumult (p. 67) • noisy confusion

ransom (p. 88) • money or goods that are demanded in exchange for setting someone free

upbraided (p. 91) • scolded

FIRST READ ▸ **Think Through the Text**

Have students cite text evidence and draw inferences to answer questions.

p. 60 • *What does Nestor ask Patroclus to do?* Nestor sends Patroclus to ask Achilles if Patroclus can wear his armor and lead his men. *Why does Nestor think that this will help?* He thinks the Trojans will think Achilles has returned to fight and be afraid because Achilles is known to be a fierce warrior. **RL 3**

pp. 74–81 • *Why does Achilles rejoin the battle?* Patroclus died, and Achilles wants revenge for his death. *What prediction does Hector make as he dies?* He tells Achilles that Paris will slay him. **RL 3**

pp. 88–89 • *So far Achilles has been a fierce warrior and rarely changes his mind about his decisions. How does he show that he can be sympathetic to others?* He listens to Thetis and stops dishonoring Hector's body. He allows Hector's father to arrange for a proper burial for his son. **RL 3**

SECOND READ ▸ **Analyze the Text**

- *On page 69, Achilles prays to Zeus to strengthen Patroclus and send him back unharmed. Which part of the prayer does Zeus answer?* Zeus strengthens Patroclus, but Patroclus dies in battle, so he does not answer the second part. *Why does Zeus not answer the second part of Achilles's prayer? Use your knowledge of story events to make an inference.* Patroclus is fighting for the Greeks, and Zeus is helping the Trojans. **RL 1**

- Reread page 90. Tell students that many of the events in Greek epic poems are foretold, or predicted, before they occur. *What is likely to happen to Achilles? How do you know?* Achilles will die in battle. The text says that Achilles knows that his own father will soon have cause for grieving. **RL 1, Grade 8 RL 9**

- Reread page 91. Ask: *How does Helen feel about her decision to leave Menelaus and go with Paris? Cite evidence from the text to support your answer.* She regrets it. She says that she wishes she had died before those years began. **RL 1**

Academic Vocabulary

Read each word with students and discuss its meaning.

omen (p. 93) • a sign or warning about the future

belittle (p. 115) • say that something has little value

amends (p. 120) • corrections for errors or wrongdoing

foreknowledge (p. 133) • something known ahead of time

FIRST READ ## Think Through the Text

Have students cite text evidence and draw inferences to answer questions.

pp. 93–104 • *Who is the beggar?* Odysseus *What does he do?* He steals the Luck of Troy. *How did this affect the Trojans?* It made them feel as though their last hope was gone. ▬RL 3

p. 112 • *How does Achilles meet the end that has been predicted for him?* Paris shoots him in the ankle. *Why is this the only spot that will kill Achilles?* It is where his mother held him when she dipped him in the protective River Styx. It is the only spot that is unprotected. ▬RL 3

pp. 134–135 • *Ask: How do the Greeks eventually defeat the Trojans?* They hide in a wooden horse. When night comes, they storm the city. ▬RL 3

SECOND READ ## Analyze the Text

• Reread page 133. Ask: *How do Cassandra's warnings follow the pattern of other events in this story?* Cassandra warns that the horse would be the death of Troy, but no one listens. Her prediction is correct. Point out that in myths, events are foretold and then come to pass. Nothing the characters do changes the outcome. ▬Grade 8 RL 9

• *What role does trickery and deception play in the Greeks' eventual victory?* Odysseus disguises himself as a beggar and steals the Luck of Troy, which lowers the Trojan morale. The Greeks build a wooden horse and hide warriors inside while the others pretend to sail home. The Trojans let their guard down, and the Greeks defeat them. ▬RL 3

• *At the beginning of the story, Menelaus is angry because Helen has left him. How is this problem resolved at the end of the story?* Helen returns as a queen to the ship of Menelaus. ▬RL 3

Independent/Self-Selected Reading

If students have demonstrated comprehension of *Black Ships Before Troy* have them read other myths to practice skills. Suggested titles:

• *D'Aulaire's Book of Greek Myths* by Ingri and Edgar Parin d'Aulaire

• *In Search of a Homeland: The Story of the Aeneid* by Penelope Lively
▬RL 10

Performance Task

WRITE & PRESENT

1. Have small groups summarize the plot of the story, discussing the series of events that leads the story to its resolution. Guide them to discuss the structure of myths, in which important events are foretold and then come to pass. ▬RL 3

2. Individual students write a summary of the story, describing the problem and the events that lead to its resolution. Ask them to cite examples of events that are foretold and then occur. ▬W 2

3. Have groups reconvene to share and edit their writing. ▬W 5

4. Students present their final summaries to their classmates. ▬SL 4

5. Students turn in their final drafts to the teacher.

See Copying Masters, pp. 164–171

STUDENT CHECKLIST

Writing

☑ Write a summary of the story, describing the problem and the events that lead to its resolution.

☑ Use appropriate transitions to clarify the relationship between story events.

☑ Cite examples from the story of events that are foretold and then occur.

Speaking & Listening

☑ Participate effectively in a collaborative discussion.

☑ Sequence events and ideas logically.

☑ Speak clearly at an understandable pace.

OBJECTIVES

- Analyze how elements of a drama interact
- Analyze how the author builds suspense
- Cite specific textual evidence to support analysis

Sorry, Wrong Number is broken into three instructional segments.

SEGMENTS

Options for Reading

Independent Students read the text independently or with a partner and then answer questions posed by the teacher.

Supported Students read a segment and answer questions with teacher support.

 **Common Core Connection**

Grade 6: RL 3 describe how a story or drama's plot unfolds and how characters respond or change

Grade 7: RL 3 analyze how particular elements of a story or drama interact

Grade 8: RL 3 analyze how dialogue or incidents in a story or drama propel action, reveal a character, or provoke a decision

Grades 6–8: RL 1 cite textual evidence to support analysis of what the text says explicitly as well as inferences drawn

Sorry, Wrong Number

by Lucille Fletcher

SUMMARY Bedridden Mrs. Stevenson is trying to call her husband, but the number keeps ringing busy. Finally, she asks an operator to try the number. When the operator connects her, she overhears two men plotting a murder. As Mrs. Stevenson desperately tries to convince the operators and police of the impending murder, she realizes that she is the intended victim.

ABOUT THE AUTHOR **Lucille Fletcher** was born in 1912. After graduating from Vassar College, she began typing up radio plays. She soon decided that she could write plays that were as good as the ones she was typing. *Sorry, Wrong Number* first aired on the radio in 1943.

Discuss Genre and Set Purpose

DRAMA Display the book, and read the title together. Show students the text features, such as the cast of characters, the technical staff, and the stage directions. Discuss how students can tell this text is a drama.

SET PURPOSE Help students set a purpose for reading, such as to find out how the playwright uses setting and dialogue to create suspense.

⚠ TEXT COMPLEXITY RUBRIC

Overall Text Complexity		*Sorry, Wrong Number* DRAMA SIMPLE
Quantitative Measures	Lexile	N/A
	Guided Reading Level	N/A
Qualitative Measures	Text Structure	simple, linear chronology
	Language Conventionality and Clarity	few unfamiliar or academic words
	Knowledge Demands	situation includes unfamiliar aspects
	Purpose/Levels of Meaning	single level of complex meaning

Academic Vocabulary

Read each word with students and discuss its meaning.

querulous (p. 7) • complaining

neurotic (p. 7) • abnormally anxious

imperious (p. 8) • bossy

high-strung (p. 11) • very nervous, easily upset

 ENGLISH LANGUAGE LEARNERS

Use Demonstration

Use gestures and facial expressions to demonstrate the character's actions and feelings as you read aloud the dialogue. Have students answer questions to demonstrate understanding. For example: *Does Mrs. Stevenson hear men talking about murder?* yes *What do the men plan to do?* murder someone *How does Mrs. Stevenson feel? Show me or tell me.*

FIRST READ ‖ **Think Through the Text**

Have students cite text evidence and draw inferences to answer questions.

pp. 7–8 • *Who is Mrs. Stevenson trying to reach?* She is trying to reach her husband. *What does she overhear when the operator rings the number?* She overhears two men planning a murder. ⬛ RL 3

pp. 10–11 • *Why can't the operators help Mrs. Stevenson?* The first operator can't figure out what Mrs. Stevenson wants her to do. The Chief Operator tells her that the call can't be traced if it has been disconnected. They also can't trace it because she is a private individual rather than the police. ⬛ RL 1

SECOND READ ‖ **Analyze the Text**

- Review page 7. Ask: *What is the setting of this play?* The setting is Mrs. Stevenson's bedroom. It is mostly dark except for one lamp. *How does the setting create a sense of suspense?* Mrs. Stevenson is alone in the dark. She seems to be sick and confined to her bed. The dark, lonely setting and Mrs. Stevenson's helplessness create a feeling of suspense. ⬛ RL 3

- Reread page 8 with students. Explain that one way an author can create tension is by giving some characters more knowledge than others. Ask: *Why is it important that Mrs. Stevenson can hear the criminals but they can't hear her?* Mrs. Stevenson has knowledge of the potential murder, but no power to do anything about it. The imbalance between what Mrs. Stevenson knows and what she can do about it creates tension. ⬛ RL 3

RESPOND TO SEGMENT 1

 Classroom Collaboration

Have partners summarize what they have read so far. Tell them to ask questions about anything they don't understand.

Use Comprehensible Input

Students may need support for idiomatic expressions, such as *tied up in red tape.* Explain that this means being made to follow a lot of rules that make things happen very slowly. Ask: *What does Mrs. Stevenson want to report?* a murder *Are people making it easy or hard for her to report it?* hard Yes, she is getting tied up in red tape. It is hard for her to report the murder.

RESPOND TO SEGMENT 2

 Classroom Collaboration

Have groups summarize what they have read so far and ask questions about what they don't understand.

 Common Core Connection

Grade 6: RL 2 determine a theme or central idea of a text/provide a summary; **RL 3** describe how a story's or drama's plot unfolds and how characters respond or change; **SL 4** present claims and findings, sequence ideas, and use details to accentuate main ideas or themes/use appropriate eye contact, volume, and pronunciation

Grade 7: RL 2 determine a theme or central idea of a text/analyze its development/provide a summary; **RL 3** analyze how particular elements of a story or drama interact

Grade 8: RL 2 determine a theme or central idea of a text/analyze its development/provide a summary; **RL 3** analyze how dialogue or incidents in a story or drama propel action, reveal a character, or provoke a decision

Grades 7–8: SL 4 present claims and findings, emphasizing points in a focused, coherent manner

Grades 6–8: RL 1 cite textual evidence that most strongly supports analysis of what text says explicitly as well as inferences drawn; **RL 10** read and comprehend literature **W 2** write informative/explanatory texts; **W 5** develop and strengthen writing by planning, revising, editing, rewriting, or trying a new approach.

Academic Vocabulary

Read each word with students and discuss its meaning.

double-takes (p. 12) • delayed reactions to an unusual remark or circumstance

stolidly (p. 13) • showing little emotion

high-handed (p. 13) • showing no regard for the concerns or feelings of others

FIRST READ **Think Through the Text**

Have students cite text evidence and draw inferences to answer questions.

pp. 12–13 • *Summarize what Mrs. Stevenson tells Duffy.* She tells him that two men are going to murder a woman at 11:15 at a house near a bridge. They are going to take her rings and bracelets and use a knife. RL 2

pp. 14–15 • *What does Duffy tell Mrs. Stevenson after listening to her talk about the call she overheard?* He says that maybe she has reason to believe that someone is planning to murder her. *Does Mrs. Stevenson agree?* No. She says that the only people she sees all day are her maid and her husband. Her maid is too lazy, and her husband adores her. RL 3

p. 15 • *Does Duffy plan to act on Mrs. Stevenson's call? How do you know?* Probably not. He looks at the pie on his desk and says that he has other matters that need his immediate attention. RL 1

SECOND READ **Analyze the Text**

• Review pages 12–13. Ask: *How does the dialogue between Duffy and Mrs. Stevenson create tension?* Mrs. Stevenson is annoyed and anxious to communicate her information. Duffy is not taking her seriously. He is relaxed and more interested in eating his lunch. Mrs. Stevenson demands an immediate response, and Duffy just tells her that they'll take care of it and not to worry. The tension mounts as Mrs. Stevenson grows more determined to convince Duffy of what she overheard. RL 3

• Ask: *What similarities are there between the location Mrs. Stevenson overheard the murderers talking about and where she lives?* She lives near a bridge, near Second Avenue, and has a private policeman on her street. *How does this add to the suspense?* Mrs. Stevenson grows more anxious as she realizes the coincidence. RL 3

Academic Vocabulary

Read each word with students and discuss its meaning.

catechizing (p. 19) • questioning

lethargic (p. 20) • lacking energy

FIRST READ Think Through the Text

Have students cite text evidence and draw inferences to answer questions.

p. 17 • *Who is trying to reach Mrs. Stevenson? What is the message?* *Western Union is trying to reach Mrs. Stevenson. They have a telegram for her that her husband is going to Boston on urgent business.* ◼RL 1

pp. 18–19 • *After Mrs. Stevenson can't reach her husband, what does she do next? Why?* *She calls Henchley Hospital. She wants a trained nurse to keep her company so that she won't have to be alone.* ◼RL 3

pp. 20–21 • *What does Mrs. Stevenson realize while she is on the phone with the hospital?* *Someone is downstairs and has picked up her phone. What happens to Mrs. Stevenson? George murders her.* ◼RL 3

SECOND READ Analyze the Text

• Review pages 16–17. Ask: *What problems is Mrs. Stevenson having with the telephone? What feeling does this create?* *The phone rings busy when Mrs. Stevenson tries to reach her husband. Then Mrs. Stevenson's phone keeps ringing, but no one is on the other end. She feels isolated, and the constant ringing of the telephone adds to the edgy mood. She can't connect to anyone in the outside world.* ◼RL 3

• Guide students to summarize the dialogue. Then ask: *What does Mrs. Stevenson's dialogue reveal about her mental state?* *She is isolated and feels superior to others. Her anxiety and inability to resolve the problem is making her lose control. She says that if someone doesn't come at once she is afraid she'll go out of her mind.* ◼RL 3

• Reread page 21. Ask: *How does the setting add to the suspense of the ending?* *There are only shadows, so readers can't really "see" or "hear" what is happening. This adds to the suspense as readers fill in the blanks and realize that what Mrs. Stevenson overheard is coming to pass.* ◼RL 3

Independent/Self-Selected Reading

If students have demonstrated comprehension of *Sorry, Wrong Number*, have them read other texts to practice skills. Suggested titles:

• *The Telltale Heart* by Edgar Allan Poe

• *And Then There Were None: A Mystery Play Script in Three Acts* by Agatha Christie ◼RL 10

Performance Task

WRITE & PRESENT

1. Have small groups discuss how the playwright uses the setting and dialogue to add dramatic tension to *Sorry, Wrong Number.* ◼RL 3

2. Individual students write an expository text that analyzes the use of setting and dialogue to create tension and give specific examples. Tell them to cite particular lines of dialogue or aspects of the setting to support their analysis. ◼W 2

3. Students work with partners to share and edit their work. ◼W 5

4. Have students present their work to the class. ◼SL 4

See Copying Masters, pp. 164–171.

STUDENT CHECKLIST

Writing

☑ Write an expository text that analyzes the playwright's use of setting and dialogue.

☑ Cite particular lines of dialogue or aspects of the setting to support analysis.

☑ Use correct language conventions.

Speaking & Listening

☑ Participate effectively in a collaborative discussion.

☑ Present analysis, sharing lines of dialogue or elements of the setting that add tension.

☑ Use language that is appropriate for the purpose.

OBJECTIVES

- Analyze how elements of a drama interact
- Analyze how lines of dialogue reveal aspects of a character
- Cite specific textual evidence to support analysis

The Diary of Anne Frank is broken into three instructional segments.

Options for Reading

Independent Students read the text independently or with a partner and then answer questions posed by the teacher.

Supported Students read a segment and answer questions with teacher support.

COMMON CORE Common Core Connection

Grade 7: RL 3 analyze how particular elements of a story or drama interact; **RL 5** analyze how a drama's or poem's form or structure contributes to its meaning

Grades 6– 8: RL 1 cite textual evidence that most strongly supports analysis of what text says explicitly as well as inferences drawn

The Diary of Anne Frank

by Frances Goodrich and Albert Hackett

SUMMARY This play adapts the diary of Anne Frank, a Dutch Jewish teenager. Anne Frank's diary details the two years her family spent hiding from the Nazis in a secret annex before eventually being captured.

ABOUT THE AUTHORS Frances Goodrich and Albert Hackett were both stage actors before they met in 1927 and began working together as a writing team. After writing many successful films, they began adapting *The Diary of Anne Frank* for the stage in 1950. The play opened on Broadway in 1955. It won a Tony Award and a Pulitzer Prize.

Discuss Genre and Set Purpose

DRAMA Display the book, and read the title together. Show students the text features of a drama, such as the cast of characters, the setting, the division into acts, and the stage directions. Discuss with students how they can tell this text is a drama.

SET PURPOSE Help students set a purpose for reading, such as to recognize how particular lines of dialogue reveal aspects of a character.

TEXT COMPLEXITY RUBRIC

Overall Text Complexity		The Diary of Anne Frank DRAMA
		COMPLEX
Quantitative Measures	Lexile	N/A
	Guided Reading Level	N/A
Qualitative Measures	Text Structure	somewhat complex story concepts
	Language Conventionality and Clarity	some unfamiliar language
	Knowledge Demands	distinctly unfamiliar situation
	Purpose/Levels of Meaning	multiple levels of meaning

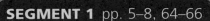

SEGMENT 1 pp. 5–8, 64–66

Academic Vocabulary

Read each word with students and discuss its meaning.

enhance (p. 5) • to make something better

authenticity (p. 5) • realness; genuineness

annex (p. 7) • a smaller building connected to a main building

---

FIRST READ ## Think Through the Text

Have students cite text evidence and draw inferences to answer questions.

p. 5 • *When should the reader pay close attention?* when Anne speaks directly to the audience and when she is heard in voiceover Grade 7 RL 5

p. 7 • *Who is the main character of this play?* Anne Frank *Where and when does the story take place?* It takes place in an annex on top of an office building in Amsterdam during the years of World War II. ⬤RL 1

SECOND READ ## Analyze the Text

- Reread page 5. Ask: *How do the authors show that they care about authenticity?* They recommend that the actors avoid using German or Dutch accents because it diminishes authenticity. However, they do emphasize the importance of proper pronunciation of foreign words and phrases. ⬤RL 1

- Ask: *How do the authors show that they care about the historical accuracy of the play?* They recommend that the historical sound materials and effects compiled for the Broadway production be used. ⬤RL 1

- Reread the list of sound effects on page 66. Ask: *How do the sound effects help you picture the setting?* Sample answer: Hitler's voice; sirens, trains, bombs, gunfire, and screams all show that this takes place during World War II. They add suspense. Grade 7 RL 3

Domain Specific Vocabulary

intermission (p. 5) • a short break in a play or performance

monologue (p. 5) • a long speech made by one person

ELL **ENGLISH LANGUAGE LEARNERS**

Use Visuals

Use visuals or demonstration to illustrate the items on the Property List. As you present visuals or demonstrations, have students repeat the names. Have them use the items to respond to questions such as: *What would you carry in the rain?* an umbrella *What would you write with?* a fountain pen

---

RESPOND TO SEGMENT 1

Classroom Collaboration

Have partners summarize what they have read so far. Tell them to ask questions about anything they don't understand.

ENGLISH LANGUAGE LEARNERS

Use Comprehensible Input

Restate text in simpler language. For example, on page 10, restate *embrace* as *hug*. Have students repeat after you. Ask: *Does Anne hug Miep? yes That's right. Anne _____ Miep. embraces*

RESPOND TO SEGMENT 2

 Classroom Collaboration

Have small groups work together to summarize what they have read so far. Have them ask questions about what they don't understand.

 Common Core Connection

Grade 6: RL 2 determine a theme or central idea of a text/provide a summary; **RL 3** describe how a story's or drama's plot unfolds and how characters respond or change; **SL 4** present claims and findings, sequence ideas, and use details to accentuate main ideas or themes/use appropriate eye contact, volume, and pronunciation

Grade 7: RL 2 determine a theme or central idea of a text/analyze its development/provide a summary; **RL 3** analyze how particular elements of a story or drama interact;

Grade 8 RL 2 determine theme or central idea of a text/analyze development/provide a summary; **RL 3** analyze how dialogue or incidents in a story or drama propel action, reveal a character, or provoke a decision

Grades 7–8: SL 4 present claims and findings, emphasizing points in a focused, coherent manner

Grades 6–8: RL 1 cite textual evidence that most strongly supports analysis of what text says explicitly as well as inferences drawn; **RL 10** read and comprehend literature; **W 2** write informative/explanatory texts; **W 5** develop and strengthen writing by planning, revising, editing, rewriting, or trying a new approach.

Academic Vocabulary

Read each word with students and discuss its meaning.

branded (p. 15) • marked with a symbol

inconceivable (p. 26) • impossible to imagine

impenetrable (p. 40) • not able to be entered

implore (p. 40) • beg

FIRST READ ## Think Through the Text

Have students cite text evidence and draw inferences to answer questions.

p. 10 • *What was life like for the Jewish people when the Germans arrived?* They had to give up their businesses. They couldn't use street-cars or go to the theatre or movies. They had to turn in their bicycles and couldn't go to the beach, swimming pool, or library. They had to wear a yellow star to show they were Jewish. **RL 1**

pp. 9–11 • *Why does Anne's family have to go into hiding? Where do they go?* Her sister Margot was ordered to go to a transit camp. The family is hiding so that she won't be taken to a concentration camp. They go to the "Secret Annex." **RL 1**

p. 28 • *What is happening to the Jewish people in Amsterdam? How does Anne feel about this news?* Jewish people are disappearing. They are being taken away on trains. Anne is very upset, especially when she hears that her friend Hanneli has been taken away. **RL 1**

SECOND READ ## Analyze the Text

- Reread pages 9–10. Ask: *How does the description of the setting set the stage for the events to come?* Sample answer: *It reveals the silence and secrecy in which the family must live. It shows the relationship between the family members—Margot and Mrs. Frank are close, as are Anne and her father.* **Grade 7 RL 3**

- Review pages 9–12. Ask: *How does Anne feel about hiding at first?* She thinks it will be fun, like a romantic and dangerous adventure. She laughs and skips around the room. *What does Anne's response to the situation tell you about her?* She is an optimist, willing to see the positives in a negative situation. **RL 3**

- Reread Anne's lines on pages 17 and 18. Ask: *How have Anne's feelings about hiding changed? Give examples.* She is frightened by the silence. Every time she hears a noise, she thinks the Nazis are coming. She feels like a songbird whose wings have been ripped off. She wants to be free but is also grateful to be hiding. *Do the other characters know what Anne is thinking? How do you know?* No, only the audience knows. These lines are spoken to the audience, not to the other characters. **RL 3**

Academic Vocabulary

Read each word with students and discuss its meaning.

plagued (p. 41) • bothered or annoyed by

exquisite (p. 42) • very beautiful

liberators (p. 60) • people who free others

FIRST READ 🟢 Think Through the Text

Have students cite text evidence and draw inferences to answer questions.

p. 41 • *How does the play show the passing of time?* Anne says that it is Saturday, January 1, 1944, and the start of a new year. She says they have been hiding for one year, five months, and twenty-five days. ▬ RL 1

p. 51 • *Why is Anne inspired to start revising her diary?* She hears a radio broadcast that says that history can't be written from official documents alone. They need diaries and letters to show what people have endured. *What does Anne hope to achieve with her diary?* She wants to be useful and bring enjoyment. She wants to go on living after she dies. ▬ RL 1

pp. 61–62 • *Summarize what happens to Anne and her family.* They are taken by the Nazis and sent to concentration camps. Only Anne's father and Anne's diary survive. ▬ RL 2

SECOND READ 🟢 Analyze the Text

- Review page 53. *How has Anne changed from the beginning of the play?* She is growing up. She doesn't want to go back to the superficial girl that she once was. *Why is writing important to Anne? Cite details from the dialogue.* Anne says that without writing, she would suffocate. She has to express what she thinks and feels. ▬ RL 3

- Ask: *What do Anne's voiceovers reveal about her? Cite specific details from the play.* Anne is an optimist. She says she still believes, in spite of everything, that people are truly good at heart. She also says that it is utterly impossible to build her life on a foundation of fear. ▬ RL 3

- Reread the last line of the play on page 63. Ask: *Did Anne's dream of her diary living on after she died come true? How do you know?* Yes. Her diary survived and has been read around the world and turned into plays, such as this one. Her life story is still being told. ▬ RL 1

Independent/Self-Selected Reading

If students have demonstrated comprehension of *The Diary of Anne Frank*, have them read other texts to practice skills. Suggested titles:

- *The Diary of Anne Frank* by Anne Frank

- *War Stories for Readers Theatre: World War II* by Suzanne I. Barchers
▬ RL 10

WRITE & PRESENT

1. Have small groups discuss the character of Anne Frank and support their analysis of her traits with examples from her dialogue. ▬ RL 1

2. Individual students write an expository paragraph that analyzes the character of Anne Frank and supports the analysis with particular lines of dialogue. ▬ W 2

3. Students work with partners to share and edit their work. ▬ W 5

4. Have students present their work to the class. ▬ SL 4

See Copying Masters, pp. 164–171.

STUDENT CHECKLIST

Writing

☑ Write expository text that analyzes the character of Anne Frank.

☑ Cite particular lines of dialogue to support analysis.

☑ Use correct language conventions.

Speaking & Listening

☑ Participate effectively in a collaborative discussion.

☑ Present analysis, sharing lines of dialogue that reveal specific character traits.

☑ Use language that is appropriate for the purpose.

▶ OBJECTIVES

- Identify the characteristics of a narrative poem
- Analyze the structural elements of a poem
- Compare and contrast a poem with a media version of the same event
- Analyze text using text evidence

"Paul Revere's Ride"
by Henry Wadsworth Longfellow

SUMMARY This narrative poem tells the story of Paul Revere's famous midnight ride to warn the colonists that the British were coming.

ABOUT THE POET Henry Wadsworth Longfellow was born on February 27, 1807, in Portland, Maine. He was the most popular American poet of his time. As the country approached the Civil War, Longfellow wrote "Paul Revere's Ride" to inspire courage in the American people.

Discuss Genre and Set Purpose

POETRY Display the poem, and discuss the elements that characterize it as a narrative poem. Explain that this text is a narrative poem because it tells a story.

TEXT FOCUS: Structural Elements Guide students to explore the poem's structural elements: a poem is arranged in lines that are grouped in stanzas that build on each other. Many poems rhyme and have a regular rhythm where the syllables follow a metered pattern.

SET PURPOSE Have students set a purpose for reading, such as to find out whether Paul Revere accomplished his mission. Tell them that they will compare and contrast the poem with a multimedia dramatization of the event.

Options for Reading

Independent Students read the poem independently or with a partner and then answer questions posed by the teacher.

Supported Students read several lines and answer questions with teacher support.

 Common Core Connection

Grade 6: RL 2 determine a theme or central idea of a text/provide a summary; **RL 4** determine the meaning of words and phrases, including figurative and connotative meanings/analyze impact of word choice; **RL 7** compare and contrast the experience of reading to listening or viewing; **SL 4** present claims and findings, sequence ideas, and use details to accentuate main ideas or themes

Grade 7: RL 4 determine the meaning of words and phrases as they are used in a text/ analyze impact of rhymes and other repetitions of sound; **RL 7** compare and contrast a written story, drama, or poem to its audio, filmed, staged, or multimedia version

Grade 8: RL 4 determine the meaning of words and phrases as they are used in a text/ analyze impact of word choices

Grades 7–8: RL 2 determine a theme or central idea of a text/analyze its development/ provide summary; **SL 4** present claims and findings, emphasizing points in a focused, coherent manner

Grades 6–8: RL 1 cite textual evidence to support analysis of what the text says explicitly as well as inferences drawn; **RL 10** read and comprehend literature; **W 2** write informative/ explanatory texts; **W 5** develop and strengthen writing by planning, revising, editing, rewriting, or trying a new approach; **SL 6** adapt speech to contexts and tasks, demonstrating command of formal English when appropriate

▲ TEXT COMPLEXITY RUBRIC		"Paul Revere's Ride" POETRY
Overall Text Complexity		COMPLEX
Quantitative Measures	Lexile	N/A
	Guided Reading Level	N/A
Qualitative Measures	Text Structure	less familiar poetic structure
	Language Conventionality and Clarity	increased unfamiliar language
	Knowledge Demands	some cultural and literary knowledge useful
	Purpose/Levels of Meaning	single level of complex meaning

Academic Vocabulary

Read each word with students and discuss its meaning.

muster (line 27) • to gather in a group before a battle

impetuous (line 62) • moving quickly and without thinking

aghast (line 99) • filled with shock

FIRST READ ## Think Through the Text

Have students cite text evidence and draw inferences to answer questions.

- *What does Paul Revere tell his friend to do?* *Hang one lantern if the British are coming by land and two if they are coming by sea.* ◼ RL 1

- *How would you summarize this poem?* *Paul Revere warns the people of Middlesex that the British are coming so they will be ready for battle.* ◼ RL 2

SECOND READ ## Analyze the Text

- Review stanza 1. Ask: *Does the speaker want to give historical facts or tell an inspiring story? How do you know?* *The speaker wants to tell an inspiring story. The speaker says, "Listen my children and you shall hear," which suggests that he is going to tell a story.* ◼ RL 1

- Reread stanzas 8 and 9. Ask: *How does the rhythm of the poem change between these stanzas?* *At the beginning of stanza 8, the rhythm is slow and ticking. Then the rhythm begins to pick up. By stanza 9, the pace matches Paul Revere's haste to start his journey.* ◼ RL 4

- Have students visit http://www.paulreverehouse.org/ride/ to view a multimedia dramatization of Paul Revere's ride. Guide them to compare and contrast the techniques used in "Paul Revere's Ride" with the techniques used in the digital map. Discuss what students found most effective about each medium. ◼ Grades 6–7 RL 7

☑ Practice Fluency

EMPHASIZE EXPRESSION Explain that the poet's choice of punctuation can influence expressive reading. In "Paul Revere's Ride," the exclamation points suggest lines that should be read with an excited expression. Echo-read the poem with students, modeling appropriate expression. ◼ SL 6

Independent/Self-Selected Reading

If students have already demonstrated comprehension of "Paul Revere's Ride," have them read other poems to practice skills. Suggested titles:

- *America at War: Poems* selected by Lee Bennett Hopkins

- *Lives: Poems About Famous Americans* selected by Lee Bennett Hopkins
  ◼ RL 10

WRITE & PRESENT

1. Have small groups discuss the effect that "Paul Revere's Ride" had on them and the effect they experienced from the interactive digital map.
   ◼ RL 1, Grades 6–7 RL 7

2. Individual students write an essay that compares and contrasts the techniques used in "Paul Revere's Ride" and the interactive digital map, and the effects the techniques created. ◼ W 2

3. Students work with partners to share and edit their work. ◼ W 5

4. Have students share their essays with the class. ◼ SL 4

See Copying Masters, pp. 164–171.

STUDENT CHECKLIST

Writing

☑ Write a paragraph that compares the techniques used in "Paul Revere's Ride" with those in the interactive digital map.

☑ Develop and strengthen writing by revising and editing.

☑ Use correct language conventions.

Speaking & Listening

☑ Participate effectively in a collaborative discussion.

☑ Present findings, emphasizing points in a focused, coherent manner.

☑ Present work using appropriate eye contact and volume, and clear pronunciation.

OBJECTIVES

- Explain the meaning of poetry
- Examine symbols, allusions, and analogies in poetry
- Analyze the impact of a poet's word choice
- Analyze text using text evidence

Options for Reading

Independent Students read the poem independently or with a partner and then answer questions posed by the teacher.

Supported Students read several lines and answer questions with teacher support.

 **Common Core Connection**

Grade 6: RL 2 determine a theme or central idea of a text/provide a summary; **RL 4** determine the meaning of words and phrases, including figurative and connotative meanings/analyze impact of word choice; **SL 4** present claims and findings, sequence ideas, and use details to accentuate main ideas or themes

Grade 7: RL 4 determine the meaning of words and phrases as they are used in a text/analyze impact of rhymes and other repetitions of sound

Grade 8: RL 4 determine the meaning of words and phrases as they are used in a text/analyze impact of word choices

Grades 7–8: RL 2 determine a theme or central idea of a text/analyze its development/provide summary; **SL 4** present claims and findings, emphasizing points in a focused, coherent manner

Grades 6–8: RL 1 cite textual evidence to support analysis of what the text says explicitly as well as inferences drawn; **RL 10** read and comprehend literature; **W 4** produce writing in which development, organization, and style are appropriate to task, purpose, and audience; **W 5** develop and strengthen writing by planning, revising, editing, rewriting, or trying a new approach; **SL 6** adapt speech to contexts and tasks, demonstrating command of formal English when appropriate

"O Captain! My Captain!"

by Walt Whitman

SUMMARY Walt Whitman wrote this poem to express his shock and sadness after Abraham Lincoln's death. In this poem, Lincoln is symbolized by the Captain, and the ship stands for the United States.

ABOUT THE POET Walt Whitman is considered one of America's most significant poets. Despite their present-day popularity, Whitman's poems received little recognition during his lifetime.

Discuss Genre and Set Purpose

POETRY Share the summary above. Explain that this poem is an elegy, a sad poem written in honor of the dead. Discuss Abraham Lincoln and the Civil War as necessary for understanding this poem.

TEXT FOCUS: Allusion and Analogy Discuss with students that a poem may refer, or allude, to other people or events. A reader must be familiar with the allusion to understand the poem. An analogy is an extended metaphor that gives several points of comparison.

SET PURPOSE Have students set a purpose for reading, such as to uncover the poem's allusions and analogies and analyze the impact of the poet's word choice.

TEXT COMPLEXITY RUBRIC

Overall Text Complexity		"O Captain! My Captain!" POETRY
		MORE COMPLEX
Quantitative Measures	Lexile	N/A
	Guided Reading Level	N/A
Qualitative Measures	Text Structure	simple, familiar poetic structure
	Language Conventionality and Clarity	figurative, symbolic language
	Knowledge Demands	cultural and literary knowledge useful
	Purpose/Levels of Meaning	multiple levels of meaning

Academic Vocabulary

Read each word with students and discuss its meaning.

exulting (line 3) • praising; rejoicing

vessel (line 4) • a large ship

mournful (line 22) • filled with sadness or grief

FIRST READ ## Think Through the Text

Have students cite text evidence and draw inferences to answer questions.

- *Who does the Captain represent?* Abraham Lincoln *What does the ship represent?* The ship represents the United States. ▬RL 2

- *What has happened to the Captain?* He has died. ▬RL 1

SECOND READ ## Analyze the Text

- *This poem describes the death of a ship's captain. What event in history does this allude to?* the assassination of Lincoln ▬RL 4

- *Why does the poet compare Lincoln to a captain?* The captain of a ship steers a boat, sometimes through rough waters, just as Lincoln led the country through a difficult war and time in history. ▬RL 4

- Reread line 2 with students. Say: *We know that the poet uses the ship to symbolize the United States. He says "The ship has weather'd every rack, the prize we sought is won." What is he alluding to?* He is alluding to the end of the Civil War. ▬RL 4

- Reread line 4 with students. *How does the word* grim *express the overall mood and tone of the poem?* Grim means "very serious" and contributes to the serious mood and tone of the poem. ▬RL 4

☑ Practice Fluency

EMPHASIZE EXPRESSION Point out that in line 1, the speaker is excited because the fearful trip is over. In line 5, he realizes that the Captain is dead. Discuss how the expression might change when reading these lines. Then have students echo-read the poem with you using appropriate expression. ▬SL 6

Independent/Self-Selected Reading

If students have already demonstrated comprehension of "O Captain! My Captain!," have them read other poems to practice skills. Suggested titles:

- *Celebrate America: In Poetry and Art* by Nora Panzer

- *My America: A Poetry Atlas of the United States* selected by Lee Bennett Hopkins ▬RL 10

WRITE & PRESENT

1. Have small groups discuss "O Captain! My Captain!" and how understanding the allusions, analogies, and word choice helps them figure out the topic, mood, and tone. ▬RL 4

2. Individual students write three paragraphs analyzing how the author used allusion, analogies, and word choice to write an elegy for Abraham Lincoln. ▬W 4

3. Students work with partners to share and edit their work. ▬W 5

4. Have students share their work with the class ▬SL 4

See Copying Masters, pp. 164–171.

STUDENT CHECKLIST

Writing

☑ Write paragraphs that analyze the poet's use of allusions, analogies, and word choice.

☑ Explain how they used the allusions, analogies, and word choice to "decode" the poem.

☑ Use correct language conventions.

Speaking & Listening

☑ Participate effectively in a collaborative discussion.

☑ Ask and answer questions about details in a poem.

☑ Present work using appropriate eye contact and volume, and clear pronunciation.

▶ OBJECTIVES

- Identify the characteristics of poems
- Explore the use of onomatopoeia
- Analyze the poet's use of invented language
- Analyze text using text evidence

Options for Reading

Independent Students read the poem independently or with a partner and then answer questions posed by the teacher.

Supported Students read several lines and answer questions with teacher support.

 Common Core Connection

Grade 6: RL 2 determine a theme or central idea of a text/provide a summary; **RL 4** determine the meaning of words and phrases, including figurative and connotative meanings/analyze impact of word choice; **RL 5** analyze how a sentence, chapter, scene or stanza fits in the overall structure; **SL 4** present claims and findings, sequence ideas, and use details to accentuate main ideas or themes

Grade 7: RL 4 determine the meaning of words and phrases as they are used in a text/analyze impact of rhymes and other repetitions of sound; **RL 5** analyze how a drama's or poem's form or structure contributes to its meaning

Grade 8: RL 4 determine the meaning of words and phrases as they are used in a text/analyze impact of word choices

Grades 7–8: RL 2 determine a theme or central idea of a text/analyze its development/provide summary; **SL 4** present claims and findings, emphasizing points in a focused, coherent manner

Grades 6–8: RL 1 cite textual evidence to support analysis of what the text says explicitly as well as inferences drawn; **RL 10** read and comprehend literature; **W 4** produce writing in which development, organization, and style are appropriate to task, purpose, and audience; **W 5** develop and strengthen writing by planning, revising, editing, rewriting, or trying a new approach; **SL 6** adapt speech to contexts and tasks, demonstrating command of formal English when appropriate

"Jabberwocky"
by Lewis Carroll

SUMMARY "Jabberwocky" is one of many nonsense poems in Lewis Carroll's novel *Through the Looking-Glass*, the sequel to *Alice's Adventures in Wonderland*. Carroll uses made-up words to tell the story of a boy who kills a fierce monster–the Jabberwock.

ABOUT THE POET **Lewis Carroll** was born Charles Lutwidge Dodgson in Cheshire, England, in 1832. He was a renowned Victorian author and poet. He is best known for his novel *Alice's Adventures in Wonderland* and its sequel, *Through the Looking-Glass*.

Discuss Genre and Set Purpose

POETRY Display the poem and discuss the elements that characterize it as a poem. Explain that this text is a nonsense poem because it uses invented language.

TEXT FOCUS: Onomatopoeia Discuss that onomatopoeia is a literary device in which words, such as *bang* and *buzz,* sound like their meanings. Poets can also invent words to express precise meaning. These words help readers hear, as well as see, what's happening in the poem.

SET PURPOSE Help students set a purpose for reading the poem, such as to appreciate Carroll's inventive language and hear, as well as envision, the boy's adventure with the Jabberwock.

▲ TEXT COMPLEXITY RUBRIC

Overall Text Complexity		"Jabberwocky" POETRY
		MORE COMPLEX
Quantitative Measures	Lexile	N/A
	Guided Reading Level	N/A
Qualitative Measures	Text Structure	simple, familiar poetic structure
	Language Conventionality and Clarity	archaic, unfamiliar language
	Knowledge Demands	distinctly unfamiliar experience
	Purpose/Levels of Meaning	single level of complex meaning

Academic Vocabulary

Read each word with students and discuss its meaning.

shun (line 7) • to deliberately avoid or ignore someone or something

foe (line 10) • enemy

sought (line 10) • looked for

FIRST READ ## Think Through the Text

Have students cite text evidence and draw inferences to answer questions.

- *What should the boy beware of?* the Jabberwock ▬ RL 1

- *What sound does the boy's blade make as he fights the Jabberwock?* snicker-snack *What kind of figurative language is this?* onomatopoeia *How do you know?* It describes the sound of the blade. ▬ RL 4

- *What happens to the Jabberwock?* The boy kills it. ▬ RL 2

SECOND READ ## Analyze the Text

- Reread stanza 1. Say: *The fun of this poem is that it allows us to play with language. For example, what do you think* Did gyre and gimble in the wabe *may mean?* Sample answer: did dance and sway in the wind ▬ RL 4

- Reread stanza 5. Ask: *How does the boy walk back after he has killed the Jabberwock?* He goes galumphing back. *Why do you think the poet chose* galumphing *instead of* walking? It helps readers picture and hear the walk. The boy is probably walking proudly but a little awkwardly because he is carrying the Jabberwock's head. ▬ RL 4

- Point to the first and last stanza. Ask: *What do you notice about these stanzas?* They are the same. Explain that the repeated stanza is a refrain. Help students recognize that "Jabberwocky" has a traditional poetic structure despite its invented language. ▬ Grades 6–7 RL 5

☑ Practice Fluency

EMPHASIZE ACCURACY Explain that this poem has nonsense words that may seem awkward or unfamiliar. Tell students to underline words they do not know and practice them to ensure accurate reading. ▬ SL 6

Independent/Self-Selected Reading

If students have already demonstrated comprehension of "Jabberwocky," have them read other poems to practice skills. Suggested titles:

- *Lewis Carroll: Poetry for Young People* edited by Edward Mendelson

- *The Complete Nonsense of Edward Lear* collected by Holbrook Jackson

  ▬ RL 10

Performance Task

WRITE & PRESENT

1. Have partners discuss how the poem uses nonsense words and onomatopoeia to tell a story. Encourage them to explain their own ideas and understanding of the words based on the text. ▬ RL 4

2. Have each student choose a stanza and rewrite it as a paragraph in standard English, citing details and quoting accurately to support the "translation." ▬ W 4

3. Students work with partners to share and edit their work. ▬ W 5

4. Have students share their paragraphs with the class. Tell them to first read the stanza from the poem and then read their prose version. ▬ SL 4

See Copying Masters, pp. 164–171.

STUDENT CHECKLIST

Writing

☑ "Translate" and rewrite a stanza of the poem as a paragraph in prose.

☑ Cite details and quote accurately to support "translations."

☑ Use correct language conventions.

Speaking & Listening

☑ Participate effectively in a collaborative discussion.

☑ Respond to questions about the translation with elaboration and details.

☑ Present work using appropriate eye contact, volume, and clear pronunciation.

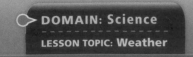

OBJECTIVES

- Identify the structure of poetry
- Explore the use of repetition in a poem
- Examine the use of figurative language
- Analyze text and identify theme using text evidence

"Twelfth Song of the Thunder"
Traditional Navajo

SUMMARY This song is a traditional Navajo chant for thunder and rain. It was sung as part of the Mountain Chant Ceremony. Rain is especially important for the Navajo, who keep livestock in desert regions.

ABOUT THE NAVAJO The **Navajo** people are the second largest Native-American tribe in North America. They live mostly in New Mexico, Arizona, and Utah and were traditionally farmers and shepherds.

Options for Reading

Independent Students read the poem independently or with a partner and then answer questions posed by the teacher.

Supported Students read several lines and answer questions with teacher support.

Discuss Genre and Set Purpose

POETRY Display the poem, and explain that it is a chant, a rhythmic poem that is recited together by a group.

TEXT FOCUS: Repetition Recall that repetition is the repeating of words, lines, or stanzas in a poem. Discuss the use of repetition to emphasize important ideas. Point out that repetition is also a main structural element of songs and chants.

SET PURPOSE Help students set a purpose for reading the poem, such as to identify the repetition and use it to determine the poem's theme.

 **Common Core Connection**

Grade 6: RL 2 determine a theme or central idea of a text/provide a summary; **RL 4** determine the meaning of words and phrases, including figurative and connotative meanings/analyze impact of word choice; **SL 4** present claims and findings, sequence ideas, and use details to accentuate main ideas or themes

Grade 7: RL 4 determine the meaning of words and phrases as they are used in a text/ analyze impact of rhymes and other repetitions of sound

Grade 8: RL 4 determine the meaning of words and phrases as they are used in a text/ analyze impact of word choices

Grades 7–8: RL 2 determine a theme or central idea of a text/analyze its development/ provide summary; **SL 4** present claims and findings, emphasizing points in focused, coherent manner

Grades 6–8: RL 1 cite textual evidence to support analysis of what the text says explicitly as well as inferences drawn; **RL 10** read and comprehend literature; **W 2** write informative/ explanatory texts; **W 5** develop and strengthen writing by planning, revising, editing, rewriting, or trying a new approach; **SL 6** adapt speech to contexts and tasks, demonstrating command of formal English when appropriate

	TEXT COMPLEXITY RUBRIC		"Twelfth Song of the Thunder" POETRY
Overall Text Complexity			SIMPLE
Quantitative Measures	Lexile		N/A
	Guided Reading Level		N/A
Qualitative Measures	Text Structure		simple, familiar poetic structure
	Language Conventionality and Clarity		clear, direct language
	Knowledge Demands		some cultural and literary knowledge useful
	Purpose/Levels of Meaning		single level of complex meaning

FIRST READ **Think Through the Text**

Have students cite text evidence and draw inferences to answer questions.

- *What lines does the poet repeat?* *"The voice that beautifies the land," "Again and again it sounds"* ⬤ RL 4

- *What are the two voices that the poet says beautify the land?* *the voice of the thunder and the voice of the grasshopper* ⬤ RL 1

SECOND READ **Analyze the Text**

- Have students reread stanza 1. Ask: *What human quality does the poet give thunder?* *The poet says the thunder has a voice.* *What type of figurative language is this?* *personification* Guide students to identify the personification in the second stanza. ⬤ RL 4

- Ask: *Why does the poet call thunder "the voice that beautifies the land?"* Sample answer: *Thunder brings rain, which makes plants, grass, and flowers grow and makes the land more beautiful.* ⬤ RL 4

- Discuss the repetition in the poem and the poem's theme. Say: *The first stanza calls thunder "the voice that beautifies the land." The last stanza says the voice of the grasshopper is the voice that beautifies the land. How are these two sounds different?* *Thunder is a big, booming sound, and a grasshopper's voice is a quiet, chirping sound.* *What theme about nature does the poem express by giving equal value to these different nature sounds?* Sample answer: *The poem expresses the idea that all of nature, big and small, is equally beautiful.* ⬤ RL 2

☑ **Practice Fluency**

EMPHASIZE RHYTHM Explain that chants such as "Twelfth Song of the Thunder" are meant to be read aloud as a group. The repeated lines give the poem its rhythm. Chorally read the poem with the class, emphasizing the rhythm. ⬤ SL 6

Independent/Self-Selected Reading

If students have demonstrated comprehension of "Twelfth Song of the Thunder," have them practice skills using another poem. Suggested titles:

- *Earth Always Endures: Native American Poems* edited by Neil Philip
- *Mother Earth Father Sky: Poems of Our Planet* by Jane Yolen ⬤ RL 10

WRITE & PRESENT

1. Have small groups discuss the repetition in "Twelfth Song of the Thunder" and analyze it to figure out the poem's theme. ⬤ RL 2

2. Individual students write an expository paragraph that identifies the theme of the poem and explains how they used the repetition and word choice to figure it out. ⬤ W 2

3. Students work with partners to share and edit their work. ⬤ W 5

4. Have students present their work to the class. ⬤ SL 4

See Copying Masters, pp. 164–171.

STUDENT CHECKLIST

Writing

☑ Write an expository paragraph that identifies the theme of the poem.

☑ Include an explanation of how students used the repetition and word choice to figure it out.

☑ Use correct language conventions.

Speaking & Listening

☑ Participate effectively in a collaborative discussion.

☑ Present claims and findings, including facts and details that support the main ideas.

☑ Use language that is appropriate for the purpose.

OBJECTIVES

- Identify the structure of poetry
- Explore the use of metaphor
- Analyze the impact of rhyme and repetition of sounds
- Analyze text using text evidence

"The Railway Train"
by Emily Dickinson

SUMMARY When trains first gained popularity as a mode of transportation, they were called "iron horses." Dickinson plays with this metaphor by comparing the movements of a train across the countryside to the movements of a horse.

ABOUT THE POET Emily Dickinson was born in 1830 in Amherst, Massachusetts. She lived most of her life in isolation, rarely leaving her home. She wrote more than 1800 poems during her lifetime, but her first book of poetry was not published until 1890, four years after her death.

Discuss Genre and Set Purpose

POETRY Remind students that poets use the sound and rhythm of words to express ideas. Discuss how the pulsing rhythm of "The Railway Train" mimics the familiar "chugga chugga" of a train.

TEXT FOCUS: Metaphor Explain that a metaphor is a kind of figurative language in which the poet compares two unlike things. Tell students that an extended metaphor is one that is continued throughout a poem.

SET PURPOSE Help students set a purpose for reading the poem, such as to understand the poet's use of metaphor and appreciate the poem's rhythmic quality.

Options for Reading

Independent Students read the poem independently or with a partner and then answer questions posed by the teacher.

Supported Students read several lines and answer questions with teacher support.

 Common Core Connection

Grade 6: RL 2 determine a theme or central idea of a text/provide a summary; **RL 4** determine the meaning of words and phrases, including figurative and connotative meanings/analyze impact of word choice; **SL 4** present claims and findings, sequence ideas, and use details to accentuate main ideas or themes

Grade 7: RL 4 determine the meaning of words and phrases as they are used in a text/analyze impact of rhymes and other repetitions of sound

Grade 8: RL 4 determine the meaning of words and phrases as they are used in a text/analyze impact of word choices

Grades 7–8: RL 2 determine a theme or central idea of a text/analyze its development/provide summary; **SL 4** present claims and findings, emphasizing points in a focused, coherent manner

Grades 6–8: RL 10 read and comprehend literature; **W 2** write informative/explanatory texts; **W 5** develop and strengthen writing by planning, revising, editing, rewriting, or trying a new approach; **SL 6** adapt speech to contexts and tasks, demonstrating command of formal English when appropriate

---

TEXT COMPLEXITY RUBRIC

Overall Text Complexity		"The Railway Train" POETRY
		COMPLEX
Quantitative Measures	Lexile	N/A
	Guided Reading Level	N/A
Qualitative Measures	Text Structure	simple, familiar poetic structure
	Language Conventionality and Clarity	sophisticated descriptions
	Knowledge Demands	perspective includes unfamiliar aspects
	Purpose/Levels of Meaning	single level of simple meaning

Academic Vocabulary

Read each word with students and discuss its meaning.

prodigious (line 4) • enormous

supercilious (line 6) • proud; scornful

docile (line 15) • calm; obedient

omnipotent (line 15) • all powerful

FIRST READ ## Think Through the Text

Have students cite text evidence and draw inferences to answer questions.

- *This poem is a riddle because it doesn't directly tell us what is described. What does this poem describe?* a train ◼ RL 2, RL 4

- *What animal is the train being compared to?* a horse *What kind of figurative language is this?* a metaphor *How do you know?* In the poem, the train is the horse. The poet doesn't use like or as. ◼ RL 4

SECOND READ ## Analyze the Text

- Review stanza 1. Ask: *What words in the first stanza give the train animal-like qualities?* lap, lick, feed itself, step Guide students to look for other words that give the train animal-like qualities. ◼ RL 4

- Reread stanza 3 with students. Ask: *What is the train doing when it is complaining and hooting?* Sample answer: *It is making a loud, shrill noise as it travels through a tunnel.* ◼ RL 4

- Reread the last stanza. Point out the words *star, stop,* and *stable.* Ask: *What do you notice about these words?* They all start with the sound of /st/. Remind students that the repetition of initial consonant sounds is called alliteration, and have them find additional examples. ◼ RL 4

☑ Practice Fluency

EMPHASIZE RHYTHM Explain that a poet's use of meter can guide rhythmic reading. In "The Railway Train," Dickinson uses a pattern of unstressed/stressed syllables to give the poem its musical qualities. Read the first line aloud, emphasizing the rhythm: *I **like** to **see** it **lap** the **miles.*** Then chorally read the poem with the class, emphasizing the rhythm. ◼ SL 6

Independent/Self-Selected Reading

If students have already demonstrated comprehension of "The Railway Train," have them read other poems to practice skills. Suggested titles:

- *Poems for Youth* by Emily Dickinson

- *Come with Me: Poems for a Journey* by Naomi Shihab Nye ◼ RL 10

WRITE & PRESENT

1. Have small groups discuss the metaphor in "The Railway Train" and how understanding the comparison helped them figure out the poem's riddle. ◼ RL 2

2. Individual students write a paragraph that identifies the subject of the poem and explains how they used the extended metaphor, rhythm, and word choice to figure it out. ◼ W 2

3. Students work with partners to share and edit their work. ◼ W 5

4. Have students present their work to the class. ◼ SL 4

See Copying Masters, pp. 164–171.

STUDENT CHECKLIST

Writing

☑ Write an expository paragraph that identifies the subject of the poem.

☑ Include an explanation of how students used the extended metaphor, rhythm, and word choice to figure it out.

☑ Use correct language conventions.

Speaking & Listening

☑ Participate effectively in a collaborative discussion.

☑ Present claims and findings, including facts and details that support the main ideas.

☑ Use language that is appropriate for the purpose.

OBJECTIVES

- Identify the structure of poetry
- Explore the use of visual imagery through precise words and figurative language
- Analyze text using evidence

Options for Reading

Independent Students read the poem independently or with a partner and then answer questions posed by the teacher.

Supported Students read each line and answer questions with teacher support.

 **Common Core Connection**

Grade 6: RL 2 determine a theme or central idea of a text/provide a summary; **RL 4** determine the meaning of words and phrases, including figurative and connotative meanings/analyze impact of word choice; **SL 4** present claims and findings, sequence ideas, and use details to accentuate main ideas or themes

Grade 7: RL 4 determine the meaning of words and phrases as they are used in a text/analyze impact of rhymes and other repetitions of sound

Grade 8: RL 4 determine the meaning of words and phrases as they are used in a text/analyze impact of word choices

Grades 7–8: RL 2 determine a theme or central idea of a text/analyze its development/provide summary; **SL 4** present claims and findings, emphasizing points in focused, coherent manner

Grades 6–8: RL 1 cite textual evidence to support analysis of what the text says explicitly as well as inferences drawn; **RL 10** read and comprehend literature; **W 4** produce writing in which development, organization, and style are appropriate to task, purpose, and audience; **W 5** develop and strengthen writing by planning, revising, editing, rewriting, or trying a new approach; **SL 6** adapt speech to contexts and tasks, demonstrating command of formal English when appropriate

"The Song of Wandering Aengus"

by W. B. Yeats

SUMMARY This poem retells a myth about the Irish god Aengus (**Een**-gus), who is on a quest to find his true love. The poem includes symbolism, rhyme, and visual imagery.

ABOUT THE POET Poet and playwright W. B. (William Butler) Yeats was born in Dublin, Ireland, in 1865. In addition to writing, he served as a senator in Ireland. Yeats won the Nobel Prize in 1923.

Discuss Genre and Set Purpose

POETRY Display the poem, and discuss elements that characterize it as a poem. Explain that it is a narrative poem; it retells an Irish myth about the god Aengus who wandered Earth looking for a girl from a dream.

TEXT FOCUS: Visual Imagery Discuss how poets choose their words carefully to create images that create a word picture in a reader's mind. Discuss how vivid verbs and adjectives can help create word pictures.

SET PURPOSE Help students set a purpose for reading, such as to find out what is happening in the poem, or to visualize Aengus as he wanders.

△ TEXT COMPLEXITY RUBRIC

Overall Text Complexity		"The Song of Wandering Aengus" POETRY
		MORE COMPLEX
Quantitative Measures	Lexile	N/A
	Guided Reading Level	N/A
Qualitative Measures	Text Structure	less familiar poetic structure
	Language Conventionality and Clarity	increased unfamiliar language
	Knowledge Demands	several references or allusions to other texts
	Purpose/Levels of Meaning	multiple levels of meaning

WRITE & PRESENT

1. Have partners discuss how the poem uses vivid words to create visual imagery. Encourage them to explain their own ideas and understanding of the images based on the text. 🔲 RL 4

2. Students write a paragraph that describes a person, a place, or an event. Challenge them to use vivid words to create an image in readers' minds. 🔲 W 4

3. Students exchange paragraphs and offer suggestions for revising and editing. 🔲 W 5

4. Students present their final paragraphs to classmates. 🔲 SL 4

5. Individual students turn in their final summaries to the teacher.

See Copying Masters, pp. 164–171.

STUDENT CHECKLIST

Writing

☑ Write a paragraph that describes a person, place, or event.

☑ Use vivid words to help readers construct an image in their minds.

☑ Use correct language conventions.

Speaking & Listening

☑ Engage effectively in collaborative conversations.

☑ Ask and answer questions about details in a poem.

☑ Speak clearly to report on a text.

Academic Vocabulary

Read each word with students and discuss its meaning.

wandering (title) • traveling without a clear destination

flickering (line 6) • shining unsteadily

rustled (line 11) • swished, crunched

glimmering (line 13) • twinkling, sparkling

dappled (line 21) • speckled

FIRST READ ## Think Through the Text

Have students cite text evidence and draw inferences to answer questions.

- *What happens in the first stanza?* Aengus is fishing. 🔲 RL 1

- *What happens in the second stanza?* The trout turns into a girl. 🔲 RL 1

- *What image do you see in your mind after reading the third stanza?* Aengus is an old man who wanders around looking for his love. 🔲 RL 1

SECOND READ ## Analyze the Text

- Ask: *Which words does Yeats use to create the image of light?* fire, stars, flickering, flame, glimmering, brightening, silver, golden, sun 🔲 RL 4

- Point out *wandering* in the title. Ask: *Why is wandering an appropriate word to use?* Aengus does not know exactly where to look for the girl. 🔲 RL 4

- Reread stanza 3. Ask: *What is the mood of Aengus in this stanza?* He is hopeful that he will find his true love and stay with her forever. 🔲 RL 1

- Remind students that the theme of a poem is the message or idea that the poet wants to convey. Ask: *What is the theme of this poem?* True love is important enough to become a life quest. 🔲 RL 2

☑ Practice Fluency

EMPHASIZE RATE Remind students that when they read poetry aloud, they should adjust their rate to match what happens in each stanza. Read the first stanza slowly to reflect what happens when Aengus first goes out. Discuss what happens in the other stanzas and how they should be read. Then read the poem chorally at an appropriate rate. 🔲 SL 6

Independent/Self-Selected Reading

If students have demonstrated comprehension of "The Song of Wandering Aengus," have them practice skills using another poem. Suggested titles:

- *Rhyme and Punishment: Adventures in Wordplay* by Brian Cleary

- *Trailblazers: Poems of Exploration* by Bobbi Katz 🔲 RL 10

OBJECTIVES

- Analyze how the poem's rhythm and meter are structured
- Explore the theme of the poem
- Analyze text using text evidence

Options for Reading

Independent Students read the poem independently or with a partner and then answer questions posed by the teacher.

Supported Students read each line and answer questions with teacher support.

 Common Core Connection

Grade 6: RL 2 determine a theme or central idea of a text/provide a summary; **RL 4** determine the meaning of words and phrases, including figurative and connotative meanings/analyze impact of word choice; **RL 5** analyze how a sentence, chapter, scene or stanza fits in the overall structure; **SL 4** present claims and findings, sequence ideas, and use details to accentuate main ideas or themes

Grade 7: RL 4 determine the meaning of words and phrases as they are used in a text/ analyze impact of rhymes and other repetitions of sound; **RL 5** analyze how a drama's or poem's form or structure contributes to its meaning

Grade 8: RL 4 determine the meaning of words and phrases as they are used in a text/ analyze impact of word choices; **RL 5** compare and contrast the structure of two or more texts/ analyze how differing structure contributes to meaning and style

Grades 7–8: RL 2 determine a theme or central idea of a text/analyze its development/ provide summary; **SL 4** present claims and findings, emphasizing points in a focused, coherent manner

Grades 6–8: RL 1 cite textual evidence to support analysis of what the text says explicitly as well as inferences drawn; **RL 10** read and comprehend literature; **W 2** write informative/ explanatory texts; **W 5** develop and strengthen writing by planning, revising, editing, rewriting, or trying a new approach; **SL 6** adapt speech to contexts and tasks, demonstrating command of formal English when appropriate

"The Road Not Taken"

by Robert Frost

SUMMARY This poem uses an extended metaphor to describe a life decision the speaker makes. The poem includes metaphor, rhyme, and visual imagery.

ABOUT THE POET Born in San Francisco in 1874, Robert Frost was a poet and a teacher. His poems are often constructed with traditional forms and deal with universal themes.

Discuss Genre and Set Purpose

POETRY Discuss theme in poetry and how poets often use metaphors to explore themes, or bigger ideas about life.

TEXT FOCUS: Rhythm and Meter Remind students that rhythm is the beat that the words in a poem create through its meter. Meter is the pattern of accented and unaccented syllables in the words of a poem. Tell students that they can hear a poem's rhythm and meter when they read the poem aloud.

SET PURPOSE Help students set a purpose for reading, such as to understand the theme of the poem, or to analyze how the rhythm and meter is structured.

TEXT COMPLEXITY RUBRIC

Overall Text Complexity		"The Road Not Taken" POETRY
		COMPLEX
Quantitative Measures	Lexile	N/A
	Guided Reading Level	N/A
Qualitative Measures	**Text Structure**	simple, familiar poetic structure
	Language Conventionality and Clarity	some unfamiliar language
	Knowledge Demands	fairly complex theme
	Purpose/Levels of Meaning	multiple levels of meaning

Academic Vocabulary

Read each word with students and discuss its meaning.

diverged (line 1) • separated

undergrowth (line 5) • bushes under the trees

trodden (line 12) • walked on

hence (line 17) • in the future

FIRST READ ## Think Through the Text

Have students cite text evidence and draw inferences to answer questions.

- *What is happening in the first two stanzas?* The poet comes to two roads and has to decide which one to take. ● RL 1

- *In the last stanza, which road does the poet say he took?* He took the road that was less traveled. ● RL 1

SECOND READ ## Analyze the Text

- Explain that the roads are a metaphor for something else. Ask: *What do the roads stand for?* Sample answers: *a decision, a life choice* ● RL 4

- *How is the theme introduced by the speaker in the first stanza developed over the course of the poem?* The speaker introduces the two roads as a metaphor for a life decision in the first stanza. The theme is making a life decision. In the next two stanzas he discusses how he thinks about the choices the roads offer. In the last stanza, he tells what his choice is and how that has made all the difference. ● RL 2, RL 5

- *How does the poet feel about his choice. Why do you think so?* Sample answer: *In the fourth stanza, he sighs. This shows that he wonders what would have happened if he had taken the other road.* ● RL 4

☑ Practice Fluency

EMPHASIZE RHYTHM Guide students to clap out the accented syllables of the first stanza as they chorally read it aloud. Discuss the rhythm and meter. Repeat with the remaining stanzas. Then guide students to analyze how the first stanza structures the rhythm and meter for the poem. Finally reread the poem chorally, emphasizing rhythm and meter. ● SL 6

Independent/Self-Selected Reading

If students have demonstrated comprehension of "The Road Not Taken," have them practice skills using another poem. Suggested titles:

- *River of Words* by Pamela Michael

- *Honeybee: Poems and Short Prose* by Naomi Shihab Nye ● RL 10

WRITE & PRESENT

1. Have small groups discuss the theme of the poem introduced in the first stanza and how it is developed over the course of the poem. ● RL 2

2. Individual students write an essay to explain how the theme of the poem is introduced in the first stanza and developed over the course of the poem. ● W 2

3. Students exchange paragraphs and offer suggestions for revising and editing. ● W 5

4. Students present their final paragraphs to classmates. ● SL 4

5. Individual students turn in their final summaries to the teacher.

See Copying Masters, pp. 164–171.

STUDENT CHECKLIST

Writing

☑ Write an essay that explains how the theme of the poem is introduced in the first stanza and developed over the course of the poem.

☑ Develop and strengthen writing by revising and editing.

☑ Use correct language conventions.

Speaking & Listening

☑ Engage effectively in collaborative conversations.

☑ Ask and answer questions about details in a poem.

☑ Speak clearly to report on a text.

OBJECTIVES

- Examine personification in poetry
- Identify the structure of poetry
- Identify the theme in poetry
- Analyze text using text evidence

Options for Reading

Independent Students read the poem independently or with a partner and then answer questions posed by the teacher.

Supported Students read each line and answer questions with teacher support.

Common Core Connection

Grade 6: RL 2 determine a theme or central idea of a text/provide a summary; **RL 4** determine the meaning of words and phrases, including figurative and connotative meanings/analyze impact of word choice; **SL 4** present claims and findings, sequence ideas, and use details to accentuate main ideas or themes

Grade 7: RL 4 determine the meaning of words and phrases as they are used in a text/analyze impact of rhymes and other repetitions of sound

Grade 8: RL 4 determine the meaning of words and phrases as they are used in a text/analyze impact of word choices

Grades 7–8: RL 2 determine a theme or central idea of a text/analyze its development/provide summary; **SL 4** present claims and findings, emphasizing points in focused, coherent manner

Grades 6–8: RL 1 cite textual evidence to support analysis of what the text says explicitly as well as inferences drawn; **RL 10** read and comprehend literature; **W 2** write informative/explanatory texts; **W 5** develop and strengthen writing by planning, revising, editing, rewriting, or trying a new approach; **SL 6** adapt speech to contexts and tasks, demonstrating command of formal English when appropriate

"Chicago"
by Carl Sandburg

SUMMARY Written in 1916, this poem presents Carl Sandburg's tribute to the city of Chicago. It is one of Sandburg's best-known works and includes personification, simile, and visual imagery.

ABOUT THE POET Carl Sandburg was born in Galesburg, Illinois, in 1878. He worked for a while as a journalist while continuing to write his poetry. His poems often celebrate the Midwestern lifestyle and work ethic. Sandburg was awarded two Nobel Prizes. He died in 1967.

Discuss Genre and Set Purpose

POETRY Display the poem and discuss the elements that characterize it as a poem. Point out that the poem's five-line first stanza describes the city of Chicago. It ends with a colon, which signals that the poet begins talking to the city in the rest of the poem. The poem is written in open verse, so the lines do not rhyme and are different lengths.

TEXT FOCUS: Personification Recall with students that personification is the use of human qualities to describe an object. Sandburg talks to the city of Chicago directly and refers to the city as "you."

SET PURPOSE Help students set a purpose for reading, such as to find out how Chicago is described, or to enjoy the open verse style.

TEXT COMPLEXITY RUBRIC

Overall Text Complexity		"Chicago" POETRY
		COMPLEX
Quantitative Measures	Lexile	N/A
	Guided Reading Level	N/A
Qualitative Measures	Text Structure	somewhat complex poetic structure
	Language Conventionality and Clarity	longer descriptions
	Knowledge Demands	some cultural and literary knowledge useful
	Purpose/Levels of Meaning	single level of complex meaning

Academic Vocabulary

Read each word with students and discuss its meaning.

husky (line 4) • heavily built

brawling (line 4) • fighting

brutal (line 10) • cruel, vicious

wanton (line 11) • excessive

cunning (line 18) • sly, sneaky

FIRST READ ## Think Through the Text

Have students cite text evidence and draw inferences to answer questions.

- *What does the first stanza describe?* It describes some of the agricultural and industrial activities that take place in Chicago. ◀RL 1

- *What kind of figurative language does the poet use in line 18?* simile *To what does he compare Chicago?* a fierce dog ◀RL 4

- *What picture of Chicago do you see in your mind after reading the poem?* Sample answer: *I see a large city full of activity.* ◀RL 1

SECOND READ ## Analyze the Text

- *What are examples of personification in this poem?* Sample answers: *big shoulders, brutal, crooked, laughing* What effect does it have? Sample answer: *It makes the city seem real and alive.* ◀RL 4

- Explain that some words in the poem have both a denotation, or dictionary meaning, and a connotation, or implied meaning. Ask: *What is the denotation of* husky? *a heavily built person* What is its connotation in the poem? *The city is large, but it is also strong and tough.* Discuss the connotations and denotations for *brawling, wicked,* and *cunning.* ◀RL 4

- What is the theme of this poem? Possible response: *The poet believes that Chicago is a strong city that will endure for a long time.* ◀RL 2

☑ Practice Fluency

EMPHASIZE EXPRESSION Remind students that when they read poetry aloud, their expression should match the events or actions in the poem. Read the poem chorally using appropriate expression. ◀SL 6

Independent/Self-Selected Reading

If students have demonstrated comprehension of "Chicago," have them practice skills using another poem. Suggested titles:

- *Monumental Verses* by J. Patrick Lewis

- *Worlds Apart: Traveling with Fernie and Me* by Gary Soto ◀RL 10

WRITE & PRESENT

1. Have partners discuss how the poem uses vivid imagery and figurative language to describe the city of Chicago. Encourage them to explain their own ideas and understanding of the images based on the text. ◀RL 1

2. Individual students write a paragraph that describes the city of Chicago based on what they know from the poem. Challenge them to create an image in the reader's mind by using vivid words, figurative language, and words with interesting connotations. ◀W 2

3. Students exchange paragraphs and offer suggestions for revising and editing. ◀W 5

4. Students present their final paragraphs to classmates. ◀SL 4

5. Individual students turn in their final summaries to the teacher.

See Copying Masters, pp.164–171.

STUDENT CHECKLIST

Writing

☑ Write a paragraph that describes the city of Chicago.

☑ Use vivid imagery, figurative language, and words with interesting connotations.

☑ Use correct language conventions.

Speaking & Listening

☑ Engage effectively in collaborative conversations.

☑ Ask and answer questions about details in a poem.

☑ Speak clearly to report on a text.

▶ OBJECTIVES

- Identify the structure of poetry
- Examine allusions in poetry
- Explore the use of visual imagery through precise words
- Analyze text and identify theme using text evidence

Options for Reading

Independent Students read the poem independently or with a partner and then answer questions posed by the teacher.

Supported Students read each line and answer questions with teacher support.

Common Core Connection

Grade 6: RL 2 determine a theme or central idea of a text/provide a summary; **RL 4** determine the meaning of words and phrases, including figurative and connotative meanings/analyze impact of word choice; **SL 4** present claims and findings, sequence ideas, and use details to accentuate main ideas or themes

Grade 7: RL 4 determine the meaning of words and phrases as they are used in a text/analyze impact of rhymes and other repetitions of sound

Grade 8: RL 4 determine the meaning of words and phrases as they are used in a text/analyze impact of word choices

Grades 7–8: RL 2 determine a theme or central idea of a text/analyze its development/provide summary; **SL 4** present claims and findings, emphasizing points in a focused, coherent manner

Grades 6–8: RL 1 cite textual evidence to support analysis of what the text says explicitly as well as inferences drawn; **RL 10** read and comprehend literature; **W 1** write arguments to support claims; **W 5** develop and strengthen writing by planning, revising, editing, rewriting, or trying a new approach; **SL 6** adapt speech to contexts and tasks, demonstrating command of formal English when appropriate

"I, Too, Sing America"

by Langston Hughes

SUMMARY This poem describes the treatment of African Americans in American society. The title is an allusion to Walt Whitman's famous poem "I Hear America Singing."

ABOUT THE POET **Langston Hughes** is recognized for his detailed and moving descriptions of African-American life from the 1920s to the 1960s. Hughes wrote fiction, plays, and his autobiography.

Discuss Genre and Set Purpose

POETRY Look at the poem with students. Guide them to distinguish it from prose. Help them note that the poem is written in lines organized into stanzas, rather than into paragraphs as prose is.

TEXT FOCUS: Allusion Explain to students that a poem may refer, or allude, to other people, stories, or events. Read aloud Walt Whitman's poem "I Hear America Singing," and guide students to conclude that Whitman's poem is what Hughes's poem alludes to.

SET PURPOSE Help students set a purpose for reading, such as to identify the allusions in the poem and figure out what they mean.

▲ TEXT COMPLEXITY RUBRIC

Overall Text Complexity		"I, Too, Sing America" POETRY
		COMPLEX
Quantitative Measures	Lexile	N/A
	Guided Reading Level	N/A
Qualitative Measures	Text Structure	less familiar poetic structure
	Language Conventionality and Clarity	clear, direct language
	Knowledge Demands	one or two references or allusions to other texts
	Purpose/Levels of Meaning	single level of complex meaning

Academic Vocabulary

Read each word with students and discuss its meaning.

company (line 4) • a visiting person or group of people

ashamed (line 17) • embarrassed, humiliated

FIRST READ # Think Through the Text

Have students cite text evidence and draw inferences to answer questions.

- *What picture do you see in your mind after reading the second stanza?* someone who is sent to the kitchen to eat **RL 1**

- *What picture do you see in your mind after reading the third stanza?* someone who is allowed to eat with the company **RL 1**

- *In the fourth stanza, how will people feel when they look at the person who had been sent away?* They will feel ashamed. **RL 1**

SECOND READ # Analyze the Text

- Ask: *What does the poet want to do?* He wants to be a part of America, to be proud of it. **RL 4**

- Encourage students to ask and answer questions about any unknown words and phrases to clarify meaning. Then ask: *What does the phrase the darker brother allude to?* African Americans **RL 4**

- Point out that Hughes contrasts the way that African Americans were treated during his time with the way he thinks they will be treated in the future. He uses a metaphor of a table to describe the treatment. Ask: *What does Hughes mean when he says he will be at the table?* African Americans will have equal rights with white Americans. **RL 4**

- Ask: *What is the theme of this poem?* African Americans are as American as white Americans and should be treated equally. **RL 2**

☑ Practice Fluency

EMPHASIZE EXPRESSION Point out that the first two stanzas describe a negative situation, but the remaining stanzas describe a positive one. Discuss how the expression might differ when reading the stanzas. Have students echo-read the poem with you using appropriate expression. **SL 6**

Independent/Self-Selected Reading

If students have demonstrated comprehension of "I, Too, Sing America," have them practice skills using another poem. Suggested titles:

- *The Dream Keeper and Other Poems* by Langston Hughes

- *Canto Familiar* by Gary Soto **RL 10**

WRITE & PRESENT

1. Have small groups discuss the theme of "I, Too, Sing America" and how understanding the allusions, metaphors, and other figurative language helps them figure out the theme. **RL 2**

2. Individuals write an argument paragraph that makes an argument about the theme of the poem and supports the argument with details from the poem, including the allusions, symbols, and other figurative language. **W 1**

3. Students work with partners to share and edit their work. **W 5**

4. Students present their final summaries to classmates. **SL 4**

5. Individual students turn in their final summaries to the teacher.

See Copying Masters, pp. 164–171.

STUDENT CHECKLIST

Writing

- ☑ Write an argument paragraph that identifies the theme of the poem.

- ☑ Include an explanation of how allusions, symbols, and other figurative language were used to figure out the theme.

- ☑ Use correct language conventions.

Speaking & Listening

- ☑ Engage effectively in collaborative conversations.

- ☑ Ask and answer questions about details in a poem.

- ☑ Speak clearly to report on a text.

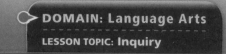
OBJECTIVES

- Identify the characteristics of a poem
- Explore the use of visual imagery in poetry
- Analyze the structure of a poem
- Analyze text using text evidence

The Book of Questions is broken into three instructional segments.

SEGMENTS

Options for Reading

Independent Students read the poems independently or with a partner and then answer questions posed by the teacher.

Supported Students read a poem and answer questions with teacher support.

 Common Core Connection

Grade 6: RL 4 determine the meaning of words and phrases, including figurative and connotative meanings/analyze impact of word choice

Grade 7: RL 4 determine the meaning of words and phrases as they are used in a text/ analyze impact of rhymes and other repetitions of sound; **RL 5** analyze how a drama's or poem's form or structure contributes to its meaning

Grade 8: RL 4 determine the meaning of words and phrases as they are used in a text/analyze impact of word choices

The Book of Questions
by Pablo Neruda

SUMMARY Pablo Neruda composed the 74 poems in *The Book of Questions* from 316 questions. Written in couplets, these unanswerable questions touch on themes such as nature, life, and death.

ABOUT THE POET **Pablo Neruda** was born in 1904 in Chile. He is widely considered to be the most influential Latin American poet of the 20th century. He won the Nobel Prize for Literature in 1971.

Discuss Genre and Set Purpose

POETRY Guide students to note that the poems are made up of questions. Explain that the poet does not expect readers to answer the questions. Instead, he poses the questions to guide readers' thinking. Point out that the poems appear in both Spanish and English.

TEXT FOCUS: Imagery Explain that poets use vivid words and figurative language to enhance imagery. Tell students that visualizing the images in the poems may help them think about the questions in new ways.

SET PURPOSE Help students set a purpose for reading, such as to think about different ways that the questions can be answered.

TEXT COMPLEXITY RUBRIC

Overall Text Complexity		The Book of Questions POETRY COMPLEX
Quantitative Measures	Lexile	N/A
	Guided Reading Level	N/A
Qualitative Measures	Text Structure	less familiar poetic structure
	Language Conventionality and Clarity	some unfamiliar language
	Knowledge Demands	somewhat unfamiliar perspective
	Purpose/Levels of Meaning	multiple levels of complex meaning

Academic Vocabulary

Read each word with students and discuss its meaning.

immense (p. 1) • extremely large; huge

brazen (p. 4) • bold; without shame

abundance (p. 9) • a great quantity

transmogrifies (p. 23) • change in a surprising way

FIRST READ **Think Through the Text**

Have students cite text evidence and draw inferences to answer questions.

p. 8 • *In poem VIII, what two images does the speaker associate with tears?* small lakes and invisible rivers *How are tears like lakes and rivers? They are all different kinds of water.* RL 4

p. 15 • *The speaker asks why spring once again offers its green clothes. What event in nature is he describing?* Sample answer: *He is describing the leaves growing back on the trees and "clothing" them in green.* RL 4

p. 17 • *What connects the questions in poem XVII?* All of the questions are about the seasons. *To what two things does the author compare autumn?* a yellow cow and a dark skeleton RL 4

p. 22 • *What poetic device does the poet use in the first two couplets, or pairs of lines?* repetition *What feeling or mood does this create?* Sample answer: *It creates a feeling of longing and reflection.* Grade 7 RL 5

SECOND READ **Analyze the Text**

• Reread the first couplet on page 6. Ask: *What picture do you get in your mind?* Possible response: *a dark, starry night* *What do you think the holes in the hat of night represent?* Sample answer: *stars* *What might be another way we could ask the poet's question here?* Sample answer: *Why is the night so full of stars?* RL 4

• Reread page 9 with students. Ask: *What picture do you get in your mind when you reread the third couplet?* a dark, black storm cloud *What do you think the black sacks of tears are?* The black sacks of tears are rain. RL 4

• Reread page 17 with students. Say: *In poem XVII, the speaker compares autumn to a yellow cow and then to a dark skeleton. How do these images help you picture the trees in autumn?* Sample answer: *When autumn first comes, the trees are full of gold and yellow leaves. As autumn changes to winter, the trees lose their leaves and their bare branches look like dark skeletons.* RL 4

ENGLISH LANGUAGE LEARNERS

Use Visuals

For poem III on page 3, draw a simple diagram of a tree and its roots underground. Say: *We can't see trees' roots. They are underground.* Chorally reread the second couplet. Ask: *Does the poet wonder why trees hide their roots? yes What do the trees hide? their roots* Repeat for similar concrete images.

RESPOND TO SEGMENT 1

Classroom Collaboration

Have partners discuss what they have read so far. Tell them to ask questions about anything they don't understand.

ENGLISH LANGUAGE LEARNERS

Use Comprehensible Input
Point to the homophones *see* and *sea* and pronounce them. Clarify the different meanings, using gestures and visuals as needed. Have students complete and read aloud the following sentence frames: *I ____ with my eyes.* see *I swim in the ____.* sea

RESPOND TO SEGMENT 2
 Classroom Collaboration

Have small groups work together to discuss what they have read so far. Have them ask questions about what they don't understand.

 Common Core Connection

Grade 6: RL 4 determine the meaning of words and phrases as they are used in a text/ analyze impact of rhymes and other repetitions of sound

Grade 7: RL 4 determine the meaning of words and phrases as they are used in a text/ analyze impact of word choices

Grade 8: RL 4 determine the meaning of words and phrases as they are used in a text/ analyze impact of word choices

Grades 6-8: RL 1 cite textual evidence to support analysis of what the text says explicitly as well as inferences drawn; **RL 10** read and comprehend literature; **W 4** produce writing in which development, organization, and style are appropriate to task, purpose, and audience; **W 5** develop and strengthen writing by planning, revising, editing, rewriting, or trying a new approach; **SL 6** adapt speech to contexts and tasks, demonstrating command of formal English when appropriate

Academic Vocabulary
Read each word with students and discuss its meaning.

melancholy (p. 29) • depression; feelings of sadness
congenial (p. 33) • pleasant; agreeable
disintegrated (p. 36) • fell apart
compassion (p. 41) • feeling sympathy for others

FIRST READ **Think Through the Text**

Have students cite text evidence and draw inferences to answer questions.

p. 26 • *What part of the eagle might the speaker compare to a dagger?* He might compare the eagle's beak to a dagger. RL 4

p. 36 • *What is the speaker wondering about in poem XXXVI? Cite evidence from the poem to support your answer.* The speaker is wondering what happens to people after they die. He asks what happens to their bones and whether their worms will become dogs or butterflies. RL 1

p. 48 • *What image does the last couplet in poem XLVIII create in your mind?* Sample answer: I pictured the shaggy petals of a chrysanthemum going every which way, rather than in a neat pattern like a daisy. RL 4

SECOND READ **Analyze the Text**

• Reread page 31 with students. Ask: *In poem XXXI, does the speaker feel sure of the life choices he has made? Cite evidence from the text to support your answer.* No, he wonders who he can ask to find out what he was supposed to make happen. He wonders why he moves without wanting to and why he migrated from Chile. RL 1

• Reread page 33 with students. Ask: *In poem XXXIII, what does the speaker realize about the sun?* He realizes that the sun that makes traveling through the desert difficult is the same sun that brightens and warms the hospital garden. The sun can be both harsh and kind. RL 1

• Reread poem XXXIX on page 39. *What is the overall tone of this poem? Cite imagery from the text that expresses this tone.* The tone is dark and threatening. The poet uses the words danger, threat, and die. He describes the poppy's red petals as bloody silk. RL 4

Academic Vocabulary

Read each word with students and discuss its meaning.

persistence (p. 56) • the quality of not giving up

decorum (p. 58) • correct or proper behavior

itinerary (p. 68) • a list of places to see on a trip

FIRST READ **Think Through the Text**

Have students cite text evidence and draw inferences to answer questions.

pp. 65–66 • *In poems LXV and LXVI, what aspect of poetry is the speaker thinking about?* the way words sound *Which word in the second couplet is an example of onomatopoeia—words that sound like what they mean?* Slithers; it sounds like the movement it describes. **RL 1; RL 4**

p. 72 • *What does the speaker question in poem LXXII?* The speaker questions the cycles of nature and how nature knows what to do. *What natural cycle does the seasons changing their shirt describe?* It describes the change of the seasons. **RL 4**

SECOND READ **Analyze the Text**

- Reread poem LX on page 60. Ask: *To what does the courtroom of oblivion refer?* Sample answer: *death* **RL 4**

- Review page 64. Ask: *In the third couplet of poem LXIV, what do you think the speaker is asking?* Sample answer: *He is asking if we learn how to be kind or if we just learn to look like we are being kind.* **RL 4**

- Reread page 74. Ask: *In the first two couplets of poem LXXIV, what does the word* it *refer to?* autumn *What does the image of the yellow trousers describe?* the yellow leaves that "clothe" the trees **RL 4**

✓ Practice Fluency

EMPHASIZE INFLECTION Review that these poems are made up of questions. Tell students that inflection is the way people change their voices as they speak. Explain that when they read a question, they should raise the pitch of their voice at the end of the sentence. Echo-read the poems with students, modeling proper inflection. **SL 6**

Independent/Self-Selected Reading

If students have demonstrated comprehension of *The Book of Questions*, have them read other poems to practice skills. Suggested titles:

- *The Dreamer* by Pam Muñoz Ryan and Peter Sís

- *Odes to Opposites* by Pablo Neruda **RL 10**

Performance Task

WRITE & PRESENT

1. Have partners discuss how the poems use vivid words and figurative language to create visual imagery. Encourage them to explain their own ideas and understanding of the questions based on the imagery. **RL 4**

2. Tell students to write their own poem of questions. Challenge them to write three couplets that use vivid words and figurative language to ask unanswerable questions. **W 4**

3. Have students exchange poems and offer suggestions for revising and editing. Have them improve their poem and correct it on the computer. **W 5**

4. Students present their final poems to the class and discuss possible answers to the questions posed. **SL 6**

See Copying Masters, pp. 164–171.

STUDENT CHECKLIST

Writing

☑ Write three couplets that ask three unanswerable questions.

☑ Use vivid words and figurative language to create strong imagery.

☑ Follow the correct poetic structure.

Speaking & Listening

☑ Participate effectively in a collaborative discussion.

☑ Pose and respond to questions

☑ Use appropriate eye contact and volume.

OBJECTIVES

- Identify the characteristics of a poem
- Explore the use of visual imagery through precise words and figurative language
- Analyze symbolism
- Analyze text using text evidence

Options for Reading

Independent Students read the poem independently or with a partner and then answer questions posed by the teacher.

Supported Students read several lines and answer questions with teacher support.

 Common Core Connection

Grade 6: RL 2 determine a theme or central idea of a text/provide a summary; **RL 4** determine the meaning of words and phrases, including figurative and connotative meanings/analyze impact of word choice; **SL 4** present claims and findings, sequence ideas, and use details to accentuate main ideas or themes

Grade 7: RL 4 determine the meaning of words and phrases as they are used in a text/ analyze impact of rhymes and other repetitions of sound

Grade 8: RL 4 determine the meaning of words and phrases as they are used in a text/ analyze impact of word choices

Grades 7–8: RL 2 determine a theme or central idea of a text/analyze its development/ provide summary; **SL 4** present claims and findings, emphasizing points in a focused, coherent manner

Grades 6–8: RL 1 cite textual evidence to support analysis of what the text says explicitly as well as inferences drawn; **RL 10** read and comprehend literature; **W 3** write narratives; **W 5** develop and strengthen writing by planning, revising, editing, rewriting, or trying a new approach; **SL 6** adapt speech to contexts and tasks, demonstrating command of formal English when appropriate

"Oranges"
by Gary Soto

SUMMARY This poem reflects on a memorable walk that a twelve-year-old boy took with a girl whom he liked. The poem includes visual imagery, figurative language, and symbolism.

ABOUT THE POET **Gary Soto,** a Mexican-American poet and author, was born in Fresno, California, in 1952. As a child, he worked in the fields of the San Joaquin Valley. In high school, he became interested in poetry. His works often reflect his culture and everyday life experiences.

Discuss Genre and Set Purpose

POETRY Look at the poem with students, and discuss that "Oranges" is free verse because it does not have a regular rhythm or rhyme. Instead it follows the rhythm of natural speech.

TEXT FOCUS: Visual Imagery Explain that poets use vivid words, as well as figurative language and symbolism, to help create a strong image in the minds of readers.

SET PURPOSE Encourage students to set a purpose for reading, such as to picture the boy's walk with the girl and how this experience made him feel.

▲ TEXT COMPLEXITY RUBRIC

Overall Text Complexity		"Oranges" POETRY
		SIMPLE
Quantitative Measures	Lexile	N/A
	Guided Reading Level	N/A
Qualitative Measures	Text Structure	less familiar poetic structure
	Language Conventionality and Clarity	contemporary, familiar language
	Knowledge Demands	common everyday experience
	Purpose/Levels of Meaning	multiple levels of meaning

Academic Vocabulary

Read each word with students and discuss its meaning.

rouge (line 15) • makeup put on the cheeks to make them look pinker

tiered (line 26) • placed in rows, one above the other

FIRST READ ## Think Through the Text

Have students cite text evidence and draw inferences to answer questions.

- *How would you summarize what the speaker is doing in this poem?* *He is going for a walk with a girl whom he likes.* **RL 2**

- *What problem does the speaker have?* *He doesn't have enough money to buy the girl a chocolate.* *How does he solve it?* *He gives the shopkeeper an orange and a nickel. The shopkeeper understands and accepts them.* **RL 1**

SECOND READ ## Analyze the Text

- Reread line 5. Ask: *How does the poet help you picture how cold the day is?* Sample answer: *The hard sound of the word* cracking *helps me picture a day that is sharp and cold, like ice.* **RL 4**

- Say: *When the speaker reaches the girl's house, the porch light burns yellow and the girl's face is bright with rouge. What feeling do these images create?* *They create a feeling of warmth and happiness. They capture the speaker's joy.* Guide students to notice and discuss additional color and color-related words that the poet uses. **RL 4**

- Say: *Sometimes poets use everyday objects to symbolize, or stand for, an idea. What do you think the orange symbolizes in the final stanza?* Sample answer: *It symbolizes the happiness that the speaker is feeling and the beginning of a new time in his life.* **RL 4**

☑ Practice Fluency

EMPHASIZE RATE Explain that a poet's choice of punctuation can influence rate. Remind students that they should take a breath at the end of each line and pause at commas and periods. Have students choral-read the poem with you, matching your rate. **SL 6**

Independent/Self-Selected Reading

If students have already demonstrated comprehension of "Oranges," have them read other poems to practice skills. Suggested titles:

- *A Fire in My Hands* by Gary Soto

- *Neighborhood Odes* by Gary Soto **RL 10**

WRITE & PRESENT

1. Have partners discuss how the poet uses vivid words to create visual imagery. Encourage them to explain their own ideas and understanding of the images based on the text. **RL 4**

2. Individual students write two or three paragraphs describing an important moment in their life. Challenge them to use vivid words and symbolism to create an image in readers' minds. **W 3**

3. Have students exchange paragraphs and offer suggestions for revising and editing. Have them improve their writing and correct it on the computer. **W 5**

4. Have students create or add a digital image to their work. Ask them to share their writing in small groups. **SL 4**

See Copying Masters, pp. 164–171.

STUDENT CHECKLIST

Writing

☑ Write two or three paragraphs that describe an important moment in students' lives.

☑ Use vivid words, imagery, and symbolism to help readers picture the moment.

☑ Use correct language conventions.

Speaking & Listening

☑ Participate effectively in a collaborative discussion.

☑ Use text evidence to explain ideas and understanding.

☑ Demonstrate a connection between the features in the poem and their own writing.

▶ OBJECTIVES

- Explain the meaning of poetry
- Examine the allusions in poetry
- Analyze text and identify theme using text evidence

"A Poem for My Librarian, Mrs. Long"

by Nikki Giovanni

Options for Reading

Independent Students read the poem independently or with a partner and then answer questions posed by the teacher.

Supported Students read several lines and answer questions with teacher support.

SUMMARY In this memoir poem, the poet shares memories from her childhood and pays tribute to a librarian who changed her life.

ABOUT THE POET Nikki Giovanni was born in 1943 and has written over 30 books. Her work often focuses on the power of the individual.

Discuss Genre and Set Purpose

POETRY Display the poem and discuss how poets are free to ignore conventions of capitalization and punctuation.

TEXT FOCUS: Allusion Discuss that a poem may refer, or allude, to other stories, people, or historical events. Explain that allusions in this poem refer to places in the poet's hometown, singers of the 1950s, books she read, and the times in which she lived, when African Americans were often not treated with respect. Work with students to look up and discuss allusions so they can better appreciate the poem.

SET PURPOSE Help students set a purpose for reading the poem, such as to identify its allusions and determine its theme.

Common Core Connection

Grade 6: RL 2 determine a theme or central idea of a text/provide a summary; **RL 4** determine the meaning of words and phrases, including figurative and connotative meanings/analyze impact of word choice; **SL 4** present claims and findings, sequence ideas, and use details to accentuate main ideas or themes

Grade 7: RL 4 determine the meaning of words and phrases as they are used in a text/ analyze impact of rhymes and other repetitions of sound;

Grade 8: RL 4 determine the meaning of words and phrases as they are used in a text/analyze impact of word choices

Grades 7–8: RL 2 determine a theme or central idea of a text/analyze its development/ provide summary; **SL 4** present claims and findings, emphasizing points in a focused, coherent manner

Grades 6–8: RL 1 cite textual evidence to support analysis of what the text says explicitly as well as inferences drawn; **RL 10** read and comprehend literature; **W 1** write arguments to support claims; **W 5** develop and strengthen writing by planning, revising, editing, rewriting, or trying a new approach; **SL 6** adapt speech to contexts and tasks, demonstrating command of formal English when appropriate

▲ TEXT COMPLEXITY RUBRIC		"A Poem for My Librarian, Mrs. Long" POETRY
Overall Text Complexity		COMPLEX
Quantitative Measures	Lexile	N/A
	Guided Reading Level	N/A
Qualitative Measures	Text Structure	less familiar poetic structure
	Language Conventionality and Clarity	less straightforward sentence structure
	Knowledge Demands	increased amount of cultural and literary knowledge useful
	Purpose/Levels of Meaning	single level of complex meaning

Academic Vocabulary

Read each word with students and discuss its meaning.

portable (line 11) • able to be carried from place to place

preference (line 20) • liking one thing better than another

humiliating (line 31) • deeply embarrassing

FIRST READ ## Think Through the Text

Have students cite text evidence and draw inferences to answer questions.

- *Is this poem set in the past or the present? How do you know?* The speaker is reflecting on the past when people had portable radios. ▬RL 1

- *Where does the speaker like to visit? Why?* She likes to visit the library and check out books because it gives her new places to dream about. ▬RL 1

SECOND READ ## Analyze the Text

- Reread stanzas 4 and 5. Ask: *What does Mrs. Long have to do to get the books the speaker requests?* She has to go to the big library uptown and risk humiliation. *What era in American history is the poet alluding to?* She is alluding to the time when white people often did not respect African Americans. ▬RL 4

- Reread the last stanza. Ask: *What does Mrs. Long do for the speaker by giving her books?* Sample answer: *Mrs. Long shows her new worlds and gives her confidence that wonderful things are waiting for her.* ▬RL 4

- *What is the theme of this poem?* Sample answer: *Books and people who care about you can change your life and open new doors.* ▬RL 2

☑ Practice Fluency

EMPHASIZE EXPRESSION Explain that this poem reflects the speaker's feelings about an important person and time in her childhood. When students read, their expression should match the speaker's emotions. Have them echo-read the poem with you with appropriate expression. ▬SL 6

Independent/Self-Selected Reading

If students have demonstrated comprehension of "A Poem for My Librarian, Mrs. Long," have them read other poems to practice skills. Suggested titles:

- *The 100 Best African American Poems* edited by Nikki Giovanni

- *I, Too, Sing America: Three Centuries of African American Poetry* by Catherine Clinton ▬RL 10

WRITE & PRESENT

1. Have small groups discuss the theme of "A Poem for My Librarian, Mrs. Long" and how understanding the allusions helped them figure out the poem's theme. ▬RL 2

2. Individual students write an argument paragraph that identifies the allusions and explains whether they were effective at conveying the theme. Tell students to support their claims with clear reasons and relevant evidence. ▬W 1

3. Students work with partners to share and edit their work. ▬W 5

4. Have students present their work to the class. ▬SL 4

See Copying Masters, pp. 164–171.

STUDENT CHECKLIST

Writing

☑ Write an argument paragraph that analyzes the effectiveness of allusions in conveying the theme.

☑ Include clear reasons and relevant evidence to support claims.

☑ Use correct language conventions.

Speaking & Listening

☑ Participate effectively in a collaborative discussion.

☑ Present claims and findings, presenting facts and details that support the main ideas.

☑ Use language that is appropriate for the purpose.

▶ OBJECTIVES

- Determine the speaker's point of view
- Analyze how a speaker distinguishes his position from an alternate point of view
- Cite text evidence to support an analysis

Options for Reading

Independent Students read the letter independently or with a partner and then answer questions posed by the teacher.

Supported Students read a segment and answer questions with teacher support.

"Letter on Thomas Jefferson"

by John Adams

SUMMARY In these excerpts from John Adams's letters, Adams describes the events leading up to Thomas Jefferson's drafting of the Declaration of Independence and shares his point of view about the document and its significance for our country.

ABOUT THE AUTHOR John Adams was born in the Massachusetts Bay Colony in 1735. He was a leader in the movement for independence and the second president of the United States, serving from 1797–1801. When he retired to his farm in Quincy, he wrote many letters to his close friend Thomas Jefferson. Both men died hours apart on July 4, 1826.

Discuss Genre and Set Purpose

LETTER Examine the selection with students. Have students scan the text to identify features that show this is a letter, such as the first-person point of view.

SET PURPOSE Help students set a purpose for reading "Letter on Thomas Jefferson," such as to determine John Adams's point of view about Thomas Jefferson and the Declaration of Independence.

COMMON CORE Common Core Connection

Grade 6: RI 6 determine the author's point of view or purpose and explain how it is conveyed; **SL 4** present claims and findings, sequence ideas, and use details to accentuate main ideas or themes

Grade 7: RI 6 determine author's point of view or purpose/analyze how author distinguishes position

Grade 8: RI 6 determine author's point of view or purpose/analyze how author responds to conflicting evidence or viewpoints

Grades 7–8: SL 4 present claims and findings, emphasizing points in a focused, coherent manner

Grades 6-8: RI 1 cite textual evidence to support analysis of what the text says explicitly as well as inferences drawn; **RI 10** read and comprehend literary nonfiction; **W 2** write informative/explanatory texts; **W 5** develop and strengthen writing by planning, revising, editing, rewriting, or trying a new approach; **SL 5** include multimedia components and visual displays in presentations

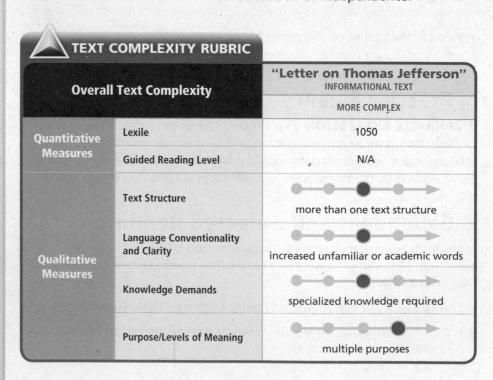

TEXT COMPLEXITY RUBRIC		"Letter on Thomas Jefferson" INFORMATIONAL TEXT
Overall Text Complexity		**MORE COMPLEX**
Quantitative Measures	Lexile	1050
	Guided Reading Level	N/A
Qualitative Measures	Text Structure	more than one text structure
	Language Conventionality and Clarity	increased unfamiliar or academic words
	Knowledge Demands	specialized knowledge required
	Purpose/Levels of Meaning	multiple purposes

Academic Vocabulary

Read each word with students and discuss its meaning.

zeal (p. 74) • energy and enthusiasm

felicity (p. 74) • a pleasing style

preceptor (p. 75) • teacher

posterity (p. 77) • future generations

rue (p. 77) • regret

WRITE & PRESENT

1. Have small groups determine John Adams's point of view in his letter and discuss how he distinguishes it from Thomas Jefferson's point of view. ⬤ RI 6

2. Individual students write an expository paragraph that uses examples and quotations from the text to analyze how Adams distinguishes his position. ⬤ W 2

3. Students work with small goups to share and edit their work. ⬤ W 5

4. Have students present their work to the class. Encourage them to incorporate visual media, such as letters, photographs, or other primary sources, into their presentation. ⬤ SL 4, SL 5

See Copying Masters, pp. 164–171.

STUDENT CHECKLIST

Writing

☑ Write an expository text that analyzes how Adams distinguishes his point of view.

☑ Cite specific examples and quotations that illustrate how Adams distinguishes his point of view.

☑ Use correct language conventions.

Speaking & Listening

☑ Participate effectively in a collaborative discussion.

☑ Present claims and findings, including examples and quotations that support the main ideas and incorporating visual media as appropriate.

☑ Use language that is appropriate for the purpose.

FIRST READ ## Think Through the Text

Have students cite text evidence and draw inferences to answer questions.

- *Why does Adams admire Jefferson even though Jefferson is silent in Congress?* *Adams admires Jefferson because he is prompt, frank, explicit, and decisive in committees and in conversation.* ⬤ RI 1

- *What does Adams like about Jefferson's draft of the Declaration of Independence?* *He likes its high tone and the flights of oratory, especially about slavery.* ⬤ RI 1

- *What is Adams's point of view about the second day of July 1776?* *He believes it will be the most memorable time in American history and will be celebrated as a day of freedom by future generations.* ⬤ Grade 6 RI 6

SECOND READ ## Analyze the Text

- *What do Jefferson and Adams disagree about?* *They disagree about who should draft the Declaration of Independence.* *How does Adams distinguish his position from Jefferson's?* *He offers three reasons why Jefferson is the more suitable—Jefferson is a Virginian; Adams is thought of as obnoxious, suspected, and unpopular while Jefferson is not; and Jefferson can write better than Adams.* ⬤ RI 6

- *How does Adams respond to those who might think that he is too enthusiastic about the Declaration?* *He acknowledges their point of view and says that he is aware of what it will cost to maintain the Declaration and defend America. However he also believes that the end is more than worth all the means.* ⬤ RI 6

Independent/Self-Selected Reading

If students have demonstrated comprehension of "Letter on Thomas Jefferson," have them practice skills using another text, such as:

- *Adams Family Papers: An Electronic Archive* at http://www.masshist. org/digitaladams/aea/index.html, Massachusetts Historical Society

- *John Adams—The Writer: A Treasury of Letters, Diaries, and Public Documents* compiled and edited by Carolyn P. Yoder ⬤ RI 10

▶ OBJECTIVES

- Determine the central idea of a text
- Analyze how key details support the central idea
- Provide an objective summary
- Analyze text using text evidence

Narrative of the Life of Frederick Douglass is broken into three instructional segments.

SEGMENTS

Options for Reading

Independent Students read the selection independently or with a partner and then answer questions posed by the teacher.

Supported Students read a segment and answer questions with teacher support.

 Common Core Connection

Grade 6: RI 2 *determine a central idea of a text/provide a summary;* **RI 3** *analyze how a key individual, event, or idea is introduced, illustrated, and elaborated;* **RI 6** *determine the author's point of view or purpose and explain how it is conveyed*

Grade 7: RI 2 *determine two or more central ideas in a text/analyze their development/ provide summary;* **RI 6** *determine author's point of view or purpose/analyze how author distinguishes position*

Grade 8: RI 2 *determine a central idea of a text/analyze its development/provide summary*

Grades 6-8: RI 1 *cite textual evidence to support analysis of what the text says explicitly as well as inferences drawn*

Narrative of the Life of Frederick Douglass an American Slave
Written by Himself

by Frederick Douglass

SUMMARY In this autobiography, abolitionist Frederick Douglass tells about his childhood, his experiences as a slave, and his escape to the North to gain freedom.

ABOUT THE AUTHOR Frederick Douglass was born a slave in 1818 in Maryland. He escaped to New York in 1838. Despite concerns that he might risk his freedom, Douglass published his autobiography in 1845.

Discuss Genre and Set Purpose

AUTOBIOGRAPHY Display the book. Explain that an autobiography is a book in which the author tells the story of his or her life.

SET PURPOSE Help students set a purpose for reading, such as to find out information about Frederick Douglass's life and slavery.

▲ TEXT COMPLEXITY RUBRIC

Overall Text Complexity		*Narrative of the Life of Frederick Douglass* INFORMATIONAL TEXT
		COMPLEX
Quantitative Measures	Lexile	1080
	Guided Reading Level	NR
Qualitative Measures	Text Structure	conventional sequential text structure
	Language Conventionality and Clarity	increased unfamiliar language
	Knowledge Demands	distinctly unfamiliar experience
	Purpose/Levels of Meaning	implied, but easy to identify from context

Academic Vocabulary

Read each word with students and discuss its meaning.

impertinent (p. 1) • disrespectful; not polite

misdemeanor (p. 6) • wrongdoing

incoherent (p. 8) • difficult to understand

benefactor (p. 14) • a person who gives money or other help

consolation (p. 17) • something that comforts or makes you feel better

FIRST READ ## Think Through the Text

Have students cite text evidence and draw inferences to answer questions.

pp. 1–2 • *Why does Douglass know little about his mother?* They were separated, as was the custom, when Douglass was an infant. He only saw her four or five times. ⬤RI 1

p. 6 • *Summarize what life was like for the slaves on the plantation.* They had a food allowance and only a few items of clothing. They had no beds, only one coarse blanket. After working in the fields all day, most had more work to do, such as washing, mending, and cooking. ⬤RI 2

pp. 16–18 • *What happened to Douglass when he was seven or eight years old?* He left Colonel Lloyd's plantation. *How does Douglass think this move changed his life?* Douglass believes that he might still have been in slavery. He sees it as the event that marked the beginning of much of his good fortune. ⬤RI 1, Grade 6 RI 3

RESPOND TO SEGMENT 1

Classroom Collaboration

Have partners summarize what they have read so far. Tell them to ask questions about anything they don't understand.

SECOND READ ## Analyze the Text

- Reread page 1. Ask: *What is the central idea of this page?* Slaves are kept in ignorance about even the most basic details of their lives. *What details support this idea?* The author says that he never knew a slave who knew his own birthday, but white children could tell their birthdays. Asking was deemed impertinent. Douglass also did not know who his father was. The means of knowing was withheld from him. ⬤RI 2

- Reread page 11. Ask: *Why did slaves rarely tell the truth about their treatment? Cite details that support your answer.* They didn't tell the truth because slave owners were known to send spies, and none wanted to risk the consequences of speaking truthfully. The author describes one man who was chained, handcuffed, and sent away. ⬤RI 1

- Reread page 14. Ask: *Why do you think the author tells readers that it wasn't considered a crime to kill a slave?* The author wants readers to understand that slaves were considered less than regular people. The fact that people could boast about brutally killing a slave shows that white people did not value the lives of slaves. ⬤Grades 6–7 RI 6

ENGLISH LANGUAGE LEARNERS

Use Comprehensible Input

After long or complex sentences, pause to paraphrase the information. For example, rephrase the fifth sentence on page 22 as: *My mistress had stopped teaching me. She would not let anyone else teach me either.* Ask questions such as: *What does Frederick Douglass want to learn how to do?* read

RESPOND TO SEGMENT 2

 Classroom Collaboration

Have small groups work together to summarize what they have read so far. Have them ask questions about what they don't understand.

 Common Core Connection

Grade 6: RI 2 determine a central idea of a text/provide a summary; **RI 6** determine the author's point of view or purpose and explain how it is conveyed; **SL 4** present claims and findings, sequence ideas, and use details to accentuate main ideas or themes

Grade 7: RI 2 determine two or more central ideas in a text/analyze their development/provide summary; **RI 6** determine author's point of view or purpose/analyze how author distinguishes positions

Grade 8: RI 2 determine a central idea of a text/analyze its development/provide summary; **RI 6** determine author's point of view or purpose/analyze how author responds to conflicting evidence or viewpoints

Grades 7–8: SL 4 present claims and findings, emphasizing points in a focused, coherent manner

Grades 6-8: RI 1 cite textual evidence to support analysis of what the text says explicitly as well as inferences drawn; **RI 10** read and comprehend literary nonfiction; **W 2** write informative/explanatory texts; **W 5** develop and strengthen writing by planning, revising, editing, rewriting, or trying a new approach

Academic Vocabulary

Read each word with students and discuss its meaning.

discord (p. 19) • disagreement; conflict

emaciated (p. 21) • very thin and sickly

emancipation (p. 24) • the act of freeing from slavery or other bond

desolate (p. 29) • very sad and lonely

benevolent (p. 33) • kindly; well-meaning

FIRST READ ## Think Through the Text

Have students cite text evidence and draw inferences to answer questions.

p. 20 • *What was Mrs. Auld teaching Douglass to do?* She was teaching him to read. *Why does she stop?* Her husband says that if Douglass learned how to read, he wouldn't be fit to be a slave. ▬ RI 1

p. 24 • *What torments Douglass after he learns to read?* The idea of freedom torments him. *What details show that it was always on his mind?* He says, "I saw nothing without seeing it, heard nothing without hearing it, and felt nothing without feeling it." ▬ RI 2

p. 27 • *What happened to Douglass when he was ten or eleven?* His master died, and he was sent to a place near where he was born. *How does he feel when he is valued with the other property? Why?* He detests slavery because it degrades him. ▬ RI 1

SECOND READ ## Analyze the Text

• Reread the last paragraph of page 19. Ask: *What central idea about slavery is expressed in this paragraph?* It is a fatal poison of irresponsible power. It turns good people into bad ones. *What details support this point?* He says of Mrs. Auld, "That cheerful eye, under the influence of slavery, soon became red with rage; that voice, made all of sweet accord, changed to one of harsh and horrid discord." ▬ RI 2

• Review page 20. Ask: *What does Douglass gain from his master's refusal to allow him to be taught to read?* Douglass gains the understanding that keeping knowledge from black people gives white people power to enslave them. It strengthens his determination to learn to read. ▬ RI 1

• Reread page 29. Ask: *What point about slavery does Douglass illustrate through the details of his grandmother's story?* Douglass shows that slaves have so little human value to their owners that when they are no longer able to work, they are left to die with no comforts. ▬ RI 2

Academic Vocabulary

Read each word with students and discuss its meaning.

cunning (p. 36) • trickiness

feeble (p. 40) • weak

presumptuous (p. 47) • arrogant; inappropriate

unanimous (p. 54) • agreed on by all

vigilance (p. 64) • carefulness; watchfulness

FIRST READ ## Think Through the Text

Have students cite text evidence and draw inferences to answer questions.

pp. 37–38 • *What was the most difficult time of slavery for Douglass? Why?* The first six months with Mr. Covey were the most difficult. He worked in all weather. The longest days were never long enough. ▬ RI 1

pp. 39–44 • *What is the turning point in Douglass's life as a slave? How does it affect him?* The battle with Mr. Covey is the turning point. It renews his self-confidence and his determination to be free. ▬ RI 1

p. 63 • *When did Douglass escape slavery?* September 3, 1838 ▬ RI 1

SECOND READ ## Analyze the Text

• Review page 38. Say: *Cite details that Douglass gives to show the effect that slavery has on slaves.* Douglass says he was broken in body, soul, and spirit. He was transformed into a brute. ▬ RI 2

• Reread page 51. Say: *Patrick Henry is famous for saying "Give me liberty, or give me death." Why does Douglass believe that slaves are going even further than Patrick Henry?* The slaves were risking their lives for doubtful liberty, and death was almost certain if they failed. *Why does Douglass believe it is worth the risk?* He says, "I should prefer death to hopeless bondage." ▬ Grades 6–7 RI 6

• Reread page 76. Ask: *What was Douglass's purpose for writing this book?* He wants to show what the American slave system is really like and speed up the day when his fellow slaves will be free. ▬ RI 6

Independent/Self-Selected Reading

If students have already demonstrated comprehension of *Narrative of the Life of Frederick Douglass*, have them read other informational texts to practice skills. Suggested titles:

• *The Underground Railroad* by Raymond Bial

• *Abraham Lincoln and Frederick Douglass: The Story Behind an American Friendship* by Russell Freedman ▬ RI 10

WRITE & PRESENT

1. Have small groups work together to summarize Frederick Douglass's narrative. Guide them to analyze how the central idea regarding the evils of slavery is conveyed through supporting ideas. ▬ RI 2

2. Ask students to write an objective summary of Frederick Douglass's narrative. Tell them to include details that convey the central idea regarding the evils of slavery. ▬ W 2

3. Have students share their summaries. Ask them to add details or elaboration to their summary based on others' suggestions. ▬ W 5

4. Individual students present their summaries. ▬ SL 4

See Copying Masters, pp. 164–171.

STUDENT CHECKLIST

Writing

☑ Write an objective summary.

☑ Provide details that convey the central idea.

☑ Discuss how the ideas are developed throughout the text.

☑ Add details or elaboration based on peer feedback.

Speaking & Listening

☑ Participate effectively in a collaborative discussion.

☑ Ask and answer questions about text details.

☑ Describe details in their writing.

▶ OBJECTIVES

- Trace the line of an argument
- Distinguish which claims are supported by facts, reasons, and evidence and which are not
- Cite text evidence to support an analysis

Options for Reading

Independent Students read the speech independently or with a partner and then answer questions posed by the teacher.

Supported Students read a segment and answer questions with teacher support.

Common Core Connection

Grade 6: RI 2 determine a central idea of a text/provide a summary; **RI 4** determine the meaning of words and phrases, including figurative, connotative, and technical meanings; **SL 4** present claims and findings, sequence ideas, and use details to accentuate main ideas or themes

Grade 7: RI 2 determine two or more central ideas in a text/analyze their development/ provide summary; **RI 4** determine the meaning of words and phrases, including figurative, connotative, and technical meanings/analyze impact of word choice

Grade 8: RI 2 determine a central idea of a text/analyze its development/provide summary; **RI 4** determine the meaning of words and phrases/analyze impact of word choice

Grades 7–8: SL 4 present claims and findings, emphasizing points in a focused, coherent manner

Grades 6-8: RI 1 cite textual evidence to support analysis of what the text says explicitly as well as inferences drawn; **RI 10** read and comprehend literary nonfiction; **W 2** write informative/explanatory texts; **W 5** develop and strengthen writing by planning, revising, editing, rewriting, or trying a new approach

"Blood, Toil, Tears, and Sweat"
Address to Parliament on May 13, 1940

by Winston Churchill

SUMMARY Winston Churchill had recently become Prime Minister when he delivered this call to arms on May 13, 1940 at the beginning of World War II. The speech was intended to rally the British people and inspire confidence in his leadership without creating a false sense of optimism.

ABOUT THE AUTHOR **Winston Churchill** was born on November 30, 1874, in Oxfordshire, England. He was the British prime minister from 1940 to 1945. During World War II, he inspired confidence in the British people and helped lead the Allies to victory.

Discuss Genre and Set Purpose

SPEECH Examine the selection with students. Have them scan the text to identify features that show this is a speech, such as direct address and repetition.

SET PURPOSE Help students set a purpose for reading "Blood, Toil, Tears, and Sweat," such as to trace Churchill's line of argument.

▲ TEXT COMPLEXITY RUBRIC

Overall Text Complexity		"Blood, Toil, Tears, and Sweat" INFORMATIONAL TEXT
		MORE COMPLEX
Quantitative Measures	Lexile	1170
	Guided Reading Level	N/A
Qualitative Measures	Text Structure	organization may be complex, but is clearly stated and generally sequential
	Language Conventionality and Clarity	increased unfamiliar or academic words
	Knowledge Demands	specialized knowledge required
	Purpose/Levels of Meaning	explicitly stated

Academic Vocabulary

Read each word with students and discuss its meaning.

summoned (paragraph 2) • called

ordeal (paragraph 4) • a difficult experience

tyranny (paragraph 4) • government by a harsh, powerful ruler

buoyancy (paragraph 4) • lightheartedness; cheerfulness

FIRST READ ## Think Through the Text

Have students cite text evidence and draw inferences to answer questions.

• *What problem is Great Britain facing at the time that Churchill delivers this speech?* *World War II has begun, and Churchill believes it is time for Great Britain to join the fight.* ◼ RI 2, RI 4

• *Paraphrase Churchill's policy on war.* *Churchill says the country will go to war by land, sea, and air, and fight as hard as it can.* ◼ RI 4

• *What does Churchill mean when he says he has nothing to offer but "blood, toil, tears, and sweat"?* *He has no solution to the problem other than to promise that he will work as hard as he possibly can.* ◼ RI 4

SECOND READ ## Analyze the Text

• Reread the first paragraph. Say: *Churchill claims that he has fulfilled Parliament's wish for a broad administration that includes both parties. Is this claim supported? If so, how?* *Yes; Churchill supports his claim by describing how he filled the positions in the War Cabinet and stating that it was filled with members of both parties.* ◼ RI 4

• *Churchill says that the tyranny they are fighting has never been surpassed. Does he offer evidence to support this claim?* no Discuss that superlatives, such as the words *never surpassed*, are examples of emotional language. Point out that these words may inspire listeners but are rarely backed up with evidence. ◼ RI 4

• *In the final paragraph, why does Churchill repeat the words* victory *and* no survival? *He wants the people to side with him and agree that war is the only option. Repeating* victory *and* no survival *emphasizes his position that Great Britain must join the war.* ◼ RI 4

Independent/Self-Selected Reading

If students have already demonstrated comprehension of "Blood, Toil, Tears, and Sweat," have them read other informational texts to practice skills. Suggested titles:

• *The Good Fight: How World War II Was Won* by Stephen E. Ambrose

• *The War to End All Wars: World War I* by Russell Freedman ◼ RI 10

WRITE & PRESENT

1. Have small groups discuss the claims Churchill makes in his speech and distinguish which ones are supported by facts, reasons, and evidence and which are not. ◼ RI 1

2. Individual students write an informational essay that traces Churchill's line of argument and evaluates his specific claims and opinions, distinguishing which ones are supported by facts, reasons, and evidence and which are not. ◼ W 2

3. Students work with partners to share and edit their work. ◼ W 5

4. Have students present their work to the class. ◼ SL 4

See Copying Masters, pp. 164–171.

STUDENT CHECKLIST

Writing

☑ Write an informational text that traces Churchill's line of argument.

☑ Cite claims that were supported by facts, reasons, and examples and those that were not.

☑ Use correct language conventions.

Speaking & Listening

☑ Participate effectively in a collaborative discussion.

☑ Present claims and findings, including facts and details that support the main ideas.

☑ Use language that is appropriate for the purpose.

▶ OBJECTIVES

- Identify and explain cause-and-effect relationships
- Determine how an author structures text
- Analyze the treatment of a key event or idea
- Analyze text using text evidence

Harriet Tubman is broken into three instructional segments.

SEGMENTS

Options for Reading

Independent Students read the book independently or with a partner and then answer questions posed by the teacher.

Supported Students read a segment and answer questions with teacher support.

COMMON CORE Common Core Connection

Grade 6: RI 3 analyze how a key individual, event, or idea is introduced, illustrated, and elaborated; **RI 5** analyze how a sentence, paragraph, or section fits into the overall structure

Grade 7: RI 3 analyze interactions between individuals, events, and ideas; **RI 5** analyze the structure an author uses to organize text

Grade 8: RI 3 analyze how text makes connections among and distinctions between individuals, ideas, or events

Grades 6-8: RI 1 cite textual evidence to support analysis of what the text says explicitly as well as inferences drawn

Harriet Tubman
Conductor on the Underground Railroad
by Ann Petry

SUMMARY This biography describes the life of Harriet Tubman, an escaped slave who returns to the South to help many other slaves escape via the Underground Railroad.

ABOUT THE AUTHOR Ann Petry wrote for both adults and children. A major theme in her works is that African Americans are an important part of American society. Petry won the Houghton Mifflin Literary Fellowship in 1946, which enabled her to complete her first novel. She traveled the country giving lectures about her works.

Discuss Genre and Set Purpose

BIORGAPHY Page through the selection with students, and help them find and identify characteristics of informational text, including chapter titles, dates, and names of real people and places. Discuss how they can tell that this book is a biography, the story of a person's life.

SET PURPOSE Help students set a purpose for reading, such as to find information about how Harriet Tubman's early years contributed to her later becoming a conductor on the Underground Railroad.

▲ TEXT COMPLEXITY RUBRIC

Overall Text Complexity		*Harriet Tubman* INFORMATIONAL TEXT
		SIMPLE
Quantitative Measures	Lexile	990
	Guided Reading Level	NR
Qualitative Measures	Text Structure	explicit sequential text
	Language Conventionality and Clarity	increased, clearly-assigned dialogue
	Knowledge Demands	some specialized knowledge required
	Purpose/Levels of Meaning	single purpose

SEGMENT 1 pp. 1–69

Academic Vocabulary

Read each word with students and discuss its meaning.

passel (p. 6) • a large group or amount

insurrection (p. 17) • rebellion

shuck (p. 59) • take something out of a husk

desultorily (p. 62) • passing from one thing to another

inertness (p. 65) • being motionless and nonreactive

Domain Specific Vocabulary

boundary (p. 1) • border; edge

plantation (p. 1) • a large farm

manumission (p. 7) • freeing from slavery

conjure (p. 64) • invoke supernatural forces

abolitionist (p. 124) • someone who opposes slavery

FIRST READ ## Think Through the Text

Have students cite text evidence and draw inferences to answer questions.

pp. 1–11 • *Describe the area where the Brodas plantation was located, including its relationship to slave and free states.* The plantation was on the Eastern Shore of Maryland, bordered on one side by the Chesapeake Bay. More slave states lie to the south, while the free states are to the north. ▬ RI 1

pp. 14–20 • *What event had the slaves and the masters worried?* Denmark Vesey, a free Negro, had planned a slave insurrection. He had been caught, but new laws restricted the slaves' movements. Masters were even more concerned that their slaves might revolt. ▬ RI 1

pp. 51–54 • *How did the story of the Underground Railroad start?* A slave named Tice Davis ran away and disappeared in front of his master's eyes. The master said he must have gone on an underground road. The rumor spread and gradually the story became mixed up with news of the new steam trains that were being used. ▬ RI 1

SECOND READ ## Analyze the Text

• Review pages 21–28. Say: *Describe the things that Harriet learned about the natural world.* She learned that the North Star was a guide to reach the North. Ben taught her about predicting the weather and the waterways that led to the Chesapeake Bay. ▬ RI 3

• Guide students to review pages 59–69. Say: *Describe Harriet's accident and the events of the several months that followed it.* An overseer threw an iron weight at her head when she helped another slave escape. She recovered from the injury but learned she was to be sold. When the master died, she was sure her prayers had killed him. ▬ RI 1

• Point out the paragraphs in italics at the end of each chapter. Ask: *How does this text fit in with the life of Harriet Tubman?* The text gives information about events regarding slavery that are going on in the rest of the country. ▬ Grades 6–7 RI 5

 ELL **ENGLISH LANGUAGE LEARNERS**

Use Peer Supported Learning

Organize students into mixed-proficiency groups. Have each group draw a web with *Harriet Tubman* in the center. Have students in the group take turns adding a word or phrase that tells something they learned about Harriet Tubman and her work with the Underground Railroad. Call on groups to share their team webs.

RESPOND TO SEGMENT 1
Classroom Collaboration

Have partners work together to create and present a summary, as well as raise questions that might be answered in the next segment.

ENGLISH LANGUAGE LEARNERS

Use Gestures

Use gestures and simplified language to help students articulate the process Harriet used to help slaves escape on the Underground Railroad. Have students complete sentence frames such as, *First Harriet used ___ to signal her presence.* song or bird calls.

RESPOND TO SEGMENT 2

 Classroom Collaboration

Have small groups work together to summarize what they have learned. Have them ask questions about what they don't understand.

 Common Core Connection

Grade 6 RI 3 analyze how a key individual, event, or idea is introduced, illustrated, and elaborated; **SL 4** present claims and findings, sequence ideas, and use details to accentuate main ideas or themes

Grade 7 RI 3 analyze interactions between individuals, events, and ideas

Grade 8 RI 3 analyze how text makes connections among and distinctions between individuals, ideas, or events

Grades 7–8: SL 4 present claims and findings, emphasizing points in a focused, coherent manner

Grades 6–8: RI 1 cite textual evidence to support analysis of what the text says explicitly as well as inferences drawn; **RI 10** read and comprehend literary nonfiction; **W 2** write informative/explanatory texts; **W 5** develop and strengthen writing by planning, revising, editing, rewriting, or trying a new approach

---

Academic Vocabulary

Read each word with students and discuss its meaning.

exultation (p. 102) • happiness, rejoicing

vigilance (p. 103) • awareness; watchfulness

censored (p. 105) • having any objectionable material removed

impromptu (p. 126) • done suddenly, without preparation

stringent (p. 128) • strict; harsh

FIRST READ Think Through the Text

Have students cite text evidence and draw inferences to answer questions.

pp. 74–75 • *What is Harriet's conflict about running away?* She is afraid that her sleeping problem might interfere with her ability to travel, and she would be found. ◖RI 1

pp. 80–87 • *How and why did Harriet's attitude about freedom change after she married John?* She found out that Old Rit should have been freed long ago, but she had been kept a slave. Harriet wanted to run away to the North so she could be free like John. He threatened to turn her in if she tried to escape, and she became afraid of him. ◖RI 1

pp. 123–125 • *How did Harriet's meeting with John Tubman change her reasons for rescuing slaves?* Her original reason was to rescue members of her family. Once she discovered that John had taken another wife and did not want to go North, she began to rescue non-family members as well. ◖RI 1

SECOND READ Analyze the Text

• Guide students to reread pages 75-77. Ask: *What new things about the woods did Harriet learn from Ben?* She learned the names of birds, which berries were safe to eat, how to identify plants that made good medicines, and how to move through the woods without noise. ◖RI 3

• Have students review Chapter 13 on pages 123–130. Ask: *How did the legend of Harriet grow?* The slaves told stories about her that were handed from generation to generation. *Why did they call her Moses?* They said she was like Moses, leading them to a better place. ◖RI 3

Academic Vocabulary

Read each word with students and discuss its meaning.

vigor (p. 217) • strength; energy

indomitable (p. 142) • not able to be conquered

FIRST READ ## Think Through the Text

Have students cite text evidence and draw inferences to answer questions.

pp. 160–163 • *Describe Harriet's meeting with Old Ben before she takes the other slaves away.* He gave her and the others food. He went with them down the road, blindfolded. Harriet told him about her other trips. *Why was he blindfolded?* If questioned, he probably wanted to be able to honestly say he had not seen them and he did not know where they had gone. 🔲 RI 1

pp. 173–175 • *How did Harriet rescue Ben and Old Rit?* She stole a wagon and used her knowledge of the woods to drive them in the dark to Wilmington. Garrett gave her money, and she got them to New York. She bought a small house for them in Auburn. 🔲 RI 3

pp. 199–200 • *How did the decision in the Dred Scott case change the situation for the slaves and for Harriet?* The decision said that slaves had to be returned and slavery was allowed in the Territories. The reward for Harriet was up to sixty thousand dollars. 🔲 RI 1

SECOND READ ## Analyze the Text

• Guide students to review pages 201–209. Ask: *How does Harriet's role change ?* She begins giving speeches about slavery and describing her trips to rescue the slaves. 🔲 RI 3

• Guide students to review pages 234–240. Ask: *What final work did Harriet do when she no longer went South to rescue slaves?* She told stories about her rescues and other abolitionists. She donated her home to a church to be used to treat the sick and homeless. 🔲 RI 1

Independent/Self-Selected Reading

If students have demonstrated comprehension of *Harriet Tubman*, have them read other informational texts to practice skills. Suggested titles:

• *George Washington Carver* by Tonya Bolden

• *Black and White Airmen* by John Fleischman 🔲 RI 10

WRITE & PRESENT

1. Have small groups refer to the text to analyze in detail how the early years of Harriet Tubman's life contributed to her later becoming a conductor on the Underground Railroad, attending to how the author introduces, illustrates, and elaborates upon the events in Tubman's life. Encourage students to take notes. 🔲 RI 3

2. Have individual students use their notes to write an analysis paragraph. 🔲 W 2

3. Small groups reconvene to share their paragraphs and edit their writing. 🔲 W 5

4. Students present their final paragraphs to classmates. 🔲 SL 4

5. Individual students turn in their final paragraphs to the teacher.

See Copying Masters, pp. 164–171.

STUDENT CHECKLIST

Writing

☑ Write a paragraph that analyzes in detail how the early years of Harriet Tubman's life contributed to her later becoming a conductor on the Underground Railroad.

☑ Describe how the author presents the information, identifying how she introduces, illustrates, and elaborates upon events.

☑ Use correct language conventions.

Speaking & Listening

☑ Engage effectively in collaborative conversations.

☑ Logically present claims and findings.

☑ Cite text evidence demonstrating relevant information.

Travels with Charley
In Search of America

by John Steinbeck

▶ **OBJECTIVES**

- Determine the figurative and connotative meaning of words and phrases
- Determine the author's point of view
- Analyze text using text evidence

Travels with Charley **is broken into three instructional segments.**

SEGMENTS

Options for Reading

Independent Students read the book independently or with a partner and then answer questions posed by the teacher.

Supported Students read a segment and answer questions with teacher support.

 Common Core Connection

Grade 6: RI 6 determine the author's point of view or purpose and explain how it is conveyed

Grade 7: RI 4 determine the meaning of words and phrases, including figurative, connotative, and technical meanings/analyze impact of word choice; **RI 6** determine author's point of view or purpose/analyze how author distinguishes position

Grade 8: RI 4 determine the meaning of words and phrases/analyze impact of word choice; **RI 6** determine author's point of view or purpose/analyze how author responds to conflicting evidence or viewpoints

Grades 6–8: RI 1 cite textual evidence to support analysis of what the text says explicitly as well as inferences drawn

SUMMARY This book describes author John Steinbeck's three-month trip with his dog, Charley, in his pick-up truck. They started in New York and traveled to Maine. From there they drove to California and back to New York. He describes the people he meets and the places he sees.

ABOUT THE AUTHOR John Steinbeck was born in 1902 and raised in Salinas, California. His works deal with the social issues of his time. *The Grapes of Wrath*, published in 1939 and dealing with the migrants from the Dust Bowl, is often called his best work. He received the Nobel Prize in Literature in 1962.

Discuss Genre and Set Purpose

TRAVELOGUE Briefly discuss the selection with students. Explain that this informational text is in the form of a travelogue. Help them find and identify characteristics of a travelogue, including dates and names of places and people.

SET PURPOSE Help students set a purpose for reading, such as to find information about where Steinbeck traveled and what he discovered on his travels.

△ **TEXT COMPLEXITY RUBRIC**

Overall Text Complexity		*Travels with Charley* INFORMATIONAL TEXT
		MORE COMPLEX
Quantitative Measures	Lexile	1020
	Guided Reading Level	N/A
Qualitative Measures	Text Structure	more unconventional sequential text structure
	Language Conventionality and Clarity	increased unfamiliar or academic words
	Knowledge Demands	some references to other texts
	Purpose/Levels of Meaning	multiple purposes

Academic Vocabulary

Read each word with students and discuss its meaning.

antidote (p. 20) • remedy; cure

desolation (p. 21) • unhappiness

laconic (p. 34) • using few words

taciturnity (p. 34) • natural silence; being reserved

spangle (p. 56) • decorate or be sprinkled throughout

anarchism (p. 84) • a theory that rejects government

Domain Specific Vocabulary

peripatetic (p. 6) • going from place to place

rig (p. 28) • truck

wayfaring (p. 33) • traveling

customs (p. 84) • a government area where taxable goods are examined

mackinaw (p. 109) • a short, heavy woolen coat

FIRST READ ## Think Through the Text

Have students cite text evidence and draw inferences to answer questions.

pp. 5–9 • *Why does Steinbeck want to take this trip?* He wants to reconnect with America. *Why does he want to use a camper?* He is reasonably famous, so he wants to avoid the recognition that might come from checking into hotels or meeting people he knows. **◼ RI 1**

pp. 23–24 • *To what does Steinbeck compare his trip? How does he feel about both of these things?* He compares his trip to starting a novel. Both give him a feeling of failure. He fears that he will never be able to complete either one. **◼ RI 1**

pp. 84–88 • *Steinbeck encounters difficulty with United States customs when he tries to enter Canada. What is his point of view about this experience?* He says that government could make a person feel small, but a person doing a good deed could restore someone's feeling of importance. **◼ RI 6**

SECOND READ ## Analyze the Text

• Guide students to reread pages 33–35 to answer the question: *How does Steinbeck's use of the word* wayfaring *and the phrase* hold his peace *help to characterize him?* The word wayfaring indicates that he is traveling; he will not stay in one place. He will also be silent and listen to others. *What image does the dialogue and Steinbeck's use of the words* laconic *and* taciturnity *create?* The words indicate that the people don't talk much, which is modeled in the short, clipped dialogue. The comment about a talkative customer is ironic, as the customer is not talkative at all. **◼ Grades 7–8 RI 4**

• *On page 57 the author uses the word* nimrod *to describe a man. Why is Steinbeck's word choice here so effective?* The denotation of the word is "hunter" but the connotation is "idiot or jerk." The man was both, as he was a hunter but shot his guide. **◼ Grades 7–8 RI 4**

ELL ENGLISH LANGUAGE LEARNERS

Use Visuals and Sentence Frames

Discuss with students the various places that Steinbeck travels. Have them point out the places on a map of the United States. Then help them complete sentence frames such as, *When Steinbeck goes to _____, he talks with people in a _____.*

RESPOND TO SEGMENT 1

Classroom Collaboration

Have partners work together to create and present a summary, as well as raise questions that might be answered in the next segment.

Use Cognates

Point out the English/Spanish cognates to aid comprehension: *restaurant/ restaurante; rifle/rifle; passport/pasaporte; population/población*. Have students use the words in sentences related to the text.

 RESPOND TO SEGMENT 2
Classroom Collaboration

Have small groups work together to summarize what they have learned. Have them ask questions about what they don't understand.

 Common Core Connection

Grade 6: RI 4 determine the meaning of words and phrases, including figurative, connotative, and technical meanings; **RI 6** determine the author's point of view or purpose and explain how it is conveyed; **SL 4** present claims and findings, sequence ideas, and use details to accentuate main ideas or themes

Grade 7: RI 4 determine the meaning of words and phrases, including figurative, connotative, and technical meanings/analyze impact of word choice; **RI 6** determine author's point of view or purpose/analyze how author distinguishes position

Grade 8: RI 4 determine the meaning of words and phrases/analyze impact of word choice; **RI 6** determine author's point of view or purpose/analyze how author responds to conflicting evidence or viewpoints

Grades 7–8: SL 4 present claims and findings, emphasizing points in a focused, coherent manner

Grades 6–8: RI 1 cite textual evidence to support analysis of what the text says explicitly as well as inferences drawn; **RI 10** read and comprehend literary nonfiction; **W 2** write informative/explanatory texts; **W 5** develop and strengthen writing by planning, revising, editing, rewriting, or trying a new approach

Academic Vocabulary

Read each word with students and discuss its meaning.

apace (p. 89) • rapidly

proportioned (p. 97) • even; balanced

abated (p. 99) • reduced

aplomb (p. 115) • assurance; composure

FIRST READ **Think Through the Text**

Have students cite text evidence and draw inferences to answer questions.

pp. 91–94 • *What is Steinbeck's feeling about long-distance truckers, especially with regard to his desire to meet and talk to local people?* He likes them, and they are friendly to him. Since they are a specialized group, if he talks only with them, he will not meet local people. He does not feel they have any real knowledge of the country. **RI 6**

pp. 98–101 • *What is Steinbeck's feeling about mobile home people?* They don't seem to want or need permanence or need roots. *After his visits with the mobile home owners, how does he feel about roots in general?* He thinks humans are restless in general, and the need for roots may not be as great as the need to be somewhere else. **RI 6**

pp. 105–107 • *What does Steinbeck say about regional speech?* It is disappearing because of television and radio. He is sad about this. **RI 1**

SECOND READ **Analyze the Text**

• Guide students to reread page 89. Ask: *What words does Steinbeck use to describe the highways?* slashes and gashes *What images do these words convey?* They convey the image of something that hurts or is unwelcome. **RI 4**

• Have students find the phrases *slice through* and *clamber over* on page 114. *What contrast do these words present?* Slice through *has a connotation of speed, while* clamber over *has a connotation of slowness.* **RI 4**

Academic Vocabulary

Read each word with students and discuss its meaning.

pariah (p. 188) • an exile or outsider

warped (p. 194) • distorted; changed

nostalgic (p. 205) • sentimental recollection

macrocosm (p. 209) • a complex system seen as a single unit

microcosm (p. 209) • a small version of something larger

FIRST READ ## Think Through the Text

Have students cite text evidence and draw inferences to answer questions.

pp. 194–199 • *How is Steinbeck's hometown of Salinas different on this visit from when he was a boy?* It used to have a small mountain road but now there is a four-lane highway. The population was four thousand but is now eighty thousand. Now there are mobile home parks. RI 1

pp. 205–208 • *What does Steinbeck realize about his visit with his old friends?* He was like a ghost to them. Since he was not there, he had not grown and changed in the same ways as his friends. RI 6

pp. 267–277 • *How does Steinbeck end his journey?* He gets lost in his hometown of New York City. RI 1

SECOND READ ## Analyze the Text

- Guide students to review the description of the sequoias on page 195. Ask: *What are the references in this paragraph?* The Indians lived on the land first, followed by the Spanish-Mexicans, and then the American settlers. Golgotha refers to the hill where Jesus was crucified. Caesar was the ruler of Rome when it fell to the barbarians. *How does the use of imagery help characterize the sequoias?* The images help show that the sequoias are very old and a part of the place where they grow.
  Grades 7–8 RI 4

- Have students reread page 211. Ask: *To what does Steinbeck compare his journey? Is his word choice effective? Why or why not?* He compares his journey to a large dinner given to a starving man. This is effective because it connects the idea of the trip with the physical feelings of hunger and fullness. Grades 7–8 RI 4

Independent/Self-Selected Reading

If students have demonstrated comprehension of *Travels with Charley*, have them read other texts to practice skills. Suggested titles:

- *Where in the World?* by Bob Raczka

- *Ain't Nothing But a Man: My Quest to Find the Real John Henry* by Scott Reynolds Nelson and Marc Aronson RI 10

WRITE & PRESENT

1. Have small groups refer to the text to determine the figurative and connotative meanings of words and phrases, and then analyze how Steinbeck's specific word choices and diction impact the meaning and tone of his writing and characterization of the individuals and places he describes. RI 4

2. Have individual students write a paragraph that analyzes how Steinbeck's word choices and diction impact the meaning and tone of his writing and the characterization of the individuals and places he describes. W 2

3. Students reconvene to share and edit their writing. W 5

4. Partners present their final paragraphs to classmates. SL 4

See Copying Masters, pp. 164–171.

STUDENT CHECKLIST

Writing

- ☑ Choose a few words and phrases from the story and write a paragraph about the author's word choice.

- ☑ Analyze how the author's word choices and diction impact the meaning and tone of his writing and the characterization of the individuals and places he describes.

- ☑ Provide a logical conclusion.

Speaking & Listening

- ☑ Engage effectively in collaborative conversations.

- ☑ Logically present claims and findings.

- ☑ Cite text evidence.

▶ OBJECTIVES

- Analyze the governmental structure of the United States
- Determine the central idea of a text
- Cite text evidence to support an analysis

Options for Reading

Independent Students read the documents independently or with a partner and then answer questions posed by the teacher.

Supported Students read a segment and answer questions with teacher support.

Preamble and First Amendment
U. S. Constitution

SUMMARY The Preamble is a brief introduction to the U. S. Constitution. It provides a general statement about the Constitution's purpose and what the country's founders hoped it would achieve. The First Amendment is part of the Bill of Rights. It protects the right to freedom of religion, expression, petition, and assembly.

ABOUT THE SOURCE The U. S. Constitution was written in Philadelphia, Pennsylvania, during the summer of 1787. Fifty-five delegates worked together to draft the framework of the United States government. James Madison, the fourth President of the United States, is sometimes called "The Father of the Constitution" for his many contributions to the document. New York statesman Gouverneur Morris wrote the Preamble.

Discuss Genre and Set Purpose

PRIMARY SOURCE Explain that a primary source is a document or object that was written or created during the time period being studied. Discuss why the Constitution is a primary source.

SET PURPOSE Help students set a purpose for reading the Preamble and First Amendment, such as to use them to analyze the structure of the United States government.

Common Core Connection

Grade 6: SL 4 present claims and findings, sequence ideas, and use details to accentuate main ideas or themes

Grades 7–8: SL 4 present claims and findings, emphasizing points in a focused, coherent manner

Grades 6–8: RI 1 cite textual evidence to support analysis of what the text says explicitly as well as inferences drawn; **RI 10** read and comprehend literary nonfiction; **W 2** write informative/explanatory texts; **W 5** develop and strengthen writing by planning, revising, editing, rewriting, or trying a new approach

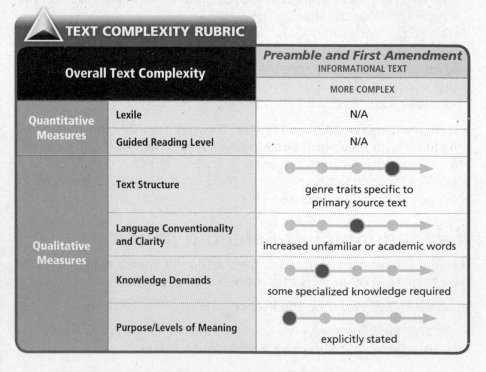

TEXT COMPLEXITY RUBRIC		Preamble and First Amendment INFORMATIONAL TEXT
Overall Text Complexity		MORE COMPLEX
Quantitative Measures	Lexile	N/A
	Guided Reading Level	N/A
Qualitative Measures	Text Structure	genre traits specific to primary source text
	Language Conventionality and Clarity	increased unfamiliar or academic words
	Knowledge Demands	some specialized knowledge required
	Purpose/Levels of Meaning	explicitly stated

Performance Task

Academic Vocabulary

Read each word with students and discuss its meaning.

tranquility (Preamble) • peacefulness

posterity (Preamble) • future generations

grievances (Amendment 1) • complaints

FIRST READ ## Think Through the Text

Have students cite text evidence and draw inferences to answer questions.

- *What is the purpose of the Constitution?* *The Preamble says that the purpose of the Constitution is to form a more perfect union, establish justice, insure domestic tranquility, provide for the common defense, promote the general welfare, and secure the blessings of liberty to ourselves and our posterity.* **RI 1**

- *What freedoms does the First Amendment protect?* *It protects the freedom of religion, the freedom of speech and press, the freedom to assemble, and the freedom to petition the government.* **RI 1**

SECOND READ ## Analyze the Text

- Reread the Preamble with students. Ask: *Who holds the most power In the United States government? Cite evidence from the Preamble to support your analysis.* *The people hold the most power. The preamble says, "We, the People, of the United States," which shows that power is vested in the people.* **RI 1**

- *Does our government place value on the rights of individuals? How do you know?* *Sample answer: The First Amendment protects individuals' rights to freedom of religion, speech, assembly, and petition. Stating the rights explicitly limits the government's ability to take them away.* **RI 1**

- Guide students to further analyze the structure of the United States government. Have them support their analysis with both primary sources, including the Preamble and the First Amendment, and secondary sources, such as *Words We Live By: Your Annotated Guide to the Constitution* by Linda R. Monk. **RI 1**

Independent/Self-Selected Reading

If students have already demonstrated comprehension of the Preamble and the First Amendment, have them read other informational texts to practice skills. Suggested titles:

- *Words We Live By: Your Annotated Guide to the Constitution* by Linda R. Monk

- *Declaring Freedom (How Government Works)* by Gwenyth Swain **RI 10**

WRITE & PRESENT

1. Have small groups analyze the governmental structure of the United States and support their analysis with textual evidence from primary and secondary sources. **RI 1**

2. Individual students write an explanatory text that analyzes the governmental structure of the United States and supports their analysis with text evidence from the Preamble, the First Amendment, and secondary sources. **W 2**

3. Students work with partners to share and edit their work. **W 5**

4. Have students present their work to the class. **SL 4**

See Copying Masters, pp. 164–171.

STUDENT CHECKLIST

Writing

☑ Write an explanatory text that analyzes the governmental structure of the United States.

☑ Cite textual evidence to support analysis.

☑ Use correct language conventions.

Speaking & Listening

☑ Participate effectively in a collaborative discussion.

☑ Present claims and findings, presenting facts and details that support the main ideas.

☑ Use language that is appropriate for the purpose.

▶ OBJECTIVES

- Identify and explain cause-and-effect relationships
- Identify and analyze the impact of word choice
- Determine how an author structures text
- Analyze text using text evidence

A Night to Remember is broken into three instructional segments.

SEGMENTS

Options for Reading

Independent Students read the book independently or with a partner and then answer questions posed by the teacher.

Supported Students read a segment and answer questions with teacher support.

COMMON CORE **Common Core Connection**

Grade 6: RI 3 analyze how a key individual, event, or idea is introduced, illustrated, and elaborated; **RI 4** determine the meaning of words and phrases, including figurative, connotative, and technical meanings; **RI 5** analyze how a sentence, paragraph, chapter, or section fits in the overall structure

Grade 7: RI 3 analyze interactions between individuals, events, and ideas; **RI 4** determine the meaning of words and phrases, including figurative, connotative, and technical meanings/ analyze the impact of word choice; **RI 5** analyze the structure an author uses to organize text

Grade 8: RI 3 analyze how text makes connections among and distinctions between individuals, ideas, or events; **RI 4** determine the meaning of words and phrases/analyze the impact of word choice

Grades 6–8: RI 1 cite textual evidence to support analysis of what the text says explicitly as well as inferences drawn

A Night to Remember
by Walter Lord

SUMMARY This book describes in great detail the events before, during, and after the luxury liner *Titanic* sank in the Atlantic Ocean on April 15, 1912.

ABOUT THE AUTHOR Walter Lord researched extensively to write *A Night to Remember*. Published in 1955, it was one of the first books to use the technique of journalistic narrative. His other books also dealt with major events in American history. Lord received the Francis Parkman Prize for Special Achievement from the Society of American Historians.

Discuss Genre and Set Purpose

INFORMATIONAL TEXT Page through the selection with students, and help them find and identify characteristics of informational text, including diagrams, exact times, direct quotations, and lifeboat numbers.

SET PURPOSE Help students set a purpose for reading, such as to find information about how and why the *Titanic* sank and what happened to the people on board.

▲ TEXT COMPLEXITY RUBRIC

Overall Text Complexity		*A Night to Remember* INFORMATIONAL TEXT
		SIMPLE
Quantitative Measures	Lexile	980
	Guided Reading Level	NR
Qualitative Measures	Text Structure	explicit sequential text structure
	Language Conventionality and Clarity	some unfamiliar or academic words
	Knowledge Demands	some specialized knowledge required
	Purpose/Levels of Meaning	single level of simple meaning

Academic Vocabulary

Read each word with students and discuss its meaning.

myriads (p. 3) • large numbers

ominous (p. 4) • threatening

jar (p. 4) • to shake or jolt violently

cascaded (p. 7) • flowed downward

listing (p. 21) • tilting to one side

paraphernalia (p. 36) • assorted objects

Domain Specific Vocabulary

crow's nest (p. 1) • a structure in the upper part of a ship that is used as a lookout

liner (p. 1) • a large passenger ship

forecastle (p. 2) • the raised deck at the bow of a ship

bow (p. 2) • the front of a ship

port (p. 2) • the left side on a ship

starboard (p. 2) • the right side on a ship

astern (p. 3) • behind the ship

aft (p. 6) • in back

FIRST READ ## Think Through the Text

Have students cite text evidence and draw inferences to answer questions.

pp. XIX–2 • *What was so special about the* Titanic *and about this voyage?* *The* Titanic *was the largest and most glamorous ship in the world. She was supposed to be unsinkable. This was her first voyage, and she was full of wealthy and important people. Also the fate of the ship had been described in a novel that had been released years earlier.* RI 1

pp. 36–37 • *How many lifeboats were on board? How many passengers could they carry, and how many passengers were on board? There were 16 lifeboats that could carry 1, 178 people. There were 2, 207 passengers. What was the procedure for getting passengers to the lifeboats? The first class women and children went first. First class men were allowed on if there was room. Lower class passengers and the restaurant staff had little or no access to the lifeboats.* RI 3

SECOND READ ## Analyze the Text

- Review basic text structures, including sequential and causal structures. Then guide students to review pages 1–60. Ask: *Which two text structures does the author primarily use? The author primarily uses a sequential structure, including giving the exact hour and minute that events occurred. He also uses cause and effect to emphasize and help explain what caused key events to occur.* Grades 6–7 RI 5

- Reread page 2 with students. Ask: *What does the author infer here about the collision?* Sample answer: *The watchman sounded the danger warning and notified the bridge. The bridge did not seem to respond, as the ship did not turn.* RI 3

- *On pages 3–6, the author uses events and quotes from passengers to describe the collision. What impact does this have for the reader? The reader is able to get a better image of just how chaotic the scene must have been, with people experiencing the collision in so many different ways.* RI 4

ELL **ENGLISH LANGUAGE LEARNERS**

Use Visuals and Sentence Frames

Discuss with students the actions that occurred during the sinking of the *Titanic*. Have them point to different sections on the illustrations of the boat deck plans. Then help them complete sentence frames such as, *At midnight on the upper deck, Lawrence Beesley notices the deck has started to _____.* tilt *At 11:50 P. M. on the bottom deck, water _____.* pours in

RESPOND TO SEGMENT 1
Classroom Collaboration

Have partners work together to create and present a summary, as well as raise questions that might be answered in the next segment.

ENGLISH LANGUAGE LEARNERS

Use Cognates

Point out the following English/Spanish cognates: *operator/operador; enthusiasm/entusiasmo; experiences/experiencias; corridor/corredor.* Have students use the words in sentences related to the text.

 RESPOND TO SEGMENT 2

Classroom Collaboration

Have small groups work together to summarize what they have learned. Have them ask questions about what they don't understand.

 Common Core Connection

Grade 6: RI 3 analyze how a key individual, event, or idea is introduced, illustrated, and elaborated; **RI 4** determine the meaning of words and phrases, including figurative, connotative, and technical meanings; **RI 5** analyze how a sentence, paragraph, chapter, or section fits in the overall structure; **SL 4** present claims and findings, sequence ideas, and use details to accentuate main ideas or themes

Grade 7: RI 3 analyze interactions between individuals, events, and ideas **RI 4** determine the meaning of words and phrases, including figurative, connotative, and technical meanings/ analyze the impact of word choice; **RI 5** analyze the structure an author uses to organize text

Grade 8: RI 3 analyze how text makes connections among and distinctions between individuals, ideas, or events; **RI 4** determine the meaning of words and phrases/analyze the impact of word choice

Grades 7–8: SL 4 present claims and findings, emphasizing points in a focused, coherent manner

Grades 6–8: RI 1 cite textual evidence to support analysis of what the text says explicitly as well as inferences drawn; **RI 10** read and comprehend literary nonfiction; **W 2** write informative/explanatory texts; **W 5** develop and strengthen writing by planning, revising, editing, rewriting, or trying a new approach

Academic Vocabulary

Read each word with students and discuss its meaning.

culprits (p. 63) • wrongdoers

prominent (p. 67) • important; well-known

maelstrom (p. 81) • turmoil

camaraderie (p. 92) • friendship

clamor (p. 99) • uproar; loud noise

FIRST READ **Think Through the Text**

Have students cite text evidence and draw inferences to answer questions.

pp. 80–83 • *What happened when the part of the ship near the fourth funnel swung up?* The slant of the deck got steeper and the people fell into the water. After that the ship went perpendicular in the water. ▬ RI 1

pp. 87–92 • *What were some of the changes to ocean liners that were put into effect after the sinking of the* Titanic? The belief that a ship was unsinkable was gone. Crews paid attention to ice messages. Governments established an ice patrol to look for icebergs. the winter ship lanes were moved further south. Wireless access was 24 hours. Every ship had enough lifeboats for all the passengers. Class distinctions on the liners ended. ▬ RI 1

p. 95 • *According to the author, what was the main effect of the* Titanic *disaster?* It marked the end of the general feeling of confidence. ▬ RI 1

SECOND READ **Analyze the Text**

- Guide students to reread page 83. *Why do you think the author included these lists of items from the* Titanic? *What impact do they have on the reader?* Sample answer: The list shows the diversity of the value of the items. It also lets the reader infer that no one's items were spared.
  ▬ Grades 7–8 RI 4

- Have students reread pages 98–99. *What are some of the words and phrases the author uses to describe the scene? What is the impact of his word choices?* Some of the words and phrases are chorus, crying, overwhelming clamor, a thousand fans at a football cup final, and the hum of locusts. All the words give the impression of a large, noisy, somewhat disorganized crowd. ▬ RI 4

SEGMENT 3 pp. 129–159

Academic Vocabulary

Read each word with students and discuss its meaning.

grieve (p. 130) • feel sad; mourn

commotion (p. 135) • noisy confusion

laconic (p. 143) • using few words

FIRST READ ## Think Through the Text

Have students cite text evidence and draw inferences to answer questions.

pp. 133–134 • *How did Ismay's life change after he was rescued?* On the Carpathia, *he stayed in the cabin and was given opiates. Once on land, he resigned from the White Star Line and lived in seclusion for the rest of his life.* ■ RI 3

pp. 129–143 • *What was the general scenario once the news of the* Titanic *started getting out?* There was a lot of confusion and misinformation. ■ RI 1

pp. 150–159 • *How did the author gather the factual information to write this book?* He interviewed survivors. *What was the major difficulty in gathering some of the facts?* Survivors' accounts varied, so some information can't be completely verified. ■ RI 1

SECOND READ ## Analyze the Text

- Guide students to review the chapter titles. Ask: *Why might the author have used quotes for the chapter titles?* Possible answer: *The quotes serve to humanize the tragedy and also add validity to the text since they are first-hand sources.* ■ Grades 7–8 RI 4

- Guide students to look back at page 148 to answer the question: *How did the label of "unsinkable" influence the events the night the* Titanic *sank?* Since no one believed the ship could sink, the crew and passengers of the Titanic were slow to react to the collision. Other ships in the area ignored some of the warning signs because the premise seemed so impossible. ■ RI 3

Independent/Self-Selected Reading

If students have demonstrated comprehension of *A Night to Remember,* have them read other informational texts to practice skills. Suggested titles:

- *Titanic* by Filson Young

- *Shadow of the Titanic: The Extraordinary Stories of Those Who Survived* by Andrew Wilson ■ RI 10

Performance Task

WRITE & PRESENT

1. Have small groups refer to the text to discuss ways the author integrates and presents information both sequentially and causally to describe the events before, during, and after the sinking of the *Titanic.* Encourage students to take notes. ■ RI 1, Grades 6–7 RI 5

2. Have individual students write a paragraph that describes how the author integrates and presents information both sequentially and causally to describe the events before, during, and after the sinking of the *Titanic.* ■ W 2

3. Students reconvene to share their paragraphs in small groups and edit their writing. ■ W 5

4. Individual students present their final paragraphs to classmates. ■ SL 4

5. Individual students turn in their final work to the teacher.

See Copying Masters, pp. 164–171.

STUDENT CHECKLIST

Writing

- ☑ Write an informational paragraph.

- ☑ Describe how the author presents the information both sequentially and causally to describe events before, during, and after the sinking of the *Titanic.*

- ☑ Use correct language conventions.

Speaking & Listening

- ☑ Engage effectively in collaborative conversations.

- ☑ Logically present claims and findings.

- ☑ Cite text evidence demonstrating sequential and causal structures.

OBJECTIVES

- Determine the author's purpose and point of view
- Identify main ideas and key details
- Analyze text using text evidence

A Short Walk Around the Pyramids and Through the World of Art is broken into three instructional segments.

Options for Reading

Independent Students read the selection independently or with a partner and then answer questions posed by the teacher.

Supported Students read a segment and answer questions with teacher support.

 Common Core Connection

Grade 6: RI 2 *determine a central idea of a text/provide a summary;* **RI 6** *determine the author's point of view or purpose and explain how it is conveyed*

Grade 7: RI 2 *determine two or more central ideas in a text/analyze their development/ provide a summary;* **RI 6** *determine author's point of view or purpose/analyze how author distinguishes position*

Grade 8: RI 2 *determine a central idea of a text/analyze its development/provide a summary;* **RI 6** *determine author's point of view or purpose/analyze how author responds to conflicting evidence or viewpoints*

Grades 6–8: RI 1 *cite textual evidence to support analysis of what the text says explicitly as well as inferences drawn*

A Short Walk Around the Pyramids and Through the World of Art

by Philip M. Isaacson

SUMMARY This book touches on all forms of art, including painting, sculpture, arts and crafts, industrial design, and city planning.

ABOUT THE AUTHOR Philip Isaacson is the art critic for the *Maine Sunday Telegram* as well as a practicing attorney.

Discuss Genre and Set Purpose

INFORMATIONAL TEXT Discuss how students can tell that this text is informational. Ask them what they predict they will learn about.

SET PURPOSE Help students set a purpose for reading, such as to find information about art and determine the author's purpose and point of view.

▲ TEXT COMPLEXITY RUBRIC

Overall Text Complexity		*A Short Walk . . . Through the World of Art* INFORMATIONAL TEXT
		COMPLEX
Quantitative Measures	Lexile	1060
	Guided Reading Level	NR
Qualitative Measures	Text Structure	more difficult art concepts
	Language Conventionality and Clarity	some unfamiliar or academic words
	Knowledge Demands	some specialized knowledge required
	Purpose/Levels of Meaning	implied, but easy to identify from context

Academic Vocabulary

Read each word with students and discuss its meaning.

mirage (p. 3) • something you think you see but that is not really there

cordial (p. 7) • friendly

primitive (p. 14) • simple and basic; unrefined

concave (p. 22) • curved inward like a spoon

hypnotic (p. 22) • mesmerizing

 ENGLISH LANGUAGE LEARNERS

Use Visuals

Use the text and photographs to develop students' oral language. Have students tell how the photographs support the ideas in the text.

FIRST READ **Think Through the Text**

Have students cite text evidence and draw inferences to answer questions.

pp. 7–11 • *Summarize what we learn about art when we look at the pyramids.* *We learn that when all the components of a work complement one another, they create an object that has harmony. The pyramids show us that simple things must be made with care. Finally they show us that light helps to shape our feelings about art.* ◖RI 2

pp. 20–21 • *Why is the Kota figure an example of abstract art? Cite evidence from the text.* *Abstract art is art that is not intended to look real. The Kota figure has triangles, cylinders, and parts of circles that remind us of eyes, a neck, and hair. Our imagination tells us that we are looking at a human.* ◖RI 1

p. 27 • *How are the pyramids like the Elgin Marbles and the Kota figure? How are they different?* *They stir up our emotions. The pyramids use their size and position, while the Elgin Marbles and Kota figure connect us with the spiritual feelings of their creators.* ◖RI 1

 RESPOND TO SEGMENT 1

Classroom Collaboration

Have small groups summarize what they have read. Have them ask questions about what they don't understand.

SECOND READ **Analyze the Text**

• Reread page 8. Ask: *How does the author develop the idea that the craftsmanship of the pyramids must be perfect?* *He says that complicated shapes can fool the eye, but with a shape as simple as a pyramid, the workmanship must be perfect.* ◖RI 2

• Discuss page 21. Ask: *What is the author's point of view about tribal art? How does he address the point of view that it is primitive?* *He says that it isn't primitive because it isn't primitive in its shape, the way it is made, or the deep feelings it expresses.* ◖RI 6

ENGLISH LANGUAGE LEARNERS

Use Visuals

Use the artwork to build students' color vocabulary. Guide them to tell what colors they see in the different works of art, either in one or two word answers or in complete sentences.

 RESPOND TO SEGMENT 2

Classroom Collaboration

Have partners work together to create and present a summary of what they have read so far.

 Common Core Connection

Grade 6: RI 2 determine a central idea of a text/provide a summary; **RI 3** analyze interactions between individuals, events, and ideas; **RI 6** determine the author's point of view or purpose and explain how it is conveyed; **SL 4** present claims and findings, sequence ideas, and use details to accentuate main ideas or themes

Grade 7: RI 2 determine two or more central ideas in a text/analyze their development/provide a summary; **RI 3** determine the meaning of words and phrases, including figurative, connotative, and technical meanings/analyze impact of word choice; **RI 6** determine author's point of view or purpose/analyze how author distinguishes position

Grade 8: RI 2 determine a central idea of a text/analyze its development/provide a summary; **RI 3** analyze how text makes connections among and distinctions between individuals, ideas, or events; **RI 6** determine author's point of view or purpose/analyze how author responds to conflicting evidence or viewpoints

Grades 7–8: SL 4 present claims and findings, emphasizing points in a focused, coherent manner

Grades 6–8: RI 1 cite textual evidence to support analysis of what the text says explicitly as well as inferences drawn; **RI 10** read and comprehend literary nonfiction; **W 2** write informative/explanatory texts; **W 5** develop and strengthen writing by planning, revising, editing, rewriting, or trying a new approach

Academic Vocabulary

Read each word with students and discuss its meaning.

throbbing (p. 30) • pulsing in a strong rhythm

influential (p. 34) • having the power to affect someone or something

radiant (p. 42) • glowing brightly

sublime (p. 47) • impressive; outstanding

FIRST READ **Think Through the Text**

Have students cite text evidence and draw inferences to answer questions.

p. 39 • *Summarize the ways Milton Avery used color in his painting of Marsden Hartley.* He used color to tell us how he felt about his friend. He used it to build form, but also gave it a life of its own. **RI 2**

p. 42 • *How is Monet's painting different from Gauguin's in its use of color?* There are no bold patterns in Monet's painting, and the colors are neither very light nor very dark. **RI 1**

p. 49 • *Why do artists invent and change forms?* They invent and change forms to express their imagination and feelings. **RI 1**

SECOND READ **Analyze the Text**

• Reread page 42. Ask: *What is the author's point of view about the works of Monet? Give examples of specific words that reveal the author's opinion.* The author admires Monet's works. He describes them as radiant and says that they have charmed the world. **RI 6**

• Reread page 57. Ask: *Does all art have to tell a story? Cite evidence from the text to support your answer.* No; artists can choose to paint to express feelings or just for the pleasure of painting. They don't have to show something exactly. **RI 1**

Academic Vocabulary

Read each word with students and discuss its meaning.

brooding (p. 62) • thinking long and deeply about something

prefabricated (p. 77) • manufactured in parts that can be put together quickly

contemporary (p. 80) • modern; of the present time

chaotic (p. 104) • in a state of disorder or confusion

FIRST READ ## Think Through the Text

Have students cite text evidence and draw inferences to answer questions.

p. 68 • *What elevates a photograph to art? It must have something more, an emotion added by the photographer that delights the viewer or shows us something about our world.* ●RI 1

pp. 76–77 • *How can things like restaurants, wristwatches, and radios be art? They can be Art Deco. They have shapes that are modern and streamlined and remind people of the future. Their design became a symbol of people's hope for better days.* ●RI 3

p. 104 • *Why does the author think of big cities as a form of art? Their chaotic energy stirs our emotions in much the same way that other art does.* ●RI 1

SECOND READ ## Analyze the Text

- Reread page 63. Ask: *Why did many artists not think of photography as art? How does the author counter their point of view? Artists thought that works of art couldn't be made with a machine. They also thought that photographs just reflected what the photographer saw, like a mirror. The author says that cameras can create images that move us and are often very different from what we see in nature.* ●RI 6

- Reread page 104. Ask: *How does the author think that art can affect us? Paraphrase his point of view. It makes us think; it can make us dream, teach us, and fill us with joy.* ●RI 6

Independent/Self-Selected Reading

If students have demonstrated comprehension of *A Short Walk Around the Pyramids and Through the World of Art*, have them read other informational texts to practice skills. Suggested titles:

- *The Vermeer Interviews: Conversations with Seven Works of Art* by Bob Raczka

- *Pyramid* by David Macaulay ●RI 10

WRITE & PRESENT

1. Have small groups refer to the text to discuss the author's point of view about art and how he develops it in the text. ●RI 6

2. Individual students write an explanatory text describing the author's point of view and how he develops it. They should include specific details, quotations, and examples from the text. ●W 2

3. Have small groups reconvene to share and edit their writing. ●W 5

4. Students present their final explanations to their classmates. Ask them to include visuals to support important points. ●SL 4

5. Individual students turn in their final drafts to the teacher.

See Copying Masters, pp. 164–171.

STUDENT CHECKLIST

Writing

☑ Write an explanatory text describing the author's point of view.

☑ Give specific details, quotations, and examples that show how the author develops his point of view.

☑ Use correct language conventions.

Speaking & Listening

☑ Participate effectively in a collaborative discussion.

☑ Provide reasons and details to support points.

☑ Use visuals to support important points.

▶ OBJECTIVES

- Identify the author's purpose in writing
- Identify aspects of the text that reveal the author's purpose
- Interpret information presented visually
- Analyze text using text evidence

The Great Fire is broken into three instructional segments.

Options for Reading

Independent Students read the book independently or with a partner and then answer questions posed by the teacher.

Supported Students read a segment and answer questions with teacher support.

 Common Core Connection

Grade 6: RI 6 determine the author's point of view or purpose and explain how it is conveyed; **RI 7** integrate information presented in different media or formats as well as in words

Grade 7: RI 4 determine the meaning of words and phrases, including figurative, connotative, and technical meanings/analyze impact of word choice; **RI 6** determine author's point of view or purpose/analyze how author distinguishes position

Grade 8: RI 4 determine the meaning of words and phrases/analyze impact of word choice; **RI 6** determine author's point of view or purpose/analyze how author responds to conflicting evidence or viewpoints

Grades 6–8: RI 1 cite textual evidence to support analysis of what the text says explicitly as well as inferences drawn

The Great Fire
by Jim Murphy

SUMMARY This book describes the Chicago fire of October 8, 1871, which was one of the worst disasters in the history of the United States. Historic photos and newspaper clippings add to the authenticity of the book. It was a Newbery Honor Book in 1995.

ABOUT THE AUTHOR **Jim Murphy** worked in publishing before he began his own writing career. He has written over thirty historical nonfiction photo essays. He spent time in Chicago doing research for *The Great Fire*. Murphy has won the Golden Kite Award and the Newbery Award twice.

Discuss Genre and Set Purpose

INFORMATIONAL TEXT Preview the selection with students, and help them find and identify characteristics of informational text, including chapter titles, photographs and illustrations with captions, and maps.

SET PURPOSE Help students set a purpose for reading, such as to find information about how and why the fire in Chicago started and what happened as a result.

▲ TEXT COMPLEXITY RUBRIC

Overall Text Complexity		*The Great Fire* INFORMATIONAL TEXT
		COMPLEX
Quantitative Measures	Lexile	1130
	Guided Reading Level	R
Qualitative Measures	Text Structure	organization of main idea and details may be complex, but is clearly stated and generally sequential
	Language Conventionality and Clarity	some unfamiliar or academic words
	Knowledge Demands	experience includes unfamiliar aspects
	Purpose/Levels of Meaning	single level of complex meaning

Academic Vocabulary

Read each word with students and discuss its meaning.

stifling (p. 13) • hot; airless

hazards (p. 19) • potential dangers

cumbersome (p. 33) • awkward or bulky

ominous (p. 49) • threatening

Domain Specific Vocabulary

embers (p. 23) • burning fragments

gusty (p. 33) • blowing hard

inflammable (p. 37) • burnable

cinder (p. 67) • burning wood

scorching (p. 73) • burning

FIRST READ ## Think Through the Text

Have students cite text evidence and draw inferences to answer questions.

pp. 14–15 • *Where did the fire start and how long did it go on? It started in the O'Leary's barn and lasted for 31 hours.* RI 1

pp. 24–25 • *What information do you learn from the map? The map shows the extent of the fire.* ▬Grade 6 RI 7

pp. 26–30 • *What were some of the errors that contributed to the fire? Bruno Goll would not unlock the alarm box. It was not clear that he ever reported the fire. The guard on duty ignored the smoke that he saw and then sent the fire trucks to the wrong location.* ▬RI 1

SECOND READ ## Analyze the Text

- Guide students to look back at pages 18–20 to answer the question: *What is the author's purpose in writing the book? What facts does he give here to support that purpose? He says that Chicago was ready to burn. Many of the buildings and sidewalks were built of wood and other flammable materials. The buildings were close together. There were many tree-lined streets. Fires were a common occurrence.* ▬RI 6

- Have students reread page 23. Ask: *What example of loaded language does the author use? How does it contribute to his purpose? The author says there were* fatal errors *in trying to put out the fire, and uses the phrase* fiery death *to describe the city. These phrases continue the idea that Chicago was ready to burn.* ▬Grades 7–8 RI 4, RI 6

- Have students reread page 43. Ask: *What example of loaded language does the author use? How does it contribute to his purpose? The author uses the phrases* fist of flame *and* ate up. *These examples of personification make the fire seem even more real and menacing.*
▬Grades 7–8 RI 4, RI 6

ELL ENGLISH LANGUAGE LEARNERS

Use Visuals and Sentence Frames

Have students use the visuals in the selection to discuss the causes and effects of the fire. Then help them complete sentence frames such as, *The fire caused some people to _____. panic, jump from buildings*

RESPOND TO SEGMENT 1

 Classroom Collaboration

Have partners work together to create and present a summary, as well as raise questions that might be answered in the next segment.

ENGLISH LANGUAGE LEARNERS

Use Peer Learning

Organize students into small groups. Have each group draw a web with the words *The Great Chicago Fire* in the center. Tell students to pass around the web, and have each student add words that describe the fire. Ask groups to share their webs.

RESPOND TO SEGMENT 2

 Classroom Collaboration

Have small groups work together to summarize what they have learned. Have them ask questions about what they don't understand.

 Common Core Connection

Grade 6: RI 4 determine the meaning of words and phrases, including figurative, connotative, and technical meanings; **RI 6** determine the author's point of view or purpose and explain how it is conveyed; **RI 7** integrate information presented in different media or formats as well as in words; **SL 4** present claims and findings, sequence ideas, and use details to accentuate main ideas or themes

Grade 7: RI 4 determine the meaning of words and phrases, including figurative, connotative, and technical meanings/analyze impact of word choice; **RI 6** determine author's point of view or purpose/analyze how author distinguishes position

Grade 8: RI 4 determine the meaning of words and phrases/analyze impact of word choice; **RI 6** determine author's point of view or purpose/analyze how author responds to conflicting evidence or viewpoints

Grades 7–8: SL 4 present claims and findings, emphasizing points in a focused, coherent manner

Grades 6–8: RI 1 cite textual evidence to support analysis of what the text says explicitly as well as inferences drawn; **RI 10** read and comprehend literary nonfiction; **W 2** write informative/explanatory texts; **W 5** develop and strengthen writing by planning, revising, editing, rewriting, or trying a new approach

---

Academic Vocabulary

Read each word with students and discuss its meaning.

torrent (p. 62) • a rush or flow

barricaded (p. 63) • put up a defensive barrier

endeavored (p. 69) • tried

boisterousness (p. 75) • disorder; unruliness

FIRST READ **Think Through the Text**

Have students cite text evidence and draw inferences to answer questions.

p. 58 • *What figure of speech is the title of Chapter 4? What image does it bring to mind?* The title is a metaphor. It brings to mind an image of a huge fire that keeps moving. **RI 4**

pp. 85–86 • *Why didn't people in the distant sections of the city know about the fire?* There were no telephones, radios, or televisions to spread the news. The people who saw the flames were not aware of the extent of the disaster. **RI 1**

pp. 78–79, 98–99 • *What can you tell about the fire now by using these two maps?* The fire has grown in all directions and has reached Lake Michigan. **Grade 6 RI 7**

SECOND READ **Analyze the Text**

• Have students reread pages 91–94. *Some of the men who wrote about the fire said the women were passive and helpless. How does Murphy counter this viewpoint?* He calls the men condescending and uses detailed examples of the things the women did, such as carrying suitcases and rescuing family members. **RI 4**

• Have students review pages 58–99. Ask: *What are some examples that further support the author's purpose in describing Chicago as a city ready to burn?* Sample answer: He uses figurative language on page 59 when he describes the rain of fiery embers. On page 63 he uses loaded language when he says that Chamberlin finally did what he should have done earlier. **RI 6**

Academic Vocabulary

Read each word with students and discuss its meaning.

rubble (p. 100) • ruins; debris

stagnant (p. 106) • foul or stale from not moving

rapport (p. 109) • relationship; connection

diatribe (p. 126) • bitter criticism

FIRST READ **Think Through the Text**

Have students cite text evidence and draw inferences to answer questions.

pp. 104–105 • *Why was the destruction of the Waterworks so devastating?* *Without the Waterworks, the people in the city did not have access to fresh water.* ◼RI 1

pp. 115–116 • *What was the meaning of the sign that William Kerfoot hung on his shack? How does the illustration add to the meaning?* Sample answer: *He wanted to show that he would recover from the losses of the fire. The illustration shows how determined people were to get back to normal.* ◼RI 4, Grade 6 RI 7

pp. 114–120 • *What were some positive effects from the fire?* *Youngsters sold some of the debris to tourists. Hotels rented out their rooms. Rebuilding provided many construction jobs.* ◼RI 1

SECOND READ **Analyze the Text**

- Have students review pages 136–138. Ask: *What are some examples that further support the author's purpose in describing Chicago as a city ready to burn?* Sample answer: *The replacement buildings were no better than the original ones. Another smaller fire broke out in 1874. It was only after the depression of 1873 that a new building style called "Chicago School" started using less flammable materials.* ◼RI 6

- Ask: *How does the author's inclusion of quotations and the experiences of specific people, such as Claire Innes, support the author's purpose in writing the book?* Sample answer: *The use of names and personal accounts makes the information more real and personal. The city becomes the people, not just a group of buildings.* ◼RI 6

Independent/Self-Selected Reading

If students have demonstrated comprehension of *The Great Fire*, have them read other informational texts to practice skills. Suggested titles:

- *Media Text: The Great Chicago Fire*, the Chicago Historical Society: http://greatchicagofire.org/great-chicago-fire

- *Planet Patrol* by Maribeth Lorbiecki ◼RI 10

Performance Task

WRITE & PRESENT

1. Have small groups discuss and evaluate aspects of the text, such as loaded language and the inclusion of particular facts, that reveal the author's purpose in writing the book: presenting Chicago as a city that was "ready to burn." ◼RI 6

2. Have individual students write a paragraph that explains how aspects of the text reveal the author's purpose: presenting Chicago as a city that was "ready to burn." ◼W 2

3. Students reconvene with their groups to share their work and edit their writing. ◼W 5

4. Students present their final paragraphs to classmates. ◼SL 4

5. Individual students turn in their final paragraphs to the teacher.

See Copying Masters, pp. 164–171.

STUDENT CHECKLIST

Writing

☑ Include a clear topic sentence.

☑ Describe how the author uses certain aspects of the text to reveal his purpose for writing.

☑ Use correct language conventions.

Speaking & Listening

☑ Engage effectively in collaborative conversations.

☑ Logically present claims and findings.

☑ Cite text evidence demonstrating the aspects of the text that reveal the author's purpose.

▶ OBJECTIVES

- Summarize main events
- Describe how the authors support and develop key events
- Determine the authors' point of view
- Analyze text using text evidence

Vincent van Gogh: Portrait of an Artist is broken into three instructional segments.

SEGMENTS

SEGMENT 1 . . . . pp. 1–38
SEGMENT 2 . . . . pp. 39–70
SEGMENT 3 . . . . . . pp. 71–110

Options for Reading

Independent Students read the selection independently or with a partner and then answer questions posed by the teacher.

Supported Students read a segment and answer questions with teacher support.

 Common Core Connection

Grade 6 RI 2 determine a central idea of a text/provide a summary

Grade 7 RI 2 determine two or more central ideas in a text/analyze their development/provide a summary; **RI 5** analyze the structure an author uses to organize text

Grade 8 RI 2 determine a central idea of a text/analyze its development/provide a summary

Grades 6–8: RI 1 cite textual evidence to support analysis of what the text says explicitly as well as inferences drawn

Vincent van Gogh
Portrait of an Artist

by Jan Greenberg and Sandra Jordan

SUMMARY Biographers Jan Greenberg and Sandra Jordan trace the life of Vincent van Gogh from his boyhood through his relatively short career as a painter. The authors describe van Gogh's complex personality, his motivations, and his techniques.

ABOUT THE AUTHORS **Jan Greenberg** and **Sandra Jordan** share a mutual love of art. Greenberg operates an art gallery in St. Louis, Missouri, while Jordan is a photographer. The two have combined their interests in art and writing in a series of books about art for young people. In addition to writing about Vincent van Gogh, they have profiled other artists including Andy Warhol and Jackson Pollock.

Discuss Genre and Set Purpose

BIOGRAPHY Have students briefly page through the book to examine the text and accompanying photographs and letters. Discuss with students how they can tell this book is informational. Then help them recall that a biography is the story of a person's life.

SET PURPOSE Have students determine a purpose for reading, such as to learn information about the life of Vincent van Gogh.

▲ TEXT COMPLEXITY RUBRIC

Overall Text Complexity		Vincent van Gogh: Portrait of an Artist INFORMATIONAL TEXT
		SIMPLE
Quantitative Measures	Lexile	1130
	Guided Reading Level	NR
Qualitative Measures	Text Structure	explicit sequential text structure
	Language Conventionality and Clarity	some unfamiliar or academic words
	Knowledge Demands	some specialized knowledge required
	Purpose/Levels of Meaning	single topic

Academic Vocabulary

Read each word with students and discuss its meaning.

obstinate (p. 6) • stubborn

tumultuous (p. 10) • noisy and confused

shirk (p. 19) • to avoid doing something that needs to be done

inferior (p. 25) • lower in quality

eccentric (p. 36) • unusual or strange

FIRST READ · **Think Through the Text**

Have students cite text evidence and draw inferences to answer questions.

pp. 5–7 • *Summarize van Gogh's childhood. Vincent shared a name with a stillborn brother, which might have been why he felt like he didn't belong. Otherwise, he had an ordinary childhood and enjoyed spending time outside.* **How did Brabant influence him?** *The strong feelings he developed for the rural landscape and the peasants remained one of his lifelong influences.* RI 2

pp. 10–24 • *What careers did van Gogh pursue before devoting his life to art? He worked in art galleries and as a teacher, and he tried to become a preacher before deciding to commit himself to his art.* ◼ RI 1

SECOND READ · **Analyze the Text**

• Reread pages 9–10. Ask: *How can you tell that van Gogh's relationship with Theo was one of the most important ones in his life? The authors describe van Gogh's relationship with Theo as an extraordinary bond that lasted the rest of their lives. Van Gogh began a correspondence with Theo that encompassed more than 600 letters, in which he chronicled almost every aspect of his life.* ◼ RI 1

• Review basic text structures, including sequential and causal structures. Then guide students to skim the text as well as the chapter titles. Ask: *What text structure did the authors primarily use? Why? The authors primarily used the sequential text structure, which takes the reader through van Gogh's life in time order.* ◼ RI 1, Grade 7 RI 5

ELL ❘ **ENGLISH LANGUAGE LEARNERS**

Use Sentence Frames

Help students generate adjectives to describe Vincent van Gogh. Have them orally complete sentence frames, such as: *Vincent van Gogh was _____ because _____.*

RESPOND TO SEGMENT 1

💬 **Classroom Collaboration**

Have small groups summarize what they have read. Have them ask questions about what they don't understand.

ENGLISH LANGUAGE LEARNERS

Use Visuals

Use the artwork in this segment to build students' vocabulary. Guide them to describe colors, shapes, or images they see in the different works of art, either in one- or two-word answers or in complete sentences.

RESPOND TO SEGMENT 2

Classroom Collaboration

Have partners work together to create and present a summary of what they have read so far.

Common Core Connection

Grade 6: RI 2 determine a central idea of a text/provide a summary; **RI 3** analyze interactions between individuals, events, and ideas; **RI 6** determine the author's point of view or purpose and explain how it is conveyed; **SL 4** present claims and findings, sequence ideas, and use details to accentuate main ideas or themes

Grade 7: RI 2 determine two or more central ideas in a text/analyze their development/ provide a summary; **RI 3** determine the meaning of words and phrases, including figurative, connotative, and technical meanings/ analyze impact of word choice

Grade 8: RI 2 determine a central idea of a text/analyze its development/provide a summary; **RI 3** analyze how a text makes connections among and distinctions between individuals, ideas, or events

Grades 7–8: SL 4 present claims and findings, emphasizing points in a focused, coherent manner

Grades 6-8: RI 1 cite textual evidence to support analysis of what the text says explicitly as well as inferences drawn; **RI 10** read and comprehend literary nonfiction; **W 2** write informative/explanatory texts; **W 5** develop and strengthen writing by planning, revising, editing, rewriting, or trying a new approach

Academic Vocabulary

Read each word with students and discuss its meaning.

ambivalent (p. 39) • having mixed feelings about a situation

taboos (p. 51) • things that are off limits

unpretentious (p. 58) • not showy; humble

nonchalance (p. 63) • calmness; casualness

elation (p. 69) • excitement; great happiness

FIRST READ ## Think Through the Text

Have students cite text evidence and draw inferences to answer questions.

pp. 39–40 • *Why was it difficult for van Gogh's parents to take him in?* He dressed like a tramp and used no social skills. *How did van Gogh's parents show their acceptance?* Mr. van Gogh wrote to Theo that they planned to let him dress how he wished and that they couldn't change the fact that he was eccentric. ◖■ RI 1

pp. 52–56 • *Summarize how the French Impressionists changed van Gogh's thinking about painting.* Van Gogh began to replace the grays he used with stronger colors and began painting a series of flowers. He imitated the style of Impressionist painters that he admired, such as Monet. He learned to combine colors with a series of short brushstrokes. ◖■ RI 2

p. 66 • *How did the people of Arles view van Gogh?* They thought he was an odd figure. They were not used to artists, and the teenage boys often made fun of him. ◖■ RI 1

SECOND READ ## Analyze the Text

• Reread pages 39–40. Ask: *Why does van Gogh compare himself to a dog?* He thinks of himself as ugly and rough. He behaves like a beast. *Why do you think the authors weave van Gogh's letters to Theo into the text?* Van Gogh's letters show his perspective about events and help readers compare his point of view with those around him. ◖■ RI 3

• Reread page 45. Ask: *Does van Gogh believe that he will one day be recognized as an artist? How do you know?* Yes. When van Gogh gives an unsigned painting to a friend, he says that he doesn't need to sign it because people will recognize his work and talk about him after he is dead. ◖■ RI 1

• Reread pages 63–69. Ask: *How does van Gogh's time in Arles change his painting?* During his time in Arles, he experiences a burst of creativity. He develops his distinctive style of jabs, dots, and hatching. He begins producing canvases in the style that would become unique to him. *What is the significance of the quote at the beginning of this chapter?* Van Gogh says he wants to produce, and produce a lot, which is exactly what he does during this period of intense creativity. ◖■ RI 2, RI 3

Academic Vocabulary

Read each word with students and discuss its meaning.

imminent (p. 78) • about to happen

enervated (p. 82) • caused to lose energy

demoralized (p. 89) • disheartened

reticent (p. 96) • reluctant to show one's thoughts and feelings

FIRST READ **Think Through the Text**

Have students cite text evidence and draw inferences to answer questions.

pp. 76–77 • *Compare and contrast the works of van Gogh and Gauguin.* *Both believed artists should move beyond imitating nature. However, van Gogh painted with thick paint and vigorous brushstrokes while Gauguin used thin, flat planes of color and simple shapes.* ▬RI 1

p. 86 • *What may have caused van Gogh's behavior?* *He may have had a rare form of epilepsy that caused attacks at infrequent intervals.* ▬RI 1

p. 105 • *How did van Gogh's work eventually reach the public?* *Theo's wife, Jo, wrote a biography of him and organized exhibitions of his work. She had his letters to Theo published.* ▬RI 1

SECOND READ **Analyze the Text**

- Reread page 86. *Do the authors believe that van Gogh was insane? How do they support their point of view?* *The authors don't believe Vincent was insane. They say that other than the weeks when he was incapacitated by an attack, he painted masterpieces and wrote intelligent, thoughtful letters about them.* ▬Grade 6 RI 6

- Reread page 101. Ask: *How does the painting Wheatfield with Crows capture the emotions of van Gogh's final days?* *The painting is filled with turbulent skies and a road leading to nowhere. The world appears to be closing in with no escape. The painting shows that van Gogh had lost hope.* ▬RI 1

Independent/Self-Selected Reading

If students have demonstrated comprehension of *Vincent van Gogh: Portrait of an Artist*, have them practice skills using another text, such as:

- *The Van Gogh Gallery* at http://www.vangoghgallery.com

- *Vincent van Gogh: The Starry Night* by Richard Thomson ▬RI 10

Performance Task

WRITE & PRESENT

1. Have small groups refer to the text to discuss how the authors use van Gogh's letters to support important points about events in his life. ▬RI 3

2. Individual students choose one event or period of van Gogh's life and write a paragraph to explain how an excerpt from one of his letters supports or develops the authors' points. ▬W 2

3. Have students share and edit their writing with others. ▬W 5

4. Students present their final explanations to their classmates. Ask them to include visuals, such as illustrative artworks, to support important points. ▬SL 4

5. Individual students turn in their final drafts to the teacher.

See Copying Masters, pp. 164–171.

STUDENT CHECKLIST

Writing

☑ Choose one event or period of van Gogh's life and write a paragraph about it.

☑ Give specific details, quotations, and examples to show how an excerpt from one of his letters supports or develops one of the authors' points about the event or period in van Gogh's life.

☑ Use correct language conventions.

Speaking & Listening

☑ Participate effectively in a collaborative discussion.

☑ Provide reasons and details to support points.

☑ Use visuals to support important points.

▷ **OBJECTIVES**

- Identify and explain cause-and-effect relationships
- Determine how an author structures text
- Interpret information presented visually
- Analyze text using text evidence

This Land Was Made for You and Me is broken into three instructional segments.

SEGMENTS

Options for Reading

Independent Students read the book independently or with a partner and then answer questions posed by the teacher.

Supported Students read a segment and answer questions with teacher support.

 Common Core Connection

Grade 6: RI 2 determine a central idea of a text/provide a summary; **RI 4** determine the meaning of words and phrases, including figurative, connotative, and technical meanings; **RI 5** analyze how a sentence, paragraph, chapter, or section fits in the overall structure

Grade 7: RI 2 determine two or more central ideas in a text/analyze their development/provide summary; **RI 4** determine the meaning of words and phrases, including figurative, connotative, and technical meanings/analyze impact of word choice; **RI 5** analyze the structure an author uses to organize text

Grade 8: RI 2 determine a central idea of a text/analyze its development/provide summary; **RI 4** determine the meaning of words and phrases/analyze impact of word choice

Grades 6–8: RI 1 cite textual evidence to support analysis of what the text says explicitly as well as inferences drawn

This Land Was Made for You and Me
The Life and Songs of Woody Guthrie

by Elizabeth Partridge

SUMMARY This book describes the life and career of folksinger and political activist Woody Guthrie and explains the inspirations for many of his songs. Lyrics of some of his songs as well as photos of Guthrie are also included in the book.

ABOUT THE AUTHOR Elizabeth Partridge interviewed folk singer Pete Seeger and Woody's adult children Arlo and Nora to write this book. Partridge won an award for her biography of photographer Dorothea Lange and has also written other books for children.

Discuss Genre and Set Purpose

BIOGRAPHY Preview the selection with students, and help them find and identify characteristics of informational text. Discuss some of the clues that help them understand that this is a biography, the story of someone's life.

SET PURPOSE Help students set a purpose for reading, such as to find information about the life of Woody Guthrie.

△ **TEXT COMPLEXITY RUBRIC**

Overall Text Complexity		This Land Was Made for You and Me INFORMATIONAL TEXT
		COMPLEX
Quantitative Measures	Lexile	1060
	Guided Reading Level	Z
Qualitative Measures	Text Structure	conventional sequential text structure
	Language Conventionality and Clarity	less straightforward sentence structure
	Knowledge Demands	some references to other texts
	Purpose/Levels of Meaning	implied, but easy to identify from context

Academic Vocabulary

Read each word with students and discuss its meaning.

excruciating (p. 23) • extremely painful

melancholy (p. 24) • depression; extreme sadness

sporadically (p. 27) • occurring irregularly

voraciously (p. 46) • eagerly; hungrily

camaraderie (p. 55) • friendship

vagrancy (p. 57) • homelessness

Domain Specific Vocabulary

ballads (p. 48) • songs that tell stories

lyrical (p. 54) • poetic

renditions (p. 94) • versions

harmonized (p. 96) • blended pleasantly

 **ENGLISH LANGUAGE LEARNERS**

Use Sentence Frames

Review the life of Woody Guthrie. Help students generate adjectives to describe him. Have them orally complete sentence frames such as, *Woody Guthrie was _____ because _____.*

FIRST READ ## Think Through the Text

Have students cite text evidence and draw inferences to answer questions.

pp. 1–3 • *How and when did Woody write "This Land is Your Land"?* He wrote it in 1940 in New York City. He had just finished a road trip there from Texas, and he had been observing people he saw along the way. ⬤ RI 1

pp. 34–42 • *What two skills did Woody develop while he was living in Pampa?* He began to draw cartoons and to play the guitar. ⬤ RI 1

pp. 47–48 • *Why was Woody most interested in songs and music?* He said they were a language for everyone. ⬤ RI 1

SECOND READ ## Analyze the Text

- Review basic text structures, including sequential, spatial, and causal structures. Then guide students to review pages 5–65. Ask: *Which two text structures did the author primarily use? Why?* Elizabeth Partridge primarily used a sequential structure, which moves through time from Guthrie's childhood to his death. She also used cause and effect to emphasize and help explain key events in Guthrie's life and how they influenced his music. An example of sequential structure is the date under each chapter head, as well as dates given throughout the chapters. An example of causal structure appears on page 31.
  ⬤ Grades 6–7 RI 5

- Reread page 34 and point out the word *exploded*. Ask: *What are the denotations of the word* exploded? *got angry, blew up* What are the connotations that make it a good word choice here? *When Nora got angry, she set Charley on fire. Charley's body exploded in fire, and the family relationships also blew up.* ⬤ RI 4

- Review pages 1–65 with students. Say: *Summarize Woody Guthrie's early life.* Woody had an unhappy childhood. His mother was ill, and his father was not able to provide a steady income. Woody learned to draw and play the guitar in his teens. At twenty-one he married Mary. He went to California, and in 1937 he got his first radio show. ⬤ RI 2

RESPOND TO SEGMENT 1
 Classroom Collaboration

Have partners work together to create and present a summary, as well as raise questions that might be answered in the next segment.

ENGLISH LANGUAGE LEARNERS

Use Visuals

Use the text visuals to develop students' oral language. Have students tell how the visuals support the ideas in the text.

RESPOND TO SEGMENT 2

 Classroom Collaboration

Have small groups work together to summarize what they have learned. Have them ask questions about what they don't understand.

 Common Core Connection

Grade 6: RI 2 determine a central idea of a text/provide a summary; **RI 4** determine the meaning of words and phrases, including figurative, connotative, and technical meanings; **RI 5** analyze how a sentence, paragraph, chapter, or section fits in the overall structure

Grade 7: RI 2 determine two or more central ideas in a text/analyze their development/ provide summary; **RI 4** determine the meaning of words and phrases, including figurative, connotative, and technical meanings/analyze impact of word choice; **RI 5** analyze the structure an author uses to organize text

Grade 8: RI 2 determine a central idea of text/analyze its development/provide summary; **RI 4** determine the meaning of words and phrases/analyze impact of word choice

Grades 6–8: RI 1 cite textual evidence that most strongly supports analysis of what text says explicitly as well as inferences drawn; **RI 10** read and comprehend literary nonfiction; **W 2** write informative/explanatory texts; **W 5** develop and strengthen writing by planning, revising, editing, rewriting, or trying a new approach; **SL 4** present claims and findings, sequence ideas, and use details to accentuate main ideas or themes/use appropriate eye contact, volume, and pronunciation

Academic Vocabulary

Read each word with students and discuss its meaning.

migrants (p. 67) • people who move from place to place
erratic (p. 71) • unreliable, unpredictable
tradition (p. 86) • a custom that is handed down
fervor (p. 109) • enthusiasm
subversive (p. 110) • planning to overthrow the government

FIRST READ ## Think Through the Text

Have students cite text evidence and draw inferences to answer questions.

pp. 66–72 • *Why did Woody get involved with the Communist party?* He felt that the migrants and other workers were being mistreated under the current system. He listened to Ed Robbins's radio program and thought it made sense. *Why didn't he join the Communist party?* He was not invited, possibly because he was too erratic and undisciplined. ◖RI 1

pp. 112–114 • *What is the origin of the word* hootenanny? There was a woman named Annie who would outshout everyone else at songfests, so they started calling her Hootin' Annie. The name spread, and people began calling songfests Hootenannies. ◖RI 4

pp. 130–131 • *What does Woody reveal to Marjorie about his dreams? How does he say he feels about her?* He dreams that he is not completely sane. He does not know why he writes as he does. His feelings for Marjorie vary greatly. ◖RI 1

SECOND READ ## Analyze the Text

• Guide students to look at the photographs and sidebars from pages 66–133. *Photographs with captions and special features, such as sidebars, are visuals that include information that is not in the main text. How do these features connect the text?* Sample answer: *The features provide information about the living conditions for the migrants, as well as Woody's companions. They help give a move complete idea of what life was like during that time.* ◖Grades 6–7 RI 5

• Have students reread pages 103–130. Ask: *What were some of the influences on Woody's music?* Performing at migrant camps, writing songs for the movie about the building of the Columbia River dam, having friends in the American Communist Party, and being a member of the Almanacs all influenced Woody's music.
◖RI 2

Academic Vocabulary

Read each word with students and discuss its meaning.

sporadically (p. 137) • occurring irregularly

ironic (p. 145) • based on contradiction

FIRST READ ## Think Through the Text

Have students cite text evidence and draw inferences to answer questions.

pp. 135–147 • *How did Woody relieve the tension on the Sea Porpoise?* He played his guitar and had the soldiers sing along. *What did Woody do about the segregation on the ship?* He ignored it and persuaded the officer to let the black and white crew members listen to the music together. ■ RI 1

pp. 146–147 • *How does the author describe Woody's thoughts about his disease?* For ten years, he knew that his Huntington's disease was getting worse, but he continued to deny it. ■ RI 1

pp. 169–172 • *How did the Weavers's recording of "So Long" affect Woody?* The Weavers paid him ten thousand dollars for the song and he and his family were finally able to live in a comfortable apartment. The news of his songwriting ability also spread. ■ RI 1

p. 198 • *How did the country pay tribute to Woody when he died?* Radio stations all over the country played "This Land Is Your Land." ■ RI 1

SECOND READ ## Analyze the Text

• Review pages 134–175. Say: *Summarize the progression of Woody's musical and writing career during this time.* Woody's biography was a success. He continued to write songs, give performances, and release albums. He worked with Pete Seeger and other folksingers to create a revival of folk music. ■ RI 2

• Review pages 187–199. Ask: *What happened with Woody's health?* Woody's health got worse. He was finally correctly diagnosed and stayed in a mental hospital. *What happened with his music?* His music became popular again, and he gave a few performances. ■ RI 2

Independent/Self-Selected Reading

If students have already demonstrated comprehension of *This Land Was Made for You and Me*, have them read other informational texts to practice skills. Suggested titles:

• *A Boy Named Beckoning* by Gina Capaldi

• *Paths to Peace* by Jane Breskin Zalben ■ RI 10

WRITE & PRESENT

1. Have small groups refer to the text to discuss ways the author integrates and presents information both sequentially and causally to describe Guthrie's life. Encourage students to take notes. ■ RI 1, Grades 6–7 RI 5

2. Have students write a paragraph that explains how the author integrates and presents information both sequentially and causally to describe Woody Guthrie's life. Tell students to cite examples from the text to support their explanations. ■ W 2

3. Small groups reconvene to share and edit their paragraphs. ■ W 5

4. Students present their final paragraphs to classmates. ■ SL 4

5. Individual students turn in their final summaries to the teacher.

See Copying Masters, pp. 164–171.

STUDENT CHECKLIST

Writing

☑ Explain how the author presents the information both sequentially and causally to describe events in Woody Guthrie's life.

☑ Cite examples from the text to support explanations.

☑ Use correct language conventions.

Speaking & Listening

☑ Engage effectively in collaborative conversations.

☑ Logically present claims and findings.

☑ Cite text evidence demonstrating sequential and causal structures.

▶ OBJECTIVES

- Analyze the governmental structure of the United States
- Determine the central idea of a secondary source
- Cite specific textual evidence to support analysis

The Words We Live By is broken into three instructional segments.

SEGMENTS

Options for Reading

Independent Students read the text independently or with a partner and then answer questions posed by the teacher.

Supported Students read a segment and answer questions with teacher support.

Common Core Connection

Grade 6: RI 2 determine a central idea of a text/provide a summary; **RI 3** analyze how a key individual, event, or idea is introduced, illustrated, and elaborated

Grade 7: RI 2 determine two or more central ideas in a text/analyze their development/provide a summary

Grade 8: RI 2 determine a central idea in a text/analyze its development/provide a summary

Grades 6–8: RI 1 cite textual evidence to support analysis of what the text says explicitly as well as inferences drawn

The Words We Live By
Your Annotated Guide to the Constitution
by Linda R. Monk

SUMMARY The Constitution is the foundation of our rights as American citizens. Author Linda R. Monk takes readers through this living document line by line. Facts, trivia, and anecdotes enliven the journey.

ABOUT THE AUTHOR Linda R. Monk is an award-winning author, a constitutional scholar, a journalist, and a museum curator. She is a two-time recipient of the American Bar Association's Silver Gavel Award for law-related media.

Discuss Genre and Set Purpose

INFORMATIONAL TEXT Display the book and read the title together. Show students the text features, such as headings, sidebars, and pullout quotes. Discuss with students how they can tell this book is informational.

SET PURPOSE Help students set a purpose for reading, such as to learn information about the U.S. Constitution and analyze the structure of the U.S. government.

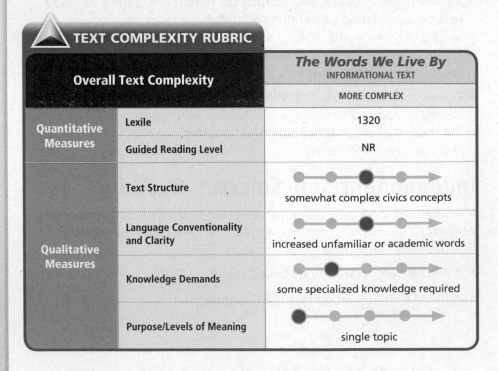

▲ **TEXT COMPLEXITY RUBRIC**

Overall Text Complexity		*The Words We Live By* INFORMATIONAL TEXT
		MORE COMPLEX
Quantitative Measures	Lexile	1320
	Guided Reading Level	NR
Qualitative Measures	Text Structure	somewhat complex civics concepts
	Language Conventionality and Clarity	increased unfamiliar or academic words
	Knowledge Demands	some specialized knowledge required
	Purpose/Levels of Meaning	single topic

Academic Vocabulary

Read each word with students and discuss its meaning.

culmination (p. 10) • the highest or final point

commerce (p. 21) • buying and selling things; business

obsolete (p. 43) • out of date; no longer in use

innovation (p. 52) • new ideas

bribe (p. 79) • money or gifts offered to someone to convince him or her to do something

Domain Specific Vocabulary

checks and balances (p. 24) • each branch of government limits the power of the others

suffrage (p. 27) • the right to vote

impeachment (p. 34) • the process by which a public official is accused of wrongdoing

veto (p. 46) • the authority to reject something that is suggested

FIRST READ ## Think Through the Text

Have students cite text evidence and draw inferences to answer questions.

p. 10 • *What is the structure of our government designed to do?* It is designed to preserve American liberty. *Why was the Constitution the most democratic document the world had ever witnessed?* The people, not the state legislatures, had to approve it. RI 1

p. 24 • *How does the Constitution limit the power of the government?* It divides governmental power among legislative, executive, and judicial branches. It creates a system of checks and balances in which each branch of government shares some powers of the other branches. RI 1

p. 64 • *What is the main focus of Article II of the Constitution?* the president; Article II tells how the president is to be selected and describes presidential powers *Is it possible to remove a president from office if he or she commits a crime? Support your response with text evidence.* Yes; Article II allows a president that has committed high crimes and misdemeanors to be impeached and removed from office. RI 1

SECOND READ ## Analyze the Text

- Review page 10. Ask: *Why is the Constitution an experiment in liberty? Cite evidence from the text.* The Constitution isn't perfect and is designed to be changed. The outcome of the Constitution still isn't certain, which makes it an experiment. RI 1

- Reread page 12. Ask: *Which three words of the Constitution are the most important?* "we the people" *Why?* They show that the people are the true rulers in American government. *What is this known as?* It is known as popular sovereignty. Grade 6 RI 3

- Reread "The Least Dangerous Branch" on page 92. Ask: *Which branch of government does Alexander Hamilton think is least dangerous to democracy? How does he support this claim?* He thinks that the judiciary is the least dangerous and that the courts are the true defenders of the will of the people. He says that, unlike the other branches, the judiciary has neither force nor will, only judgment. RI 2

ELL ### ENGLISH LANGUAGE LEARNERS

Use Comprehensible Input

Read aloud the Preamble. Then restate the text in simpler language. For example, rephrase "insure domestic tranquility" as "make sure our country has peace." Have students repeat after you. Ask questions to confirm understanding. For example, ask: *Do we want to have peace in our country?* yes *What else do want to have?* Elicit responses such as freedom, justice, and defense.

RESPOND TO SEGMENT 1

Classroom Collaboration

Have partners summarize what they have read so far. Tell them to ask questions about anything they don't understand.

ENGLISH LANGUAGE LEARNERS

Use Cognates

As students read, point out cognates such as *liberty/libertad* and *constitution/constitución*.

RESPOND TO SEGMENT 2

 Classroom Collaboration

Have small groups work together to summarize what they have read so far. Have them ask questions about what they don't understand.

COMMON CORE **Common Core Connection**

Grade 6: RI 2 determine a central idea of a text/provide a summary; **RI 4** determine the meaning of words and phrases, including figurative, connotative, and technical meanings; **RI 6** determine the author's point of view or purpose and explain how it is conveyed

Grade 7: RI 2 determine two or more central ideas in a text/analyze their development/provide a summary; **RI 4** determine the meaning of words and phrases, including figurative, connotative, and technical meanings/analyze impact of word choice; **RI 6** determine author's point of view or purpose/analyze how author distinguishes position

Grade 8: RI 2 determine a central idea of a text/analyze its development/provide a summary; **RI 4** determine the meaning of words and phrases/analyze impact of word choice

Grades 6-8: RI 1 cite textual evidence to support analysis of what the text says explicitly as well as inferences drawn; **RI 10** read and comprehend literary nonfiction; **W 1** write arguments to support claims; **W 5** develop and strengthen writing by planning, revising, editing, rewriting, or trying a new approach; **SL 4** present claims and findings, sequence ideas, and use details to accentuate main ideas or themes

---

Academic Vocabulary

Read each word with students and discuss its meaning.

amending (p. 126) • correcting; making changes to

abridging (p. 137) • shortening or lessening

infringed (p. 151) • overstepped

infamous (p. 164) • having a bad reputation

impartial (p. 175) • treating all people and opinions equally

---

FIRST READ ## Think Through the Text

Have students cite text evidence and draw inferences to answer questions.

p. 126 • *What are the first ten amendments known as?* The Bill of Rights *What is the purpose of the Bill of Rights? Cite text evidence.* The Bill of Rights protects individual liberties that Americans feared would be weakened under the new Constitution. ◼ RI 1

p. 139 • *What kinds of speech are included in free speech?* pure speech, such as word and debates; speech-plus, which includes words and actions; and symbolic speech, which is actions that deliver a message ◼ RI 1

p. 157 • *What is the purpose of the Fourth Amendment?* The Fourth Amendment protects people's privacy against the government. ◼ RI 1

p. 167 • *What does "taking the Fifth" mean?* It means that if you are being tried for a crime, you have the right not to testify against yourself. People say they are "taking the Fifth" when they refuse to answer questions. ◼ RI 4

SECOND READ ## Analyze the Text

• Ask: *What is the author's point of view about the First Amendment? Why does she feel this way?* She thinks it is the most important amendment in the Bill of Rights. The five freedoms protected in the First Amendment make up freedom of expression. Without these freedoms, we could not stand up for other rights that we have. ◼ Grade 6–7 RI 6

• Reread pages 152 and 153. Ask: *Has the Supreme Court officially ruled that individuals have the right to bear arms?* no *What are the opposing viewpoints on this issue?* Some people think that individuals should have the right to bear arms because it gives people the right to live free from fear. Others think that the right to bear arms should only be connected to service in a well-regulated, part-time military organization. They think weapons are not for personal use. ◼ RI 2

• Reread page 173. Ask: *What is the purpose of the Sixth Amendment? How does it protect individual liberties? Cite text evidence to support your answer.* The Sixth Amendment protects the individual's right to a trial by jury in a criminal case. It attempts to balance the enormous power of the state against the power of the individual. ◼ RI 1

Academic Vocabulary

Read each word with students and discuss its meaning.

inferior (p. 207) • lower in rank or importance

reparations (p. 210) • payments for damages

instrumental (p. 239) • helpful in accomplishing something

resignation (p. 255) • the act of giving up one's job or responsibilities

Performance Task

WRITE & PRESENT

1. Have small groups discuss the governmental structure of the United States and support their analysis with textual evidence from primary and secondary sources, including *The Words We Live By* and the U.S. Constitution, with the Preamble and the Bill of Rights. ▬ RI 1

2. Individual students write an argument that analyzes the effectiveness of the governmental structure of the United States and support the analysis with text evidence from *The Words We Live By* and the U.S. Constitution. ▬ W 1

3. Students work with partners to share and edit their work. ▬ W 5

4. Have students present their work to the class. ▬ SL 4

See Copying Masters, pp. 164–171.

STUDENT CHECKLIST

Writing

☑ Write an argument that analyzes the effectiveness of the governmental structure of the United States.

☑ Cite textual evidence to support analysis.

☑ Use correct language conventions.

Speaking & Listening

☑ Participate effectively in a collaborative discussion.

☑ Present claims and findings, presenting facts and details that support the argument.

☑ Use language that is appropriate for the purpose.

FIRST READ ## Think Through the Text

Have students cite text evidence and draw inferences to answer questions.

pp. 208–209 • *When was the Thirteenth Amendment passed?* 1865 *What did it accomplish?* It freed almost four million slaves. ▬ RI 1

p. 213 • *Which amendment do scholars believe created a new Constitution? Why?* Scholars believe the Fourteenth Amendment created a new Constitution because it has a wide scope and promise of equality. ▬ RI 1

pp. 238–241 • *Which amendment gave women the right to vote?* the Nineteenth Amendment *How did women show they wanted this right?* Women held rallies, got involved in politics, and chained themselves to the White House fence to show they wanted the right to vote. ▬ RI 1

p. 260 • *Why did the Twenty-Sixth Amendment lower the voting age from 21 to 18?* During the Vietnam War, young people said that if they were old enough to be sent to war and die for their country, they were old enough to vote. ▬ RI 1

SECOND READ ## Analyze the Text

• Reread pages 209 and 240 with students. Ask: *How is Susan B. Anthony's argument similar to Frederick Douglass's argument?* Like Douglass, Anthony asserts that "We the people" refers to all people, not just a select group. ▬ Grades 6–7 RI 6

• Reread page 263. *What is the author's point of view about the Constitution?* She thinks it gives the great gift of deciding for ourselves what freedom is. *How does the Constitution demonstrate that we are a government in which the people rule?* It lets us decide what words we will live by. ▬ Grades 6–7 RI 6

Independent/Self-Selected Reading

If students have demonstrated comprehension of *The Words We Live By*, have them read other texts to practice skills. Suggested titles:

• U.S. Constitution, including the Preamble and First Amendment

• *Declaring Freedom (How Government Works)* by Gwenyth Swain ▬ RI 10

▶ OBJECTIVES

- Identify main ideas and supporting details
- Describe how an author structures a text
- Analyze text using text evidence

Freedom Walkers is broken into three instructional segments.

Options for Reading

Independent Students read the book independently and then answer questions posed by the teacher.

Supported Students read a segment and answer questions with teacher support.

 Common Core Connection

Grade 6: RI 3 analyze how a key individual, event, or idea is introduced, illustrated, and elaborated

Grades 7: RI 3 analyze interactions between individuals, events, and ideas; **RI 5** analyze the structure an author uses to organize text

Grade 8: RI 3 analyze how text makes connections among and distinctions between individuals, ideas, or events

Grades 6–8: RI 1 cite textual evidence to support analysis of what the text says explicitly as well as inferences drawn

Freedom Walkers
The Story of the Montgomery Bus Boycott
by Russell Freedman

SUMMARY Late in 1955, the entire African-American community in Montgomery, Alabama, rose up behind Rosa Parks when she was arrested and jailed after refusing to give up her seat on a bus to a white man. The resulting boycott of the Montgomery bus system led to landmark civil rights victories and the end of public segregation.

ABOUT THE AUTHOR Russell Freedman is the author of more than fifty nonfiction titles. His careful choice of period photographs illustrates and deepens meaning for the reader. He has received numerous awards for his work, including the Laura Ingalls Wilder Award.

Discuss Genre and Set Purpose

INFORMATIONAL TEXT Have students briefly page through the book to examine the text and accompanying photographs. Discuss with students how they can tell that this book is informational.

SET PURPOSE Have students determine a purpose for reading, such as to learn information about the Montgomery Bus Boycott.

▲ TEXT COMPLEXITY RUBRIC

Overall Text Complexity		*Freedom Walkers* INFORMATIONAL TEXT
		COMPLEX
Quantitative Measures	Lexile	1110L
	Guided Reading Level	Z
Qualitative Measures	Text Structure	some unfamiliar language, but mostly clear and direct; somewhat complex sentence structures
	Language Conventionality and Clarity	some unfamiliar or academic words
	Knowledge Demands	some specialized knowledge required
	Purpose/Levels of Meaning	implied, but easy to identify from context

Academic Vocabulary

Read each word with students and discuss its meaning.

segregation (p. 1) • the enforced separation of different racial groups in a country, community, or establishment

grievances (p. 3) • actual or supposed wrongs that are cause for complaint or protest

boycott (p. 12) • a way to express protest by refusing to buy or use something

submission (p. 15) • the act of accepting or yielding to a superior force or authority

galvanized (p. 17) • shocked or excited into taking action

Domain Specific Vocabulary

Jim Crow (p. 1) • ethnic discrimination, particularly against African Americans

NAACP (p. 17) • National Association for the Advancement of Colored People; an African American civil rights organization formed in 1909

FIRST READ ## Think Through the Text

Have students cite text evidence and draw inferences to answer questions.

pp. 1–5 • *What was the reason for segregation in the American South? African Americans were not viewed as equal to whites. How did segregation laws affect African Americans in the South? Segregation was used to keep the races separate.* RI 1

pp. 17–20 • *What event caught the attention of E. D. Nixon? the arrest of Claudette Colvin What did he and others hope to do? E. D. Nixon and others wanted to show that segregation on buses was unconstitutional.* RI 3

SECOND READ ## Analyze the Text

• Read aloud the last paragraph on page 20. Then ask: *How can you tell that leaders like E. D. Nixon had thought deeply and carefully about how to win a case against bus segregation in court? The text describes the drawbacks of using Claudette Colvin's case and notes that the court process would require strong and costly support. This shows that the idea of bringing a case against bus segregation to court was not frivolous or based simply on anger.* RI 1

• Review basic text structures, including sequential, spacial, and causal structures. Then guide students to look at pages 1–7. Ask: *Which two text structures did the author primarily use? Why? Russell Freedman primarily used a sequential structure, which moves the text through time and follows a historical time line. However, he also used cause and effect to emphasize and help explain what caused key events to occur. An example of sequential structure appears on pages 4–7; an example of causal structure appears on pages 2–3.* Grade 7 RI 5

ENGLISH LANGUAGE LEARNERS

Use Visuals

Use the text photographs to develop students' oral language. Have students tell how the photographs support the ideas in the text.

RESPOND TO SEGMENT 1

Classroom Collaboration

Have small groups work together to create and present a summary, as well as raise questions that might be answered in the next segment.

ENGLISH LANGUAGE LEARNERS

Use Sentence Frames
Help students generate adjectives to describe Martin Luther King, Jr. Have them orally complete sentence frames, such as: *Martin Luther King, Jr., was _____ because _____.*

 RESPOND TO SEGMENT 2

Classroom Collaboration

Have small groups work together to summarize what they have learned and ask questions about anything they don't understand.

 Common Core Connection

Grade 6: RI 2 determine a central idea of a text/provide a summary; **RI 3** analyze how a key individual, event, or idea is introduced, illustrated, and elaborated; **RI 5** analyze how a sentence paragraph, chapter, or section fits in the overall structure

Grade 7: RI 2 determine two or more central ideas in a text/analyze their development/ provide summary; **RI 3** analyze interactions between individuals, events, and ideas; **RI 4** determine the meaning of words and phrases, including figurative, connotative, and technical meanings/analyze impact of word choice; **RI 5** analyze the structure an author uses to organize text

Grade 8: RI 2 determine a central idea of text/ analyze its development/provide summary; **RI 3** analyze how text makes connections among and distinctions between individuals, ideas, or events; **RI 4** determine the meaning of words and phrases/analyze impact of word choice

Grades 6–8: RI 1 cite textual evidence to support analysis of what the text says explicitly as well as inferences drawn; **RI 10** read and comprehend literary nonfiction; **W 2** write informative/ explanatory texts; **W 5** develop and strengthen writing by planning, revising, editing, rewriting, or trying a new approach; **SL 1** engage in a range of collaborative discussions; **SL 4** present claims and findings, emphasizing points in focused, coherent manner

---

Academic Vocabulary

Read each word with students and discuss its meaning.

violating (p. 30) • breaking a law or failing to follow one

momentous (p. 31) • of great importance or significance

eminent (p. 38) • distinguished or high-ranking

oppression (p. 46) • cruel or unjust treatment or control

advocating (p. 46) • recommending or speaking in favor of

FIRST READ **Think Through the Text**

Have students cite text evidence and draw inferences to answer questions.

pp. 23–35 • *Based on what you learned about Rosa Parks, what words would you use to describe her character?* Possible responses: *determined, dignified, hard-working* ▬ Grade 6 RI 3, RI 1

pp. 32–33 • *What did Parks have to consider before agreeing to make her arrest a test case against bus segregation? She had to think about the real dangers she and her family might face.* ▬ RI 1

pp. 45–47 • *What key points did King want to get across in his speech?* Possible responses: *It was time to bring the oppression of blacks to an end; that people needed to rise up together; that protests must be civil and nonviolent.* ▬ RI 2

SECOND READ **Analyze the Text**

• Ask: *What factors made Martin Luther King, Jr., a good choice to head the organization that would plan the boycott? He was a religious leader and somewhat new to the area, so he had not yet been intimidated or pressured by white community leaders. At the meeting he had declared that he was not afraid.* ▬ Grades 6–7 RI 3

• Read aloud the paragraph that begins at the end of p. 45 and continues on p. 46. Then ask: *Why did King want his audience to think about their oppression? In his speech, King wants his audience to realize how badly they have been treated for so long. By using the word* tired *repeatedly, he is helping the audience connect to how tired they are of being oppressed.* ▬ RI 3

• Guide students to look back at the second paragraph on p. 47. Ask: *What word does King use repeatedly in this paragraph? Why? By repeating the word* wrong, *King sparks and builds on the idea that protest is not wrong.* ▬ RI 1, Grades 7–8 RI 4

Academic Vocabulary

Read each word with students and discuss its meaning.

compromise (p. 49) • an agreement to settle a dispute in which both sides accept less than they want

indicted (p. 69) • accused of or charged with a crime

FIRST READ Think Through the Text

Have students cite text evidence and draw inferences to answer questions.

pp. 49–53 • *What strategies did the boycott organizers come up with to help blacks avoid using buses?* *They studied how another bus boycott worked; they asked car owners to volunteer their vehicles to transport others; they created a communications network.* ◀ RI 1

pp. 59–63 • *How did white city leaders respond to the boycott?* *The mayor attempted to discredit black leaders. Police officers ticketed car pool drivers and harassed people waiting for rides.* ◀ RI 1

pp. 67–76 • *What was the effect of indicting 115 blacks under an old law that prohibited boycotts?* *Black leaders who had been indicted decided to turn themselves in; these actions became a source of pride.* ◀ RI 1

SECOND READ Analyze the Text

• Have students review the text on pp. 54–55. Then ask: *Which of the boycotters' demands did city leaders find threatening?* *City officials were most threatened by the demand regarding bus seating, because it was illegal at the time. They didn't want to challenge these long-standing laws.* ◀ RI 1

• Guide students to look back at pp. 84–95 to answer the question: *Why did King's insistence on nonviolence become so important?* *The success of the nonviolent protest showed civil rights activists how powerful it was in challenging segregation and effecting change. It lead to the spread of nonviolent protests across the country.* ◀ RI 3

Independent/Self-Selected Reading

If students have demonstrated comprehension of *Freedom Walkers*, have them read other informational texts to practice skills. Suggested titles:

• *Boycott Blues* by Andrea Davis Pinkney

• *I've Seen the Promised Land* by Walter Dean Myers ◀ RI 10

WRITE & PRESENT

1. Have small groups refer to the text to discuss ways the author integrates and presents information both sequentially and causally in order to explain how the civil rights movement started. Encourage students to take notes.
◀ RI 3, Grades 6-7 RI 5

2. Individual students write a paragraph that describes how the author integrates and presents information both sequentially and causally. ◀ W 2

3. Small groups reconvene to share their paragraphs with each other and edit their writing.
◀ W 5, SL 1

4. Groups present their final ideas and examples to classmates.
◀ SL 4

5. Individual students turn in their final drafts to the teacher.

See Copying Masters, pp. 164–171.

STUDENT CHECKLIST

Writing

☑ Include a clear topic sentence.

☑ Describe how the author presents information both sequentially and causally to explain how the civil rights movement started.

☑ Provide a logical conclusion.

Speaking & Listening

☑ Engage effectively in collaborative discussions.

☑ Logically present claims and findings.

☑ Cite text evidence demonstrating sequential and causal structures.

▶ OBJECTIVES

- Integrate information presented in different formats to develop understanding of a topic
- Identify main ideas and key details
- Analyze text using text evidence

Cathedral is broken into three instructional segments.

SEGMENTS

SEGMENT 1 . . . . pp. 5–25
SEGMENT 2 . . . . pp. 26–50
SEGMENT 3 . . . . pp. 51–78

Options for Reading

Independent Students read the selection independently or with a partner and then answer questions posed by the teacher.

Supported Students read a segment and answer questions with teacher support.

 Common Core Connection

Grade 6: RI 2 determine a central idea of a text/provide a summary; **RI 7** integrate information presented in different media or formats as well as in words

Grade 7: RI 2 determine two or more central ideas in a text/analyze their development/ provide summary

Grade 8: RI 2 determine a central idea of a text/analyze its development/provide summary

Grades 6–8: RI 1 cite textual evidence to support analysis of what the text says explicitly as well as inferences drawn

Cathedral
The Story of Its Construction
by David Macaulay

SUMMARY Pen-and-ink drawings illustrate this step-by-step description of the building of a Gothic cathedral. Macaulay provides details about every part of the cathedral, from floor to ceiling.

ABOUT THE AUTHOR David Macaulay was born in England in 1946 and studied architecture at Rhode Island School of Design. His first idea for a book was about a gargoyle beauty pageant. Though this book never became a reality, the drawing of a cathedral he made for it became the basis for *Cathedral*, which went on to win a Caldecott Honor Award.

Discuss Genre and Set Purpose

INFORMATIONAL TEXT Have students read the title and skim the text and illustrations. Discuss with students how they can tell that this text is informational. Ask them to predict what they will learn about, based on the illustrations.

SET PURPOSE Help students set a purpose for reading, such as to use the text, drawings, and diagrams to gain information about how a cathedral is built.

◭ TEXT COMPLEXITY RUBRIC		*Cathedral* INFORMATIONAL TEXT
Overall Text Complexity		**COMPLEX**
Quantitative Measures	Lexile	1120
	Guided Reading Level	Z
Qualitative Measures	Text Structure	somewhat complex science concepts
	Language Conventionality and Clarity	some unfamiliar or academic words
	Knowledge Demands	some specialized knowledge required
	Purpose/Levels of Meaning	single topic

SEGMENT 1 pp. 5–25

Academic Vocabulary

Read each word with students and discuss its meaning.

prospered (p. 5) • succeeded; thrived

summoned (p. 7) • requested or ordered someone to appear

elevation (p. 13) • a drawing that shows one side of a structure or building

extracted (p. 17) • took out; removed

FIRST READ ## Think Through the Text

Have students cite text evidence and draw inferences to answer questions.

pp. 12–13 • *What do the diagrams on pages 12 and 13 show?* They show a floor plan and wall elevation. *Where is the Romanesque Crypt located?* It is located in the center of the cathedral below the ground. *What is the middle section of the wall called?* It is called the triforium. ▬ RI 1, Grade 6 RI 7

pp. 14–20 • *Summarize what had to happen before construction of the cathedral could begin.* Wood had to be cut down, stone had to be cut, and the site had to be cleared. Workshops were built for the workers. ▬ RI 2

SECOND READ ## Analyze the Text

• Reread page 5. Ask: *Why did the people of Chutreaux want a new cathedral?* They wanted to thank God, build a resting place for relics, and not be outdone by the people of the nearby cities. ▬ RI 1

• Say: *Look again at the illustrations on pages 10–11. What is a template used for?* It is used as a pattern to copy a design. *What is an auger used for?* It is used to bore holes in wood. *How does the author communicate this information without words?* He illustrates people using the tools. ▬ RI 1, Grade 6 RI 7

• Say: *Look again at the illustrations on pages 12–13. Why would these drawings have to be created before work could begin?* They show the basic design of the building and help people picture what the finished building will look like. ▬ RI 1, Grade 6 RI 7

ENGLISH LANGUAGE LEARNERS

Use Visuals

Use the illustrations on pages 10–11 to develop students' oral language. Read each word and have students repeat it. Ask them to demonstrate or explain how to use each tool.

RESPOND TO SEGMENT 1
Classroom Collaboration

Have small groups summarize what they have read. Have them ask questions about what they don't understand.

ENGLISH LANGUAGE LEARNERS

Use Visuals

Use the illustrations to describe the steps for building a cathedral. Ask questions to check understanding. *Is the foundation above ground or below ground?* below. *What gets built next?* walls

---

RESPOND TO SEGMENT 2

 Classroom Collaboration

Have partners work together to create and present a summary of what has happened so far, as well as make predictions about what they might learn in the next segment.

 Common Core Connection

Grade 6: RI 2 determine a central idea of a text/provide a summary; **RI 3** analyze how a key individual, event, or idea is introduced, illustrated, and elaborated; **RI 7** integrate information presented in different media or formats as well as in words; **SL 4** present claims and findings, sequence ideas, and use details to accentuate main ideas or themes

Grade 7: RI 2 determine two or more central ideas in a text/analyze their development/provide summary; **RI 3** analyze interactions between individuals, events, and ideas

Grade 8: RI 2 determine a central idea of a text/analyze its development/provide summary; **RI 3** analyze how a text makes connections among and distinctions between individuals, ideas, or events

Grades 7–8: SL 4 present claims and findings, emphasizing points in a focused, coherent manner

Grades 6-8: RI 1 cite textual evidence to support analysis of what the text says explicitly as well as inferences drawn; **RI 10** read and comprehend literary nonfiction; **W 2** write informative/explanatory texts; **W 5** develop and strengthen writing by planning, revising, editing, or trying a new approach

---

Academic Vocabulary

Read each word with students and discuss its meaning.

hoisted (p. 32) • lifted something heavy

dismantled (p. 40) • took apart, piece by piece

seeping (p. 44) • flowing or leaking slowly

FIRST READ **Think Through the Text**

Have students cite text evidence and draw inferences to answer questions.

pp. 26–29 • *When was the first foundation stone laid? April 14, 1253. What happened after the foundation was built? The walls were built. Why were the walls built in pieces and cemented together? It was too expensive to build walls of solid stone.* RI 3

pp. 33–46 • *Summarize the progress of the cathedral between summer of 1270 through 1280. During the summer of 1270, the chapels in the apse and most of the piers and buttresses in the choir were finished. The centering was mostly in place. In 1275, the walls of the choir and aisle were completed and work began on the roof. By 1280, the choir was ready for the construction of the vaulted ceiling, and the foundation of the transept was begun.* RI 2

SECOND READ **Analyze the Text**

- Ask: *How do the illustrations help you visualize the progress of the cathedral? The author describes each step of building the cathedral. The illustrations show what each piece looks like as it is being built and then what the cathedral looks like as each piece is added.* RI 1, Grade 6 RI 7

- Reread page 30. Ask: *How did flying buttresses influence the kinds of windows the cathedral could have? Because force was transferred through the flying buttress to the buttress and then to the foundation, the main piers could remain thin in proportion to their height. This allowed more space for the windows between them.* RI 3

- Review page 31. Ask: *How were workers able to build up high in the cathedral? Refer to the text and the illustration. They used scaffolding and permanent spiral staircases.* RI 1, Grade 6 RI 7

Academic Vocabulary

Read each word with students and discuss its meaning.

resumed (p. 52) • started doing something again after stopping

simultaneously (p. 55) • at the same time as

molten (p. 60) • melted at high temperature

niches (p. 75) • hollow places in walls

FIRST READ ## Think Through the Text

Have students cite text evidence and draw inferences to answer questions.

pp. 55–56 • *What two parts of the cathedral were built at the same time?* *the vaulting over the choir and the aisle* 🔊 RI 3

pp. 60–61 • *Summarize the process for making the glass windows.* *Glass was made from ash and melted sand. Metal was added for color. The molten glass was put on the end of a pipe, blown into a balloon, and spun into a flat, circular shape. The cooled glass was cut, joined by lead strips, and inserted between mullions and reinforcing bars.* 🔊 RI 2

p. 75 • *When was the cathedral finally completed?* *in 1338* 🔊 RI 1

SECOND READ ## Analyze the Text

• Review page 63. Ask: *How do you know that details were important to the workers?* *They painted lines on the stones of the web to make them appear to be the same size, even though no one would see them.* 🔊 RI 1

• Say: *Look again at the illustration on page 73. What does this illustration show?* *It shows workers filling in the rose window's diameter with glass.* *What does the illustration help you visualize?* Sample answer: *It helps me visualize how many tiny pieces of glass were needed to fill the rose window.* 🔊 RI 1, Grade 6 RI 7

• Say: *Look at the illustration on page 76. What does this illustration show?* *It shows what the cathedral looks like from inside. Why do you think the author chose to illustrate this scene rather than describe it?* Sample answer: *The illustration gives viewers a better sense of the height and space inside the cathedral than words could. It helps them imagine what it would be like to stand inside.* 🔊 RI 1, Grade 6 RI 7

Independent/Self-Selected Reading

If students have already demonstrated comprehension of *Cathedral*, have them read other texts to practice skills. Suggested titles:

• *Castle* by David Macaulay

• *Medieval Cathedral* by Fiona Macdonald 🔊 RI 10

WRITE & PRESENT

1. Have small groups integrate the quantitative and technical information in the text with the information conveyed in the diagrams and models to discuss how these elements help them develop a deeper understanding of Gothic architecture.
🔊 RI 1, Grade 6 RI 7

2. Individual students write an explanatory text describing how one part of the cathedral was built, citing details from the text and the illustrations, diagrams, or models to explain the process.
🔊 W 2

3. Have small groups reconvene to share and edit their writing.
🔊 W 5

4. Students present their final explanations to their classmates. Ask them to show visuals from the book to illustrate important points.
🔊 SL 4

See Copying Masters, pp. 164–171.

STUDENT CHECKLIST

Writing

☑ Write an explanatory text describing how one part of the cathedral was built.

☑ Give specific details and examples from the text and illustrations.

☑ Use correct language conventions.

Speaking & Listening

☑ Participate effectively in a collaborative discussion.

☑ Organize information in a logical order.

☑ Integrate visuals into the presentation.

▶ OBJECTIVES

- Determine main ideas
- Analyze how key details support the central idea
- Integrate information presented in different formats
- Compare and contrast information about the same topic

The Building of Manhattan is broken into three instructional segments.

SEGMENTS

Options for Reading

Independent Students read the selection independently or with a partner and then answer questions posed by the teacher.

Supported Students read a segment and answer questions with teacher support.

 COMMON CORE **Common Core Connection**

Grade 6: RI 2 determine a central idea of a text/provide a summary; **RI 7** integrate information presented in different media or formats as well as in words

Grade 7: RI 2 determine two or more central ideas in a text/analyze their development/ provide summary

Grade 8: RI 2 determine a central idea of a text/analyze its development/provide summary

Grades 6–8: RI 1 cite textual evidence to support analysis of what the text says explicitly as well as inferences drawn

The Building of Manhattan

by Donald A. Mackay

SUMMARY With line drawings and text, author and illustrator Donald A. Mackay traces the building of Manhattan from the ground up. He describes the city's architects, its construction methods, and city services.

ABOUT THE AUTHOR Donald A. Mackay was born in Halifax, Nova Scotia. He grew up in Boston and spent most of his career working as an artist. The excavation of a Wall Street bank, as well as his research into his family's roots in New York City, inspired Mackay to write *The Building of Manhattan*.

Discuss Genre and Set Purpose

INFORMATIONAL TEXT Display the book and read the title together. Show students the illustrations and diagrams. Discuss how students can tell this book is informational.

SET PURPOSE Help students set a purpose for reading, such as to compare and contrast information about how Manhattan was built.

▲ TEXT COMPLEXITY RUBRIC

Overall Text Complexity		*The Building of Manhattan* INFORMATIONAL TEXT MORE COMPLEX
Quantitative Measures	Lexile	1230
	Guided Reading Level	N/A
Qualitative Measures	Text Structure	sophisticated graphics, essential to understanding the text, may also provide information not otherwise conveyed in the text
	Language Conventionality and Clarity	increased unfamiliar or academic words
	Knowledge Demands	some specialized knowledge required
	Purpose/Levels of Meaning	implied, but easy to infer

Academic Vocabulary

Read each word with students and discuss its meaning.

formidable (p. 10) • frightening; awe-inspiring

contentious (p. 12) • argumentative

grid (p. 20) • a network of evenly spaced horizontal and vertical lines that form squares

squalid (p. 34) • dirty and miserable because of poverty or neglect

ingenuity (p. 37) • the ability to use original thinking to solve a problem

ENGLISH LANGUAGE LEARNERS

Use Visuals

Use the visuals to name and describe city features such as skyscrapers and bridges. Then use them to build vocabulary. Point to the illustration on page 35. Have students turn to a partner and talk about what they see. Students may name or describe the objects.

FIRST READ **Think Through the Text**

Have students cite text evidence and draw inferences to answer questions.

pp. 6–7 • *Who built the first permanent settlement on the island of Manhattan? What was it called and why was it built?* The Dutch built the first permanent settlement in Manhattan. It was called New Amsterdam, and its whole purpose was business. **RI 1**

pp. 10–13 • *How did New Amsterdam become New York?* The English demanded surrender and the Dutch did not have enough defenses to fight, so the English took over and renamed the town New York. **RI 1**

pp. 21–23 • *What problems did the growing city face?* The city needed clean drinking water, a safe sewage system, and a means of getting around more easily. *How were some of these problems solved?* The construction of the Croton Reservoir and Aqueduct brought clean water to the city. A horse-drawn "railroad" began carrying passengers. **RI 1**

SECOND READ **Analyze the Text**

- Review pages 22–27. Ask: *What two things changed how tall buildings could be built?* Cast iron construction made it possible to build above five or six floors, but people still had to walk up and down stairs. Safety elevators made it possible to build even higher. **RI 1**

- Have students reread page 29. Ask: *What is the main idea of this page?* Technology can tell you how to build something but it requires a unique person to actually build it. *What details support this idea?* The author says master builders build to the limits of their knowledge and the capabilities of their time and then go beyond them. Manhattan was built by people who rose to challenges and transformed the city. **RI 2**

- Have students look at the diagram on page 46. Ask: *What is the purpose of this diagram?* The diagram shows how the derrick works. *What raises and lifts the boom?* the top lift cable *What keeps the derrick upright and steady?* the guy wires **Grade 6 RI 7**

RESPOND TO SEGMENT 1

Classroom Collaboration

Have partners summarize what they have read so far. Tell them to ask questions about anything they don't understand.

ENGLISH LANGUAGE LEARNERS

Use Visuals

Use the diagrams and visuals to support comprehension. For example, on page 92, read each caption and point to the corresponding part of the illustration. Check comprehension: *What caps the hole? a wooden plug What holds the blasting wire in place? a rock*

RESPOND TO SEGMENT 2

Classroom Collaboration

Have small groups work together to summarize what they have read so far. Have them ask questions about what they don't understand.

COMMON CORE
Common Core Connection

Grade 6: RI 2 determine a central idea of a text/provide a summary; **RI 7** integrate information presented in different media or formats as well as in words; **RI 9** compare and contrast one author's presentation of events with that of another

Grade 7: RI 2 determine two or more central ideas in a text/analyze their development/ provide summary; **RI 9** analyze how two or more authors writing about the same topic shape their presentations

Grade 8: RI 2 determine a central idea of a text/analyze its development/provide summary; **RI 9** analyze a case in which two or more texts provide conflicting information/identify where texts disagree; **SL 5** integrate multimedia and visual displays into presentations

Grades 6–7: SL 5 include multimedia components and visual displays in presentations

Grades 6–8: RI 1 cite textual evidence to support analysis of what the text says explicitly as well as inferences drawn; **RI 10** read and comprehend literary nonfiction; **W 2** write informative/explanatory texts; **W 5** develop and strengthen writing by planning, revising, editing, rewriting, or trying a new approach

---

Academic Vocabulary

Read each word with students and discuss its meaning.

rational (p. 62) • logical and sensible

renovates (p. 69) • repairs; makes new again

homogenous (p. 87) • all of the same kind

compressed (p. 88) • flattened to fit into a small space

detonation (p. 92) • the setting off of an explosion

FIRST READ **Think Through the Text**

Have students cite text evidence and draw inferences to answer questions.

pp. 52–53 • *What effect did coming out of the Depression and World War II have on New York City? Support your answer with text evidence. The city was ready for dramatic change. Private apartment complexes were built, the city sponsored public housing, the United Nations headquarters were built, and the city became more prosperous.* ▬RI 1

p. 63 • *What is the main idea of page 63? Building a skyscraper in Manhattan is a complex and risky task. What details support it? Every bit of land already has something built on it, so you have to buy all the buildings that occupy the area you want. Plans must be filed, permits sought, variances asked for, fees paid, and forms filled out. Every delay costs money.* ▬RI 2

p. 96 • *Look at the diagram on page 96. What is the subcontractor's job? Subcontractors do the construction for all of the various trades. What is an example of a subcontractor? The steel fabricator is an example of a subcontractor.* ▬Grade 6 RI 7

SECOND READ **Analyze the Text**

- Have students skim page 62. Ask: *What do zoning laws do? Why are they needed? Zoning laws control the height and form of buildings and the amount of land to be built upon. They create commercial and residential districts. Zoning laws are needed to assure that the surroundings are livable for city inhabitants.* ▬RI 1

- Review pages 66–69. Ask: *Why is the subway system essential to New York City? It provides swift transportation. It enabled the above-ground tracks to come down and made way for skyscrapers and corporate headquarters.* ▬RI 1

- Reread page 97. Ask: *What inference can you make about what would happen if there were no surveyors? Support your inference with details. Buildings would not be aligned vertically. As a building rises, the surveyor notes any deviation from the vertical as the building is built and construction workers must correct them.* ▬RI 1

Academic Vocabulary

Read each word with students and discuss its meaning.

cumbersome (p. 114) • heavy and bulky; difficult to move around

preeminent (p. 120) • outstanding; best of all

claustrophobia (p. 137) • fear of being in an enclosed space

imperceptible (p. 138) • very slight or gradual; hard to notice

FIRST READ Think Through the Text

Have students cite text evidence and draw inferences to answer questions.

p. 101 • *Why are archeologists part of the excavation process?* They are looking for artifacts from Manhattan's Dutch and Colonial period. *What are the costs and benefits of having archeologists as part of the process?* It costs the developer time and money to cooperate with archeological digs, but much cultural material has been recovered. ⬤RI 1

p. 109 • *If you saw an irregularly shaped or curved building, what is it most likely made of? Why?* It is most likely made of concrete. Irregular shapes and curved surfaces are easier to make in concrete. ⬤RI 1

p. 142 • *How does the author describe the experience of standing on top of a skyscraper?* He says you are no longer conscious of the sounds of the street. You hear only a humming, murmuring sound. You are awed by the view and amazed by the city of imagination and wonder. ⬤RI 1

SECOND READ Analyze the Text

• Have students review pages 105–133. Ask: *If you were going to build a skyscraper, would you choose concrete or steel? Explain.* Steel; it is the material that is best at spanning great distances with a minimum of volume, which is what a skyscraper requires. ⬤RI 1

• Have students visit the multimedia sources available on the "Manhattan on the Web" portal hosted by the New York Public Library. Guide them to compare and contrast the information in *The Building of Manhattan* with the information in the multimedia sources. ⬤RI 9

Independent/Self-Selected Reading

If students have demonstrated comprehension of *The Building of Manhattan,* have them read other informational texts to practice skills. Suggested texts:

• "Manhattan on the Web," http://legacy.www.nypl.org/branch/manhattan

• *The Historical Atlas of New York City* by Eric Homberger ⬤RI 9, RI 10

Performance Task

WRITE & PRESENT

1. Have small groups work together to compare and contrast the information in *The Building of Manhattan* with the information in "Manhattan on the Web" to construct a holistic picture of the history of the city. ⬤RI 9

2. Ask students to each write an expository text that describes a holistic picture of the history of Manhattan through comparing and contrasting the information gained from the two texts. ⬤W 2

3. Have students share their writing in small groups. Ask them to make revisions based on others' suggestions. ⬤W 5

4. Individual students present their writing to classmates, using multimedia examples to support important points. ⬤SL 5

See Copying Masters, pp. 164–171.

STUDENT CHECKLIST

Writing

☑ Write an expository text that describes a holistic picture of the history of Manhattan.

☑ Analyze the information presented in two different sources.

☑ Make revisions based on peer feedback.

Speaking & Listening

☑ Participate effectively in a collaborative discussion.

☑ Demonstrate understanding of multiple perspectives.

☑ Include multimedia components to clarify information.

▶ OBJECTIVES

- Determine main ideas and key details
- Analyze how a text makes connections among ideas
- Analyze text using text evidence

The Number Devil: A Mathematical Adventure is broken into three instructional segments.

Options for Reading

Independent Students read the selection independently or with a partner and then answer questions posed by the teacher.

Supported Students read a segment and answer questions with teacher support.

The Number Devil
A Mathematical Adventure

by Hans Magnus Enzensberger

SUMMARY In a series of twelve dreams, math-hating Robert meets the Number Devil, who teaches him a variety of number tricks while explaining mathematical theory.

ABOUT THE AUTHOR Hans Magnus Enzensberger was born in Germany in 1929. Though he primarily writes poetry and essays, he has also dabbled in theater, film, opera, radio drama, translation, and novels for adults and children.

Discuss Genre and Set Purpose

INFORMATIONAL TEXT Have students read the title and page through the text and illustrations. Explain that this text is fictional but also gives information. Ask students what they predict they will learn about, based on the diagrams and examples.

SET PURPOSE Help students set a purpose for reading, such as to find information about different kinds of numbers.

 Common Core Connection

Grade 6: RI 2 determine a central idea of a text/provide a summary; **RI 3** analyze how a key individual, event, or idea is introduced, illustrated, and elaborated

Grade 7: RI 2 determine two or more central ideas in a text/analyze their development/ provide summary; **RI 3** analyze interactions between individuals, events, and ideas

Grade 8: RI 2 determine a central idea of a text/analyze its development/provide summary; **RI 3** analyze interactions between individuals, events, and ideas

Grades 6–8: RI 1 cite textual evidence to support analysis of what the text says explicitly as well as inferences drawn

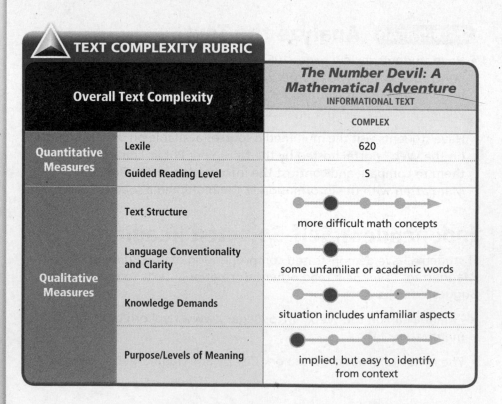

TEXT COMPLEXITY RUBRIC

Overall Text Complexity		*The Number Devil: A Mathematical Adventure* INFORMATIONAL TEXT
		COMPLEX
Quantitative Measures	Lexile	620
	Guided Reading Level	S
Qualitative Measures	Text Structure	more difficult math concepts
	Language Conventionality and Clarity	some unfamiliar or academic words
	Knowledge Demands	situation includes unfamiliar aspects
	Purpose/Levels of Meaning	implied, but easy to identify from context

Academic Vocabulary

Read each word with students and discuss its meaning.

hoax (p. 10) • a trick that fools people into believing something that isn't true

bluffing (p. 22) • trying to fool someone by acting more confident than you are

crotchety (p. 63) • irritable

contrary (p. 83) • opposite

ELL **ENGLISH LANGUAGE LEARNERS**

Use Visuals

Use the example problems to build students' knowledge of math function words. Read example problems, pointing to and naming plus signs, minus signs, and square root signs. Have students repeat. Then ask them to write and read aloud their own sample math problems.

FIRST READ ▶ ## Think Through the Text

Have students cite text evidence and draw inferences to answer questions.

pp. 16–17 • *Summarize what the number devil tells Robert about infinite numbers.* There are infinitely large numbers. There are infinitely small numbers. There are infinite numbers of infinitely small numbers. **◖RI 2**

pp. 32–41 • *Why are roman numerals so complicated?* The Romans did not have zero, so they had to give each number a different letter. *Why is zero important?* It lets you keep a place and produce any number you please. **◖RI 1**

p. 56 • *What are prima donna numbers?* Prima donna numbers are numbers that can only be divided by one and themselves. **◖RI 1**

RESPOND TO SEGMENT 1

 Classroom Collaboration

Have small groups summarize what they have read. Have them ask questions about what they don't understand.

SECOND READ ▶ ## Analyze the Text

- Have students skim page 18. Ask: *How does the number devil explain infinite numbers?* He compares them to dividing a piece of chewing gum into smaller and smaller pieces. *How does this comparison illustrate his point?* It shows that numbers can get smaller and smaller, and no matter how small they get, they can keep getting smaller. **◖RI 3**

- Review page 83. Ask: *To what does the number devil compare unreasonable numbers?* He compares them to grains of sand. *What point about infinite numbers is he trying to make?* He is trying to show that there are as many infinite numbers as there are grains of sand. Though they seem troublesome, they are more common than any other kind of number. **◖RI 3**

ENGLISH LANGUAGE LEARNERS

Use Visuals

Reread the surrounding text for each visual number problem. Use the visuals to explain and reinforce the math concepts that Robert and the number devil discuss in the text.

RESPOND TO SEGMENT 2

 Classroom Collaboration

Have partners work together to create and present a summary of what has happened so far, as well as make predictions about what might happen in the next segment.

 Common Core Connection

Grade 6: RI 2 determine a central idea of a text/provide a summary; **RI 3** analyze how a key individual, event, or idea is introduced, illustrated, and elaborated; **RI 7** integrate information presented in different media or formats as well as in words; **SL 4** present claims and findings, sequence ideas, and use details to accentuate main ideas or themes

Grade 7: RI 2 determine two or more central ideas in a text/analyze their development/ provide summary; **RI 3** analyze interactions between individuals, events, and ideas

Grade 8: RI 2 determine a central idea of a text/analyze its development/provide summary; **RI 3** analyze how text makes connections among and distinctions between individuals, ideas, or events

Grades 7–8: SL 4 present claims and findings, emphasizing points in a focused, coherent manner

Grades 6-8: RI 1 cite textual evidence to support analysis of what the text says explicitly as well as inferences drawn; **RI 10** read and comprehend literary nonfiction; **W 1** write arguments to support claims; **W 5** develop and strengthen writing by planning, revising, editing, rewriting, or trying a new approach

---

Academic Vocabulary

Read each word with students and discuss its meaning.

oasis (p. 90) • a place in the desert where there is water above ground

marshaling (p. 92) • gathering; pulling together

hefty (p. 136) • a very large amount

exhausted (p. 151) • used up all of something

FIRST READ **Think Through the Text**

Have students cite text evidence and draw inferences to answer questions.

pp. 93–99 • *What is the pattern that triangle numbers have when they are lined up next to each other?* *The differences between them are like counting from one to ten, and the pattern goes on and on.* ◉ RI 1

pp. 108–111 • *Summarize how Bonacci numbers work.* *You start with 1 + 1. The sequence continues by adding together the last two numbers.* *Why are Bonacci numbers important?* *Every living thing uses numbers or behaves as if it did.* ◉ RI 2

p. 160 • *How can making diagrams help you solve problems?* *Drawing lines, as in the example, can help you avoid adding everything up and gives you a visual representation. Then you can just count.* ◉ RI 1

SECOND READ **Analyze the Text**

• Review page 94. Ask: *What does the number devil want Robert to understand about mathematics?* *He wants him to understand that anything in mathematics can make a clean pattern.* *What point does he make about the coconuts? What might he be trying to tell readers about solving math problems?* *He says that it doesn't matter that he is using coconuts for the model. He is trying to help Robert understand that it doesn't matter what is being used as a model. It only matters what the model stands for.* ◉ RI 3

• Reread page 104. Ask: *What messages about math does the image of Robert swimming through the pool express?* *Math is exciting and the numbers go on and on.* *How have Robert's feelings about math started to change?* *He is starting to think it is exciting rather than boring.* ◉ RI 1

• Look at the diagram on page 122. Ask: *How does the diagram illustrate the concept of Bonacci numbers?* *The branches of the tree correspond to the sequence of Bonacci numbers. For example, the pattern of Bonacci numbers begins 1,1, 2, 3, 5, 8. On lines 1 and 2, the tree has 1 branch. On line 3, it has 2 branches. On line 4, it has 3 branches, and so on. It illustrates how natures behaves as if it understands numbers.* ◉ Grade 6 RI 7

Academic Vocabulary

Read each word with students and discuss its meaning.

interminable (p. 174) • endless

unheeded (p. 175) • paid no attention to

lolling (p. 191) • leaning lazily against something

conjecture (p. 219) • to guess

eccentric (p. 242) • unusual or strange

FIRST READ ## Think Through the Text

Have students cite text evidence and draw inferences to answer questions.

pp. 174–175 • *Are there more ordinary numbers than odd numbers?* *There are equal numbers of ordinary and odd numbers because there are infinite numbers of both.* **RI 1**

p. 196 • *What is an unreasonable number?* *It's a number that goes on forever. You can take it as far as you like, but it never ends.* **RI 1**

pp. 227–229 • *Why does the number devil give Robert the example of the tour problem?* *The number devil wants to show Robert that even problems that seem simple can be difficult or nearly impossible to solve. Does that mean the problem is impossible to solve?* *No; mathematicians have also not proven that no perfect solution exists.* **RI 3**

SECOND READ ## Analyze the Text

- Review pages 218–219. Ask: *How are mathematical proofs like crossing a stream?* *The rocks are ideas that are tested and slip-resistant. When you have a new idea, you look for the nearest rock and then keep leaping with caution. In other words, proofs are like the stepping stones you use to cross a stream. You connect ideas and proceed cautiously until you arrive at an answer.* **RI 3**

- Reread page 223. Ask: *What is the importance of proof in mathematics?* *Formulas collapse without proof. Sometimes formulas can work most of the time, but if they don't work all the time, they aren't good enough.* **RI 1**

Independent/Self-Selected Reading

If students have demonstrated comprehension of *The Number Devil*, have them read other texts to practice skills. Suggested titles:

- *The Man Who Counted: A Collection of Mathematical Adventures* by Malba Tahan

- *Mathematicians Are People, Too: Stories from the Lives of Great Mathematicians* by Luetta and Wilbert Reimer **RI 10**

WRITE & PRESENT

1. Have small groups refer to the text to discuss how the author uses comparisons and analogies to illustrate mathematical concepts. **RI 3**

2. Individual students write an argument text that describes one comparison or analogy and evaluates how effective it was at explaining the concept. **W 1**

3. Have small groups reconvene to share and edit their writing. **W 5**

4. Students present their final arguments to their classmates. They may want to include visuals from the text if they are relevant. **SL 4**

5. Individual students turn in their final drafts to the teacher.

See Copying Masters, pp. 164–171.

STUDENT CHECKLIST

Writing

☑ Write an argument text that describes one comparison or analogy and evaluates how effective it was at explaining the concept.

☑ Support arguments with reasons, examples, and details.

☑ Use correct language conventions.

Speaking & Listening

☑ Participate effectively in a collaborative discussion.

☑ Provide reasons and details to support points.

☑ Use visuals to support important points.

▶ OBJECTIVES

- Gain understanding of mathematical topics
- Identify main ideas and key details
- Follow multistep procedures
- Analyze text using text evidence

Math Trek is broken into three instructional segments.

SEGMENTS

Options for Reading

Independent Students read the selection independently or with a partner and then answer questions posed by the teacher.

Supported Students read a segment and answer questions with teacher support.

 Common Core Connection

Grade 6: RI 2 determine a central idea of a text/provide a summary; **RI 3** analyze how a key individual, event, or idea is introduced, illustrated, and elaborated; **RI 4** determine the meaning of words and phrases, including figurative, connotative, and technical meanings; **RI 7** integrate information presented in different media or formats as well as in words

Grade 7: RI 2 determine two or more central ideas in a text/analyze their development/provide summary; **RI 3** analyze interactions between individuals, events, and ideas; **RI 4** determine the meaning of words and phrases, including figurative, connotative, and technical meanings/analyze impact of word choice

Grade 8: RI 2 determine a central idea of text/analyze its development/provide summary; **RI 3** analyze interactions between individuals, events, and ideas; **RI 4** determine the meaning of words and phrases/analyze impact of word choice

Grades 6–8: RI 1 cite textual evidence to support analysis of what the text says explicitly as well as inferences drawn

Math Trek
Adventures in the Math Zone

by Ivars Peterson and Nancy Henderson

SUMMARY Readers travel through a math amusement park called the MathZone. Each trek invites readers to think like mathematicians to solve problems and puzzles.

ABOUT THE AUTHORS **Ivars Peterson** is the Director of Publications and Communications for the Mathematical Association of America. His wife **Nancy Henderson** is a freelance writer and editor. The two have collaborated on two mathematics books for middle school-aged students.

Discuss Genre and Set Purpose

INFORMATIONAL TEXT Have students read the title and page through the text and illustrations. Discuss with students how they can tell that this text is informational.

SET PURPOSE Help students set a purpose for reading, such as to find information about different kinds of mathematics and follow directions to complete math activities.

⬆ TEXT COMPLEXITY RUBRIC

Overall Text Complexity		*Math Trek* INFORMATIONAL TEXT
		COMPLEX
Quantitative Measures	Lexile	1050
	Guided Reading Level	N/A
Qualitative Measures	Text Structure	somewhat complex math concepts
	Language Conventionality and Clarity	some unfamiliar or academic words
	Knowledge Demands	some specialized knowledge required
	Purpose/Levels of Meaning	multiple levels of meaning

SEGMENT 1 pp. 1–28

Academic Vocabulary

Read each word with students and discuss its meaning.

phony (p. 3) • not the real thing; fake

clamoring (p. 8) • making noise in demand for something

prominent (p. 15) • famous; important

savoring (p. 20) • enjoying something slowly to make it last

ELL **ENGLISH LANGUAGE LEARNERS**

Use Demonstration

As you read the steps for the project, use demonstration to clarify each step. Confirm understanding by having students demonstrate the step or complete sentence frames such as *First, I _____*.

FIRST READ ## Think Through the Text

Have students cite text evidence and draw inferences to answer questions.

pp. 1–8 • *What is the difference between a knot and an unknot?* A knot cannot be untangled. An unknot can be untangled to form a circle. *How are granny knots and square knots alike and different?* Granny knots and square knots both have six crossings, but they have different crossing patterns. ⬤RI 1

pp. 15–17 • *What is the main idea of this section? Give details that support it.* Sometimes a simple mathematical idea calls for an incredibly complicated proof. The proof for the map problem was one of the longest mathematical proofs anyone had come up with. It filled hundreds of pages and relied on a computer to calculate and verify facts. ⬤RI 2

p. 24 • *What is topology?* Topology is the study of the features that various shapes have in common, even when the shapes are twisted or stretched. ⬤RI 4

SECOND READ ## Analyze the Text

• Discuss the information on page 6. Ask: *How can scientists use math to help them solve problems? Cite details and examples from the text.* One way scientists can use math is by applying knot theory to help them understand DNA and how viruses work. ⬤RI 3

• Reread page 24. Ask: *Why do topologists think of coffee cups and doughnuts as the same thing? Integrate information from the diagram to help you answer.* You can expand the coffee cup's handle while shrinking its bowl to make them the same shape. ⬤Grade 6 RI 7

RESPOND TO SEGMENT 1

 Classroom Collaboration

Have small groups summarize what they have read. Have them ask questions about what they don't understand.

ENGLISH LANGUAGE LEARNERS

Use Visuals

Use the text visuals to develop students' oral language. Have students tell how the illustrations and diagrams support the ideas in the text.

RESPOND TO SEGMENT 2

 Classroom Collaboration

Have partners work together to create and present a summary of each trek.

 Common Core Connection

Grade 6: RI 2 determine a central idea of a text/provide a summary; **RI 4** determine the meaning of words and phrases, including figurative, connotative, and technical meanings; **RI 6** determine the author's point of view or purpose and explain how it is conveyed; **SL 4** present claims and findings, sequence ideas, and use details to accentuate main ideas or themes

Grade 7: RI 2 determine two or more central ideas in a text/analyze their development/ provide summary; **RI 4** determine the meaning of words and phrases, including figurative, connotative, and technical meanings/analyze impact of word choice

Grade 8: RI 2 determine a central idea of text/analyze its development/provide summary; **RI 4** determine the meaning of words and phrases/analyze impact of word choice

Grades 7–8: SL 4 present claims and findings, emphasizing points in a focused, coherent manner

Grades 6-8: RI 1 cite textual evidence to support analysis of what the text says explicitly as well as inferences drawn; **RI 10** read and comprehend literary nonfiction; **W 2** write informative/explanatory texts; **W 5** develop and strengthen writing by planning, revising, editing, rewriting, or trying a new approach

Academic Vocabulary

Read each word with students and discuss its meaning.

baffled (p. 30) • puzzled; confused

infinite (p. 32) • endless

conjectures (p. 37) • guesses

meanderings (p. 43) • winding paths

tedious (p. 48) • tiring and boring

FIRST READ ## Think Through the Text

Have students cite text evidence and draw inferences to answer questions.

pp. 31–33 • *What are prime numbers? Prime numbers are numbers that can't be evenly divided by any number except 1 and the number itself. What are factors? The numbers a divisible number can be divided by. What are composite numbers? They are numbers that are not primes.* **RI 4**

pp. 43–44 • *What are fractals? Fractals are shapes that repeat themselves within an object. Fluffy clouds, jagged rocks, indented shorelines, and bare trees form fractal-like shapes.* **RI 4**

pp. 55–61 • *What does the Tilt-A-Whirl illustrate? It illustrates the phenomenon of chaos. What is chaos? Chaos occurs when systems governed by physical laws undergo transitions to a highly irregular form of behavior.* **RI 2**

SECOND READ ## Analyze the Text

- Review pages 42–43. Ask: *What is the relationship between steps and the distance traveled along a ragged coastline? The shorter the steps you take, the longer the distance you travel.* **RI 1**

- Ask students to reread the directions on pages 46–47. Ask: *To generate the Koch snowflake curve, what should you do after you draw an equilateral triangle with each side measuring 9 cm? Divide each 9 cm side into three parts, each measuring 3 cm. At the middle of each side, draw an equilateral triangle that is 1/3 the size of the original, facing outward. How will you know whether you have completed this step correctly? You should see a six-pointed star made up of 12 line segments.* **RI 1**

- Reread page 56. Ask: *How does chaos make the Tilt-A-Whirl more exciting? The mixture of rotations and spins never repeats itself exactly.* **RI 2**

Academic Vocabulary

Read each word with students and discuss its meaning.

accumulated (p. 64) • acquired an increasing amount of something

paradox (p. 71) • a statement that appears to contradict itself but might actually be true

decipher (p. 77) • to figure something out that is puzzling or written in code

ricochets (p. 84) • bounces off a hard surface

emerge (p. 94) • come into view

FIRST READ ## Think Through the Text

Have students cite text evidence and draw inferences to answer questions.

pp. 75–78 • *How are numbers used for secrecy?* In a computer, each letter of the alphabet is assigned a number. Using a key, the computer scrambles the numbers so much that the only way to understand them is by using a computer programmed with the correct key for deciphering the words. ▬ RI 1

pp. 81–89 • *What happens on an elliptical pool table?* No matter which direction you hit the ball, it will bounce off the edge and head directly to the other ball. ▬ RI 1

SECOND READ ## Analyze the Text

• Review page 88. Ask: *What is the author's purpose for having you draw an ellipsis?* As you draw, it will give you clues about what type of movement to expect on an elliptical pool table. ▬ Grade 6 RI 6

• Reread page 96. Ask: *Which gate should you take to exit? How do you know?* You should take Gate 10 because when you decode the message, it says "Way Out." ▬ RI 1

Independent/Self-Selected Reading

If students have already demonstrated comprehension of *Math Trek,* have them read other informational texts to practice skills. Suggested titles:

• *Math Trek 2: A Mathematical Space Odyssey* by Ivars Peterson and Nancy Henderson

• *Secrets of Mental Math: The Mathemagician's Guide to Lightning Calculation and Amazing Math Tricks* by Arthur Benjamin and Michael Shermer ▬ RI 10

WRITE & PRESENT

1. Have small groups read and summarize the directions for generating the Koch snowflake curve on pages 46-47. ▬ RI 2

2. Individual students follow the multi-step directions to make their own Koch snowflake curve. Then they write a summary that describes what they did and what they learned. ▬ W 2

3. Have small groups reconvene to share their snowflakes and compare their results. Then they share and edit their summaries. ▬ W 5

4. Students present their snowflakes and summaries to classmates. ▬ SL 4

See Copying Masters, pp. 164–171.

STUDENT CHECKLIST

Writing

☑ Write a summary that describes what students did to make their own Koch snowflake curve.

☑ Include information in the summary about what was learned.

☑ Include a clear topic sentence and a logical conclusion.

Speaking & Listening

☑ Participate effectively in a collaborative discussion.

☑ Retell steps in the correct sequence.

☑ Use visuals to enhance presentation.

OBJECTIVES

- Analyze how key individuals and ideas are introduced and elaborated in a text
- Determine the author's point of view
- Analyze text using text evidence

Geeks is broken into three instructional segments.

SEGMENTS

Options for Reading

Independent Students read the selection independently or with a partner and then answer questions posed by the teacher.

Supported Students read a segment and answer questions with teacher support.

Common Core Connection

Grade 6: RI 3 analyze how a key individual, event, or idea is introduced, illustrated, and elaborated; **RI 6** determine the author's point of view or purpose and explain how it is conveyed

Grade 7: RI 3 analyze interactions between individuals, events, and ideas; **RI 6** determine author's point of view or purpose/analyze how author distinguishes position

Grade 8: RI 3 analyze how text makes connections among and distinctions between individuals, ideas, or events

Grades 6-8: RI 1 cite textual evidence to support analysis of what the text says explicitly as well as inferences drawn

Geeks
How Two Lost Boys Rode the Internet Out of Idaho
by Jon Katz

SUMMARY Inspired by an email from self-professed geek Jesse Dailey, author Jon Katz chronicles the journey of Jesse and his friend Eric as they use their technology skills to flee their dead-end jobs in Idaho in search of a brighter future in Chicago.

ABOUT THE AUTHOR Jon Katz is a journalist and author. He is well-known for his articles for the online magazine *HotWired* and the technology website *Slashdot*. He has also written novels, short story collections, and nonfiction books.

Discuss Genre and Set Purpose

INFORMATIONAL TEXT Have students page through the selection. Discuss text features such as the emails and letters that bookend each chapter. Have students tell how they can tell this book is informational.

SET PURPOSE Help students set a purpose for reading, such as to find information about careers in technology and determine the author's point of view.

TEXT COMPLEXITY RUBRIC

Overall Text Complexity		*Geeks* INFORMATIONAL TEXT
		SIMPLE
Quantitative Measures	Lexile	1080
	Guided Reading Level	N/A
Qualitative Measures	Text Structure	organization of main idea and details may be complex, but is clearly stated and generally sequential
	Language Conventionality and Clarity	contemporary, familiar language
	Knowledge Demands	everyday knowledge required
	Purpose/Levels of Meaning	single topic

Academic Vocabulary

Read each word with students and discuss its meaning.

trivial (p. 3) • not important

pundits (p. 41) • people who are experts on a subject

veneer (p. 50) • outer surface

fervent (p. 72) • showing strong feeling

discernible (p. 74) • able to be seen clearly

Use Visuals and Cognates

Use classroom computers to clarify computer parts such as monitors, hard drives, scanners, and printers. Point out that *Internet* is the same word in English and Spanish. Ask: *Is the Internet important to Jesse and Eric?* yes *Jesse and Eric work on _____.* computers

FIRST READ ## Think Through the Text

Have students cite text evidence and draw inferences to answer questions.

p. 11 • *Why is the Internet so important to Jesse? He says it is his safety and his community. It is his life.* RI 1

p. 14 • *What inspires Jesse and Eric to leave Idaho? Katz tells them that they can get a job almost anywhere. People everywhere need people who can maintain, repair, and understand computers.* RI 3

pp. 23–34 • *Who saved Jesse and Eric? How? Mr. Brown saved Jesse and Eric by starting the Geek Club. It gave them a place to talk about their ideas. They had some power and a way to fight back. It gave them a community.* RI 3

RESPOND TO SEGMENT 1

Classroom Collaboration

Have small groups summarize what they have learned. Have them ask questions about what they don't understand.

SECOND READ ## Analyze the Text

- Have students review the first chapter. Ask: *How does the author describe his first meeting with Jesse? He says Jesse is skinny and unsmiling. He glances at Katz and then looks away. His face was like a mask. He is pale, like the underbelly of a fish. He wears black-rimmed glasses and is slightly stooped.* **What can you infer about Jesse from these details?** *He is shy and nervous around people. He spends a lot of time inside, bent over a computer.* RI 3

- Review pages 16–23. Ask: *What is the author's point of view about the opportunities for white, working-class kids? Support your response with text evidence. The author thinks that there is little opportunity for them. He says they are invisible in the media, and nobody worries about them. If they want more education, they have to work to pay for it.* Grades 6–7 RI 6

- Reread page 61 with students. Ask: *What words does the author use to describe Jesse? How does he support his word choice? He says Jesse is internal and anxious, and weighs every word. Jesse panics when he is outside of his familiar geek existence. He also says Jesse is brave because change doesn't come easily for him, but he is doing it anyway.* RI 3

ENGLISH LANGUAGE LEARNERS

Use Peer Supported Learning

Pair proficient speakers with less proficient speakers. Have partners work together to read the emails and letters at the beginnings and ends of the chapters and summarize each email or letter in a sentence or two.

 RESPOND TO SEGMENT 2

Classroom Collaboration

Have partners work together to create and present a summary, as well as raise questions that might be answered in the next segment.

 Common Core Connection

Grade 6: RI 3 analyze how a key individual, event, or idea is introduced, illustrated, and elaborated; **RI 6** determine the author's point of view or purpose and explain how it is conveyed; **SL 4** present claims and findings, sequence ideas, and use details to accentuate main ideas or themes/use appropriate eye contact, volume, and pronunciation

Grade 7: RI 3 analyze interactions between individuals, events, and ideas; **RI 6** determine author's point of view or purpose/analyze how author distinguishes position

Grade 8: RI 3 analyze how text makes connections among and distinctions between individuals, ideas, or events; **RI 6** determine author's point of view or purpose/analyze how author responds to conflicting evidence or viewpoints

Grades 7–8: SL 4 present claims and findings, emphasizing points in focused, coherent manner

Grades 6–8: RI 1 cite textual evidence to support analysis of what the text says explicitly as well as inferences drawn; **RI 10** read and comprehend literary nonfiction; **W 2** write informative/explanatory texts; **W 5** develop and strengthen writing by planning, revising, editing, rewriting, or trying a new approach

Academic Vocabulary

Read each word with students and discuss its meaning.

ephemeral (p. 83) • lasting for a short time
stymied (p. 109) • blocked; stuck
mediocre (p. 113) • average; not very good
impetus (p. 122) • driving force
dubious (p. 125) • showing doubts

FIRST READ **Think Through the Text**

Have students cite text evidence and draw inferences to answer questions.

pp. 81–91 • *How have Jesse and Eric changed? How have they stayed the same?* They live in a new place and have new jobs, but they live almost exactly the same way they lived before. Their lives are shaped around computing, technology, and the Net. **RI 1**

pp. 98–119 • *Why do Jesse and Eric realize they need college degrees?* They realize that without them, they will be stuck in a cubicle working dead-end jobs in taller buildings. Now that they knew they could earn a decent living, they wanted more. **RI 1**

p. 127 • *How are Jesse and Eric different?* Jesse is energized by challenges. Eric is discouraged by them. He feels depressed instead of being excited by the new experiences. **RI 3**

SECOND READ **Analyze the Text**

• Say: *On page 86, the author says that Jesse sees himself as a "citizen of the Net." How is this different from being a citizen of the real world?* The Net has rules, boundaries, and traditions of its own. Unlike the real world, citizens of the Net are free to go where they like and take what they want with no rules or regulations. **RI 1**

• Reread Jesse's email on page 96. Ask: *What point is the author trying to make about education by including this email from Jesse?* He is showing that smart people without resources may not see college as an opportunity that is available to them. **Grades 6–7 RI 6**

• Reread Jesse's poem on pages 111 and 112. Ask: *How does the author use this poem to elaborate on Jesse? What does it tell us about him that the author's own words can't?* The author uses the poem as a way to elaborate on Jesse's life story in Jesse's own words. Up to this point, we have only heard the author's impression of Jesse's upbringing and personal goals. Jesse's poem reveals a young man who wants to go beyond the limits that his upbringing set for him. **RI 3**

Academic Vocabulary

Read each word with students and discuss its meaning.

camaraderie (p. 150) • sharing one's interests and activities with others

articulate (p. 160) • able to express ideas clearly

abeyance (p. 181) • the state of being stopped for a time

commodity (p. 190) • something useful or valuable

FIRST READ ## Think Through the Text

Have students cite text evidence and draw inferences to answer questions.

pp. 144–153 • *After the Columbine shootings, the media talked about how the Internet creates dislocated, isolated kids. What is the author's point of view?* The author disagrees. He thinks that the Internet attracts these kids, not creates them. He says it is a way for them to keep in touch with others just like them. ▬RI 6

pp. 185–186 • *What happens to Jesse?* He is accepted into the University of Chicago. *On what did the university base its decision?* They based it on Jesse's words and actions. ▬RI 1

pp. 194–197 • *How are things different for Eric than they are for Jesse?* Eric does not change as much. He often feels overwhelmed and awkward in social situations. He decides not to apply to college. ▬RI 1

SECOND READ ## Analyze the Text

• Have students review chapter 10. Ask: *How does the author illustrate his point of view that the Net gives geeks power?* He explains that after Columbine, geeks were being profiled and isolated even more. The Net gave these kids a way to get their message out and change the direction of a major story. He includes emails from kids who want to share their stories. ▬RI 6

• Say: *In the epilogue, the author says that the geek had ascended. What does he mean?* He means that for many years, those who were different or misfits were just alienated. With the rise of the Internet, geeks suddenly had a place in the world with job opportunities and a community that they never had before. ▬RI 6

Independent/Self-Selected Reading

If students have demonstrated comprehension of *Geeks*, have them read other informational texts to practice skills. Suggested texts:

• *Steve Jobs: The Man Who Thought Different* by Karen Blumenthal

• *The Young and the Digital* by S. Craig Watkins ▬RI 10

WRITE & PRESENT

1. Have small groups refer to the text to discuss the author's point of view about geeks or the Internet and how he conveys it in the text. ▬RI 6

2. Have students write an expository text describing the author's point of view about geeks or the Internet and cite relevant facts, definitions, quotations, or examples from the text. ▬W 2

3. Have groups reconvene to share and edit their writing. ▬W 5

4. Students present their final work to their classmates. ▬SL 4

5. Individual students turn in their final writing to the teacher.

See Copying Masters, pp. 164–171.

STUDENT CHECKLIST

Writing

☑ State the author's point of view about one of the topics.

☑ Develop the topic with relevant facts, definitions, quotations, or examples.

☑ Use transitions to clarify the relationships among ideas and concepts.

Speaking & Listening

☑ Participate effectively in a collaborative discussion.

☑ Cite specific text evidence that supports the point of view statement.

☑ Ask and answer questions about text details.

OBJECTIVES

- Determine an author's point of view
- Analyze how a key idea is introduced and elaborated on in a text
- Determine the meaning of phrases as used in the text
- Cite text evidence to support an analysis

Options for Reading

Independent Students read the article independently or with a partner and then answer questions posed by the teacher.

Supported Students read a segment and answer questions with teacher support.

 Common Core Connection

Grade 6: RI 2 determine a central idea of a text/provide a summary; **RI 3** analyze how a key individual, event, or idea is introduced, illustrated, and elaborated; **RI 4** determine the meaning of words and phrases, including figurative, connotative, and technical meanings; **RI 6** determine the author's point of view or purpose and explain how it is conveyed; **SL 4** present claims and findings, sequence ideas, and use details to accentuate main ideas or themes

Grade 7: RI 2 determine two or more central ideas in a text/analyze their development/provide a summary; **RI 3** analyze interactions between individuals, events, and ideas; **RI 4** determine the meaning of words and phrases, including figurative, connotative, and technical meanings/analyze impact of word choice

Grade 8: RI 2 determine a central idea of a text/analyze its development/provide a summary; **RI 3** analyze how text makes connections among and distinctions between individuals, ideas, or events; **RI 4** determine the meaning of words and phrases/analyze impact of word choice

Grades 7–8: SL 4 present claims and findings, emphasizing points in a focused, coherent manner

Grades 6-8: RI 1 cite textual evidence to support analysis of what the text says explicitly as well as inferences drawn; **RI 10** read and comprehend literary nonfiction; **W 2** write informative/explanatory texts; **W 5** develop and strengthen writing by planning, revising, editing, rewriting, or trying a new approach

"The Evolution of the Grocery Bag"
by Henry Petroski

SUMMARY Henry Petroski describes the invention of the square-bottomed grocery bag and explains why, when it comes to design, perfection is never truly reached.

ABOUT THE AUTHOR Henry Petroski is a professor of civil engineering and history at Duke University. He has written a number of books and articles about the design of everyday objects such as silverware, paper clips, and pencils.

Discuss Genre and Set Purpose

INFORMATIONAL TEXT Examine the selection with students. Have them briefly scan the text, noting the title of the article and the journal in which it was published. Discuss with students how they can tell this article is informational.

SET PURPOSE Help students set a purpose for reading "The Evolution of the Grocery Bag," such as to find out how grocery bags have changed over time.

◣ TEXT COMPLEXITY RUBRIC

Overall Text Complexity		"The Evolution of the Grocery Bag" INFORMATIONAL TEXT
		SIMPLE
Quantitative Measures	Lexile	1400
	Guided Reading Level	N/A
Qualitative Measures	Text Structure	clearly stated and sequential organization of main ideas and details
	Language Conventionality and Clarity	some unfamiliar or academic words
	Knowledge Demands	everyday knowledge required
	Purpose/Levels of Meaning	single topic

Academic Vocabulary

Read each word with students and discuss its meaning.

reviled • hated

versatile • able to be used in many different ways

paradigm • an example or model of how something should be done

preclude • prevent

FIRST READ ## Think Through the Text

Have students cite text evidence and draw inferences to answer questions.

• *Would the Universal Product Code and decoding laser scanner have been effective without the square-bottomed paper bag? Why or why not?* No. *Without the square-bottomed bag, they would have only led to a faster pileup of cans and boxes down the line where the bagger works.* **RI 1**

• *Summarize how the "Machine for Making Bags of Paper" changed the way bags were made.* Before the machine, bags were created on *demand by storekeepers who cut, folded, and pasted sheets of paper into versatile containers. After the machine, bags were produced at the rate of eighteen hundred per hour.* **RI 2**

SECOND READ ## Analyze the Text

• *What is the author's point of view about the bags and the machine? How does he explain it?* The author says that the bags and machine *weren't perfect. The history of design has yet to see a perfect object because there is always room for improvement.* **Grade 6 RI 6**

• *What does the expression "build a better mousetrap" mean?* It means *to invent something that is better than a product that is widely used.* What is significant about the use of the word better *in the expression?* It doesn't say best, which leaves room for improvement. **RI 4**

• *How does the author develop the idea of "building a better mousetrap?"* He describes the evolution of the grocery bag, a widely used product, *and shows how people found ways to make it better and how other inventions depend on it.* **RI 3**

Independent/Self-Selected Reading

If students have already demonstrated comprehension of "The Evolution of the Grocery Bag," have them practice skills using another text, such as:

• *They All Laughed . . .From Light Bulbs to Lasers: The Fascinating Stories Behind the Great Inventions that Have Changed Our Lives* by Ira Flatow

• *Brainstorm! The Stories of Twenty American Kid Inventors* by Tom Tucker **RI 10**

WRITE & PRESENT

1. Have small groups discuss how the author develops the idea that inventors are always trying to "build a better mousetrap." **RI 3**

2. Individual students write an expository paragraph that analyzes how the author develops this idea. Tell them to include details, examples, or quotes from the text. **W 2**

3. Students work with partners to share and edit their work. **W 5**

4. Have students present their work to the class. **SL 4**

See Copying Masters, pp. 164–171.

STUDENT CHECKLIST

Writing

☑ Write an expository text that analyzes how the author develops the idea that inventors are always trying to "build a better mousetrap."

☑ Cite specific examples and quotations that illustrate how the author develops this idea.

☑ Use correct language conventions.

Speaking & Listening

☑ Participate effectively in a collaborative discussion.

☑ Present claims and findings, including examples and quotations that support the analysis.

☑ Use language that is appropriate for the purpose.

▶ OBJECTIVES

- Determine central ideas and key details
- Objectively summarize information
- Determine the meaning of words and phrases
- Cite text evidence to support an analysis

Options for Reading

Independent Students read the article independently or with a partner and then answer questions posed by the teacher.

Supported Students read the article and answer questions with teacher support.

 Common Core Connection

Grade 6: RI 2 determine a central idea of a text/provide a summary; **RI 4** determine the meaning of words and phrases, including figurative, connotative, and technical meanings; **SL 4** present claims and findings, sequence ideas, and use details to accentuate main ideas or themes

Grade 7: RI 2 determine two or more central ideas in a text/analyze their development/ provide summary; **RI 4** determine the meaning of words and phrases, including figurative, connotative, and technical meanings/analyze impact of word choice

Grade 8: RI 2 determine a central idea of a text/analyze its development/provide summary; **RI 4** determine the meaning of words and phrases/analyze impact of word choice

Grades 7–8: SL 4 present claims and findings, emphasizing points in a focused, coherent manner

Grades 6-8: RI 1 cite textual evidence to support analysis of what the text says explicitly as well as inferences drawn; **RI 10** read and comprehend literary nonfiction; **W 2** write informative/explanatory texts; **W 5** develop and strengthen writing by planning, revising, editing, rewriting, or trying a new approach

"Geology"
from U*X*L Encyclopedia of Science

SUMMARY This article defines geology and describes the two main categories of study: physical geology and historical geology. It also describes the work that different types of geologists do.

ABOUT THE SOURCE The *U*X*L Encyclopedia of Science* gives information about physical, life, and earth sciences, engineering, technology, math, environmental science, anthropology, and psychology. In 2002, it was named one of the 20 Best Bets for Student Researchers in the Booklist/Reference Books Bulletin.

Discuss Genre and Set Purpose

INFORMATIONAL TEXT Examine the article with students. Have students scan the title and the text to determine what this article will be about. Ask them how they can tell it is an informational text.

SET PURPOSE Help students set a purpose for reading "Geology," such as to find and summarize information about the different categories of geology.

⏶ TEXT COMPLEXITY RUBRIC

Overall Text Complexity		"Geology" INFORMATIONAL TEXT
		COMPLEX
Quantitative Measures	Lexile	1120
	Guided Reading Level	N/A
Qualitative Measures	Text Structure	somewhat complex science concepts
	Language Conventionality and Clarity	general academic and domain specific language
	Knowledge Demands	some specialized knowledge required
	Purpose/Levels of Meaning	single purpose

Academic Vocabulary

Read each word with students and discuss its meaning.

domain (paragraph 1) • an area controlled by a person, government, or group

dormant (paragraph 2) • not active

chronology (paragraph 3) • the organization of events in time order

configuration (paragraph 3) • the arrangement of the pieces or parts of something

FIRST READ ## Think Through the Text

Have students cite text evidence and draw inferences to answer questions.

paragraph 1 • *What do geologists study?* Geologists study the planet, including its formation, its internal structure, its materials, its chemical and physical processes, and its history. **RI 1**

paragraphs 1–3 • *Into what two categories is geology divided? Define them.* Physical geology, which is concerned with the processes occurring on or below the surface of the Earth and the materials on which they operate, and historical geology, which is concerned with the chronology of events, both physical and biological, that have taken place in Earth's history. **RI 1**

SECOND READ ## Analyze the Text

• *What is the main idea of paragraph 4?* Many other sciences also contribute to geology. *What details support it?* Students may list details about chemistry, physics, botany, zoology, or climatology. **Grade 6 RI 2, Grade 8 RI 2**

• Reread the end of paragraph 4. Ask: *What does the root* paleo *mean?* It means old or ancient. *How do you know?* Paleobotanists study fossil plants. Paleozoologists study fossil animals. Paleoclimatologists study ancient climates. All these scientists study old or ancient things. **RI 4**

• *How do environmental geologists help the planet?* They try to reduce the impact of pollution. They try to find the minerals and fossil fuels we need. **RI 1**

Independent/Self-Selected Reading

If students have already demonstrated comprehension of "Geology," have them read other informational texts to practice skills. Suggested titles:

• *A Field Manual for the Amateur Geologist* by Alan M. Cvancara

• *Sedimentary Rock* by Rebecca Faulkner **RI 10**

WRITE & PRESENT

1. Have small groups work together to objectively summarize the information about geology. **RI 2**

2. Individual students write an objective summary of the article that includes only the main ideas and most important details. **W 2**

3. Students work with their groups to share and edit their work. **W 5**

4. Have students present their work to the class. **SL 4**

See Copying Masters, pp. 164–171.

STUDENT CHECKLIST

Writing

☑ Write an objective summary.

☑ Include main ideas and key details.

☑ Use correct language conventions.

Speaking & Listening

☑ Participate effectively in a collaborative discussion.

☑ Present information in a logical order, using transitions to connect ideas.

☑ Use language that is appropriate for the purpose.

OBJECTIVES

- Determine central ideas and key details
- Objectively summarize information
- Describe how an author structures a text
- Cite text evidence to support an analysis

Options for Reading

Independent Students read the article independently or with a partner and then answer questions posed by the teacher.

Supported Students read the article and answer questions with teacher support.

"Space Probe"
from *Astronomy & Space*

SUMMARY This article describes space probes and explains the role they have played in space exploration and what we have learned from these unpiloted spacecraft.

ABOUT THE SOURCE *Astronomy & Space* is a three-volume encyclopedia that addresses space topics. Biographies of famous astronauts and astronomers, descriptions of space objects and space missions, and the history of astronomy are among the topics covered in this 300-article set.

Discuss Genre and Set Purpose

INFORMATIONAL TEXT Examine the article with students. Have them scan the title and the text to determine what this article will be about. Ask them how they can tell it is an informational text.

SET PURPOSE Help students set a purpose for reading "Space Probe," such as to find and summarize information about space probes.

 Common Core Connection

Grade 6: RI 2 determine a central idea of a text/provide a summary

Grade 7: RI 2 determine two or more central ideas in a text/analyze their development/ provide summary; **RI 5** analyze the structure an author uses to organize text

Grade 8: RI 2 determine a central idea of text/analyze its development/provide summary

Grades 6-8: RI 1 cite textual evidence to support analysis of what the text says explicitly as well as inferences drawn; **RI 10** read and comprehend literary nonfiction; **W 2** write informative/explanatory texts; **W 5** develop and strengthen writing by planning, revising, editing, rewriting, or trying a new approach; **SL 5** include multimedia components and visual displays in presentations

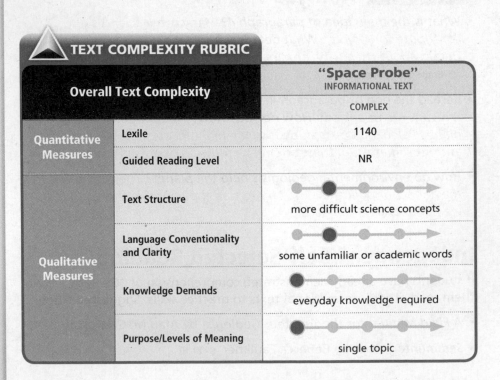

TEXT COMPLEXITY RUBRIC

Overall Text Complexity		"Space Probe" INFORMATIONAL TEXT
		COMPLEX
Quantitative Measures	Lexile	1140
	Guided Reading Level	NR
Qualitative Measures	Text Structure	more difficult science concepts
	Language Conventionality and Clarity	some unfamiliar or academic words
	Knowledge Demands	everyday knowledge required
	Purpose/Levels of Meaning	single topic

Academic Vocabulary

Read each word with students and discuss its meaning.

extraterrestrial (p. 579) • outside Earth or its atmosphere

sophisticated (p. 580) • more complicated or advanced

vast (p. 580) • very great in size or extent

incinerated (p. 580) • burned up

FIRST READ ## Think Through the Text

Have students cite text evidence and draw inferences to answer questions.

p. 579 • *What is a space probe and what is its purpose?* *A space probe is an unpiloted spacecraft that leaves Earth's orbit to explore the moon, other planets, or outer space. Its purpose is to make scientific observations, such as taking pictures and collecting soil samples.* **RI 1**

p. 579 • *What did* Viking 1 *and* Viking 2 *do?* *Viking 1 made the first successful soft landing on Mars on July 20, 1976. Viking 2 landed on the opposite side of the planet soon after. They made reports on the Martian weather and photographed almost the entire surface of the planet.* **RI 2**

p. 580 • *Summarize the journey of* Voyager 2. *It was launched in 1977. Two years later, it flew by Jupiter and took pictures of its colors, moon, and ring. Then it went to Saturn and sent back photos of its rings and moons in 1980 and 1981. Finally, it reached Neptune in 1989.* **RI 2**

SECOND READ ## Analyze the Text

- Review basic text structures with students, including sequential, causal, and comparison. Then guide students to look at the article. Ask: *Which text structure did the author primarily use? Why?* *The author primarily used a sequential text structure. It describes the history of space probes and how they became more sophisticated over time.* **Grade 7 RI 5**

- *How did the United States and the Soviet Union diverge in their use of space probes between 1970 and 1983?* *The United States explored Mars and the outer planets during these years, while the Soviet Union largely concentrated on exploring Venus.* **RI 1**

Independent/Self-Selected Reading

If students have demonstrated comprehension of "Space Probe," have them read other informational texts to practice skills. Suggested titles:

- *Postcards from Mars: The First Photographer on the Red Planet* by Jim Bell

- *The Mighty Mars Rovers: The Incredible Adventures of Spirit and Opportunity* by Elizabeth Rusch **RI 10**

WRITE & PRESENT

1. Have small groups work together to summarize the information about space probes. **RI 2**

2. Individual students write an objective summary of the missions of one family of space probes, such as the *Mariners, Vikings, Pioneers,* or *Voyagers.* **W 2**

3. Students work with their small groups to share and edit their work. **W 5**

4. Have students present their work to the class. Ask them to include media, such as photographs of the probes or of the planet or planets they visited, to clarify information. **SL 5**

See Copying Masters, pp. 164–171.

STUDENT CHECKLIST

Writing

☑ Write an objective summary.

☑ Include main ideas and key details.

☑ Use correct language conventions.

Speaking & Listening

☑ Participate effectively in a collaborative discussion.

☑ Present information in a logical order, using dates and transitions to connect ideas.

☑ Include multimedia components to clarify information.

▶ OBJECTIVES

- Summarize key ideas
- Integrate information presented in different formats
- Determine the meanings of words and phrases
- Cite text evidence to support an analysis

Options for Reading

Independent Students read the article independently or with a partner and then answer questions posed by the teacher.

Supported Students read the article and answer questions with teacher support.

Common Core Connection

Grade 6: RI 2 determine a central idea of a text/provide a summary; **RI 4** determine the meaning words and phrases, including figurative, connotative, and technical meanings; **RI 7** integrate information presented in different media or formats as well as in words; **SL 4** present claims and findings, sequence ideas, and use details to accentuate main ideas or themes

Grades 7: RI 2 determine two or more central ideas in a text/analyze their development/ provide summary; **RI 4** determine the meaning of words and phrases, including figurative, connotative, and technical meanings/analyze impact of word choice

Grade 8: RI 2 determine a central idea of text/analyze its development/provide summary; **RI 4** determine the meaning of words and phrases/analyze impact of word choice

Grades 7–8: SL 4 present claims and findings, emphasizing points in focused, coherent manner

Grades 6–8: RI 1 cite textual evidence to support analysis of what the text says explicitly as well as inferences drawn; **RI 10** read and comprehend literary nonfiction; **W 2** write informative/explanatory texts; **W 5** develop and strengthen writing by planning, revising, editing, rewriting, or trying a new approach

"Elementary Particles"

from *New Book of Popular Science*

SUMMARY This article explains elementary particles and anti-particles and describes their properties. It also explains how these particles relate to Einstein's formula $E = mc^2$ and its application to nuclear physics, astronomy, and cosmology.

ABOUT THE SOURCE *New Book of Popular Science* includes articles about science, technology, and medicine, appropriate for students in middle school and high school. Photos, maps, and technical illustrations are included to clarify scientific processes.

Discuss Genre and Set Purpose

INFORMATIONAL TEXT Examine the article with students. Have students scan the title and the section headings to determine what this article will be about. Ask them how they can tell it is an informational text.

SET PURPOSE Help students set a purpose for reading "Elementary Particles," such as to find out what elementary particles are and what role they play in the fields of science.

▲ TEXT COMPLEXITY RUBRIC		"Elementary Particles" INFORMATIONAL TEXT
Overall Text Complexity		MORE COMPLEX
Quantitative Measures	Lexile	N/A
	Guided Reading Level	N/A
Qualitative Measures	Text Structure	complex science concepts
	Language Conventionality and Clarity	many unfamiliar or high academic words
	Knowledge Demands	extensive knowledge of physical science required
	Purpose/Levels of Meaning	explicitly stated

Academic Vocabulary

Read each word with students and discuss its meaning.

properties (p. 1) • a quality or characteristic of something

equivalence (p. 2) • having equal value or importance

annihilation (p. 2) • complete destruction

emit (p. 2) • to send out something

convert (p. 4) • to change one thing into another

FIRST READ ## Think Through the Text

Have students cite text evidence and draw inferences to answer questions.

p. 1 • *What are the three most basic elementary particles?* electron, proton, and neutron ▬ RI 2

p. 1 • *What is a molecule?* The smallest unit of a substance, such as water, that retains the chemical properties of that substance. ▬ RI 4

pp. 2–3 • *Summarize how mass and energy can be transformed into one another.* Mass and energy can be transformed into the other one as long as the energy produced or lost and the mass produced or lost are related by $E = mc^2$. ▬ RI 2

SECOND READ ## Analyze the Text

• Reread "Atoms and Molecules" with students. Then ask: *What is the difference between a substance such as water and an element?* The smallest unit that water can be broken down into is a molecule. If you broke apart a water molecule, it would no longer be water. It would be hydrogen and oxygen. The smallest unit of an element is the atom. Elements can't be broken down into other materials. ▬ RI 2

• Review the tables in "The Properties of Elementary Particles" and "Particles and Anti-Particles." *What do these tables show?* They show the charges, the mass in kg, and the mass in amus. *Look at the tables. What is one similarity between protons and anti-protons?* They have the same mass. ▬ RI 1; Grade 6 RI 7

Independent/Self-Selected Reading

If students have already demonstrated comprehension of "Elementary Particles," have them read other texts to practice skills. Suggested titles:

• *Atomic Structures: Great Ideas of Science* by Rebecca L. Johnson

• *The Mystery of the Periodic Table* by Benjamin D. Walker ▬ RI 10

WRITE & PRESENT

1. Have small groups work together to ask and answer questions about particles and anti-particles. Guide them to integrate information from the text and the tables to answer the questions. ▬ RI 1; Grade 6 RI 7

2. Individual students write an explanatory text comparing and contrasting particles and anti-particles. Tell them to integrate information from the text and the tables. ▬ W 2

3. Students work with partners to share and edit their work. As they revise, have them add words, phrases, and clauses to clarify the connections between their ideas. ▬ W 5

4. Have students share their writing in small groups. ▬ SL 4

See Copying Masters, pp. 164–171.

STUDENT CHECKLIST

Writing

☑ Write an explanatory text comparing and contrasting particles and anti-particles.

☑ Include details from the text and the tables.

☑ Use transition words and phrases to clarify the relationship between ideas.

Speaking & Listening

☑ Participate effectively in a collaborative discussion.

☑ Present information in a logical order.

☑ Use appropriate eye contact, volume, and clear pronunciation.

OBJECTIVES

- Use text features to gain information
- Determine a central idea and key details
- Integrate information presented in different formats
- Analyze text using text evidence

Invasive Plant Inventory is broken into three instructional segments.

Options for Reading

Independent Students read the selection independently or with a partner and then answer questions posed by the teacher.

Supported Students read a segment and answer questions with teacher support.

Common Core Connection

Grade 6: RI 2 determine a central idea of a text/provide a summary; **RI 6** determine the author's point of view or purpose and explain how it is conveyed; **RI 7** integrate information presented in different media or formats as well as in words

Grade 7: RI 2 determine two or more central ideas in a text/analyze their development/provide summary

Grade 8: RI 2 determine a central idea of a text/analyze its development/provide summary

Grades 7-8: RI 6 determine author's point of view or purpose/analyze how author distinguishes position

Grades 6-8: RI 1 cite textual evidence to support analysis of what the text says explicitly as well as inferences drawn

Invasive Plant Inventory
by California Invasive Plant Council

SUMMARY The Inventory summarizes the impact, spreading potential, and distribution of over 200 non-native plants that are taking over California's natural areas.

ABOUT THE AUTHOR The **California Invasive Plant Council** was formed in 1992 to address the threat of invasive plants. The Council is committed to protecting California's wildlands through science, education, and policy.

Discuss Genre and Set Purpose

INFORMATIONAL TEXT Display the inventory and read the title together. Have students identify the features of informational texts that they observe, such as sidebars, photographs with captions, maps, and tables.

SET PURPOSE Help students set a purpose for reading, such as to find out the impact that invasive plants are having on California's natural areas.

◢ TEXT COMPLEXITY RUBRIC

Overall Text Complexity		Invasive Plant Inventory INFORMATIONAL TEXT
		MORE COMPLEX
Quantitative Measures	Lexile	1360
	Guided Reading Level	N/A
Qualitative Measures	Text Structure	multiple text structures
	Language Conventionality and Clarity	general academic and domain specific language
	Knowledge Demands	specialized knowledge required
	Purpose/Levels of Meaning	explicitly stated

SEGMENT 1 pp. 1–5

Academic Vocabulary

Read each word with students and discuss its meaning.

invasive (p. 1) • spreading freely into places where it is not wanted

native (p.1) • a plant or animal that naturally belongs in a certain place

dispersal (p. 3) • the scattering or spreading of something

threshold (p. 4) • the point at which something starts to change

restoration (p. 5) • the act of bring back to original condition

cumulative (p. 5) • getting bigger in amount by one addition after another

Domain Specific Vocabulary

ecosystem (p. 1) • all the living things in one place

biodiversity (p. 1) • a wide variety of species living in one area

hybridize (p. 2) • breed one species with another

floristic (p. 4) • referring to the plants of an area

FIRST READ ## Think Through the Text

Have students cite text evidence and draw inferences to answer questions.

p. 1 • *What is the purpose of this Inventory? to summarize the impact, potential for spread, and distribution of more than 200 non-native plants* ◼ RI 6

p. 2 • *What are invasive, non-native plants? plants that are not native and can spread into ecosystems, displacing native plants and altering the native plants and ecosystem* ◼ RI 2

p. 5 • *What can't the Inventory address? The Inventory cannot address the range of geographic variation in California or the regional nature of invasive species impacts.* ◼ RI 1

SECOND READ ## Analyze the Text

- Reread paragraph 1 on page 1. *What is the main idea? Invasive plants damage ecosystems around the world. What details support this main idea? Invasive plants displace native species, change the plant community structure, reduce habitat values, disrupt physical ecosystem processes, and clog lakes, streams, and waterways.* ◼ RI 2

- Show students the photograph and caption on page 1. Ask: *What inference can you make about invasive plants? Support your inference with text evidence. Invasive plants cost the state of California a lot of money. In the past 15 years, the state has spent approximately $15 million to control Arundo donax.* ◼ RI 1

- Reread the bulleted list on page 4. Ask: *If a plant gets a C for Ecological Impact, what does that mean? It means that it has limited ecological impact.* ◼ Grade 6 RI 7

ELL ENGLISH LANGUAGE LEARNERS

Use Gestures

Use gestures and simplified language to restate complex terms. For example, restate *invasive* as "spreading." Use your hands to show something spreading. Have students complete frames such as: *Some plants are ____ where they don't belong. spreading* Reinforce students' response with the domain specific word. Say, "That's right. Some plants are spreading where they don't belong. They are *invasive*."

RESPOND TO SEGMENT 1

 Classroom Collaboration

Have partners summarize what they have read so far. Tell them to ask questions about anything they don't understand.

ENGLISH LANGUAGE LEARNERS

Use Gestures

Use gestures to help students understand the rating words. For example, hold your hand down low and say, *A limited risk is a low risk. It is a small risk. Is a limited risk a big risk?* no *Which is a big risk—a high risk or a moderate risk?* high Encourage students to use these words to describe the different plants.

RESPOND TO SEGMENT 2

 Classroom Collaboration

Have small groups work together to summarize what they have read so far. Have them ask questions about what they don't understand.

 Common Core Connection

Grade 6: RI 5 analyze how a sentence, paragraph, chapter, or section fits in the overall structure; **RI 6** determine the author's point of view or purpose and explain how it is conveyed; **RI 7** integrate information presented in different media or formats as well as in words; **SL 4** present claims and findings, sequence ideas, and use details to accentuate main ideas or themes

Grade 7: RI 5 analyze the structure an author uses to organize text; **RI 6** determine author's point of view or purpose/analyze how author distinguishes position

Grade 8: RI 5 analyze structure of a specific paragraph, including role of particular sentences; **RI 6** determine author's point of view or purpose/analyze how author responds to conflicting evidence or viewpoints

Grades 7–8: SL 4 present claims and findings, emphasizing points in a focused, coherent manner

Grades 6–8: RI 1 cite textual evidence to support analysis of what the text says explicitly as well as inferences drawn; **RI 10** read and comprehend literary nonfiction; **W 2** write informative/explanatory texts; **W 5** develop and strengthen writing by planning, revising, editing, rewriting, or trying a new approach

---

FIRST READ ## Think Through the Text

Have students cite text evidence and draw inferences to answer questions.

p. 6 • *Which type of plant presents a high risk to coastal dunes?* *European beachgrass* **RI 1, Grade 6 RI 7**

p. 20 • *What kinds of plants are listed in Table 2?* *plants that are native to California but invasive in regions outside their natural range* **RI 1, Grade 6 RI 7**

p. 21 • *Do the plants in Table 3 have a high ecological impact?* *No; the plants in this table have a limited ecological impact.* **RI 1**

p. 23 • *Why were the species in Table 4 not listed?* *Either they are not known to escape into wildlands or there was not sufficient information.* **RI 1**

SECOND READ ## Analyze the Text

- Revisit the table on page 6. Say: *Would the Council be more concerned with black acacia or barb goatgrass? Explain.* *They would be more concerned with barb goatgrass because it has a higher ecological impact, which means it causes more harm.* **RI 1, Grade 6 RI 7**

- Revisit the table on page 20. Ask: *Why was the Council unable to score the common reed?* *Genetic issues make it unclear which strains are native to California.* **RI 1**

- *Which plants present a greater risk to the environment, the plants in Table 1 or the plants in Table 3? How do you know?* *The plants in Table 1 present a greater risk because they have a higher ecological impact.* **RI 1, Grade 6 RI 7**

SEGMENT 3 pp. 24–35

FIRST READ ## Think Through the Text

Have students cite text evidence and draw inferences to answer questions.

p. 24 • *What does the diamond symbol stand for?* alert *How are the species organized in Appendix 1?* by category, and alphabetically within each category ▬ RI 5

p. 27 • *What is the purpose of Appendix 2?* It allows those familiar with other common rating systems to compare their lists to the Cal-IPC ratings. ▬ RI 6

pp. 28–35 • *In which Appendix would you find species listed by their common names?* Appendix 4 ▬ RI 5

SECOND READ ## Analyze the Text

- Review Appendices 1 and 2 on pages 25–27. Ask: *How could you use these appendices together?* After looking at Appendix 2, you could look back at Appendix 1 to see how the Cal-IPC categorized the plant. ▬ RI 5

- Look at page 29. Ask: *Do the different groups always agree on how a plant should be categorized? Cite an example from Appendix 2 to support your answer.* No; Crupina vulgaris was considered to be a high threat by the Cal-EPPC and the CDFA but a medium/low risk by NatureServe. *What is the common name for Crupina vulgaris?* common crupina *Where did you find this information?* Appendix 4 ▬ RI 1, RI 5

Independent/Self-Selected Reading

If students have already demonstrated comprehension of *Invasive Plant Inventory*, have them read other informational texts to practice skills. Suggested titles:

- *Science Warriors: The Battle Against Invasive Species* by Sneed B. Collard III

- *Alien Invaders: Species that Threaten Our World* by Jane Drake and Ann Love ▬ RI 10

WRITE & PRESENT

1. Have small groups work together to ask and answer questions about invasive plants. Guide them to integrate information from the text and the tables to answer the questions. ▬ RI 1, Grade 6 RI 7

2. Ask students to write an explanatory text telling why invasive plants are harmful. Tell them to support their explanation with relevant, well-chosen facts and details. ▬ W 2

3. Have students exchange texts and offer suggestions for revising and editing. Have them improve their writing and correct it on the computer. ▬ W 5

4. Have students share their writing in small groups. ▬ SL 4

See Copying Masters, pp. 164–171.

STUDENT CHECKLIST

Writing

☑ Write an explanatory text explaining why invasive species are harmful.

☑ Support main points with relevant facts and details.

☑ Add details based on peer feedback.

Speaking & Listening

☑ Participate effectively in a collaborative discussion.

☑ Use text evidence to explain ideas and understanding.

☑ Respond to specific questions with elaboration and detail.

"O Captain! My Captain!"

by Walt Whitman

O Captain! my Captain! our fearful trip is done;
The ship has weather'd every rack, the prize we sought is won;
The port is near, the bells I hear, the people all exulting,
While follow eyes the steady keel, the vessel grim and daring:
    But O heart! heart! heart!
     O the bleeding drops of red,
      Where on the deck my Captain lies,
       Fallen cold and dead.

O Captain! my Captain! rise up and hear the bells;
Rise up—for you the flag is flung—for you the bugle trills;
For you bouquets and ribbon'd wreaths—for you the shores a-crowding;
For you they call, the swaying mass, their eager faces turning;
    Here Captain! dear father!
     This arm beneath your head;
      It is some dream that on the deck,
       You've fallen cold and dead.

My Captain does not answer, his lips are pale and still;
My father does not feel my arm, he has no pulse nor will;
The ship is anchor'd safe and sound, its voyage closed and done;
From fearful trip, the victor ship, comes in with object won;
    Exult, O shores, and ring, O bells!
     But I, with mournful tread,
      Walk the deck my Captain lies,
       Fallen cold and dead.

"Twelfth Song of the Thunder"

Traditional Navajo

The voice that beautifies the land!
The voice above,
The voice of the thunder
Within the dark cloud
Again and again it sounds,
The voice that beautifies the land.

The voice that beautifies the land!
The voice below,
The voice of the grasshopper
Among the plants
Again and again it sounds,
The voice that beautifies the land.

"The Railway Train"

by Emily Dickinson

I like to see it lap the miles,
And lick the valleys up,
And stop to feed itself at tanks;
And then, prodigious, step

Around a pile of mountains,
And, supercilious, peer
In shanties by the sides of roads;
And then a quarry pare

To fit its sides, and crawl between,
Complaining all the while
In horrid, hooting stanza;
Then chase itself down hill

And neigh like Boanerges;
Then, punctual as a star,
Stop—docile and omnipotent—
At its own stable door.

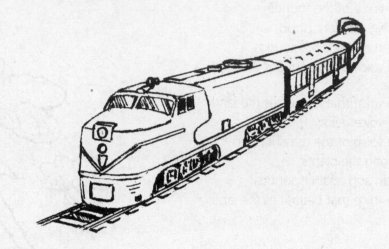

"The Song of Wandering Aengus"

by W. B. Yeats

I went out to the hazel wood,
Because a fire was in my head,
And cut and peeled a hazel wand,
And hooked a berry to a thread;
And when white moths were on the wing,
And moth-like stars were flickering out,
I dropped the berry in a stream
And caught a little silver trout.

When I had laid it on the floor
I went to blow the fire a-flame,
But something rustled on the floor,
And someone called me by my name:
It had become a glimmering girl
With apple blossom in her hair
Who called me by my name and ran
And faded through the brightening air.

Though I am old with wandering
Through hollow lands and hilly lands,
I will find out where she has gone,
And kiss her lips and take her hands;
And walk among long dappled grass,
And pluck till time and times are done,
The silver apples of the moon,
The golden apples of the sun.

"The Road Not Taken"

by Robert Frost

Two roads diverged in a yellow wood,
And sorry I could not travel both
And be one traveler, long I stood
And looked down one as far as I could
To where it bent in the undergrowth;

Then took the other, as just as fair,
And having perhaps the better claim,
Because it was grassy and wanted wear;
Though as for that the passing there
Had worn them really about the same,

And both that morning equally lay
In leaves no step had trodden black.
Oh, I kept the first for another day!
Yet knowing how way leads on to way,
I doubted if I should ever come back.

I shall be telling this with a sigh
Somewhere ages and ages hence:
Two roads diverged in a wood, and I—
I took the one less traveled by,
And that has made all the difference.

Academic Vocabulary

Little Women

apprehensively
ballast
calamity
consoler
constitution
detriment
gravity
impertinent
inconsolable
meddle
mortification
prudence
relish
remorseful
skirmishes
tranquilly
voraciously
vortex

The Adventures of Tom Sawyer

alacrity
circumstantial
cogitating
conjectured
consternation
derision
diligence
inclination
industry
inveterate
pariah
plausibilities
prodigious
quiver
ransacked

A Wrinkle in Time

apprehension
delinquent
dignity
dilapidated
dwindled
furtive
malignant
ominous
omnipotent
permeating
prodigious
serenely
tangible
tractable

The Dark Is Rising

amiably
apprehension
auspicious
begrudgingly
contemplating
derisively
disconcerted
grotesque
hindrances
inexorably
lugubriously
stoical
vanquishing
writhing

Dragonwings

boycott
confrontation
contemptuously
contraption
dictate
ethnic
exasperation
groping
immigrants
pagan
prudent
reluctantly
rubble
sprightlier
tenement
typical
unperturbed

Roll of Thunder, Hear My Cry

admonished
condescending
crescendo
despondently
flaunting
indignation
interest
lethargically
malevolently
maverick
meticulously
persnickety
shunned
tarpaulin
undaunted

"The People Could Fly"
misery
soothe

The Tale of the Mandarin Ducks
abolish
capital punishment
defense
drake
luster
mischief
oppose
plumage

"Eleven"
nonsense
raggedy

Black Ships Before Troy:
The Story of the Illiad
amends
belittle
discord
foreknowledge
mortal
omen
ransom
siege
summons
torrent
tumult
upbraided
vengeance

Sorry, Wrong Number
catechizing
double-takes
high-handed
high-strung
imperious
lethargic
neurotic
querulous
stolidly

The Diary of Ann Frank
annex
authenticity
branded
enhance
exquisite
impenetrable
implore
inconceivable
liberators
plagued

"Paul Revere's Ride"
aghast
impetuous
muster

"O Captain! My Captain!"
exulting
mournful
vessel

"Jabberwocky"
foe
shun
sought

"The Railway Train"
docile
omnipotent
prodigious
supercilious

"The Song of Wandering
Aengus"
dappled
flickering
glimmering
rustled
wandering

"The Road Not Taken"
diverged
hence
trodden
undergrowth

"Chicago"
brawling
brutal
cunning
husky
wanton

"I, Too, Sing America"
ashamed
company

The Book of Questions
abundance
brazen
compassion
congenial
decorum
disintegrated
immense
itinerary
melancholy
persistence
transmogrifies

"Oranges"
rouge
tiered

"A Poem for My Librarian,
Mrs. Long"
humiliating
portable
preference

"Letter on Thomas Jefferson"
felicity
posterity
preceptor
rue
zeal

Narrative of the Life of Frederick Douglass, An American Slave, Written by Himself
benefactor
benevolent
consolation
cunning
desolate
discord
emaciated
emancipation
feeble
impertinent
incoherent
misdemeanor
presumptuous
unanimous
vigilance

"Blood, Toil, Tears, and Sweat: Address to Parliament on May 13, 1940"
buoyancy
ordeal
summoned
tyranny

Harriet Tubman: Conductor on the Underground Railroad
abolitionist
boundary
conjure
desultorily
inertness
insurrection
manumission
passel
plantation
shuck
vigor

Travels with Charley: In Search of America
anarchism
antidote
customs
desolation
laconic
mackinaw
macrocosm
microcosm
nostalgic
pariah
peripatetic
rig
spangle
taciturnity
warped
wayfaring

Preamble and First Amendment to the U. S. Constitution
grievances
posterity
tranquility

A Night to Remember
camaraderie
cascaded
clamor
commotion
culprits
grieve
jar
laconic
listing
maelstrom
myriads
ominous
paraphernalia
prominent

A Short Walk Around the Pyramids and Through the World of Art
brooding
chaotic
concave
contemporary
cordial
hypnotic
influential
mirage
prefabricated
primitive
radiant
sublime
throbbing

The Great Fire

barricaded
boisterousness
cumbersome
diatribe
endeavored
hazards
ominous
rapport
rubble
stagnant
stifling
torrent

Vincent van Gogh: Portrait of an Artist

ambivalent
demoralize
eccentric
elation
enervated
imminent
inferior
nonchalant
obstinate
reticent
shirk
taboos
tumultuous
unpretentious

This Land Was Made for You and Me: The Life and Songs of Woody Guthrie

camaraderie
erratic
excruciating
fervor
ironic
melancholy
migrants
sporadically
subversive
tradition
vagrancy
voraciously

Words We Live By: Your Annotated Guide to the Constitution

abridging
amending
bribe
commerce
culmination
impartial
infamous
inferior
infringed
innovation
instrumental
obsolete
reparations
resignation

Freedom Walkers: The Story of the Montgomery Bus Boycott

advocating
boycott
compromise
eminent
galvanized
grievances
indicted
momentous
oppression
perpetuate
segregation
submission
violating

Cathedral: The Story of Its Construction

dismantle
elevation
extracted
hoisted
molten
niches
prospered
resumed
seeping
simultaneous
summoned

The Building of Manhattan

claustrophobic
compressed
contentious
cumbersome
detonation
formidable
grid
homogenous
imperceptible
ingenuity
preeminent
rational
renovates
squalid

The Number Devil: A Mathematical Adventure

bluffing
conjecture
contrary
crotchety
eccentric
exhausted
hefty
hoax
interminable
lolling
marshaling
oasis
unheeded

Math Trek: Adventures in the Math Zone

accumulated
baffled
clamoring
conjecture
decipher
emerge
infinite
meandering
paradox
phony
prominent
ricochets
savoring
tedious

Geeks: How Two Lost Boys Rode the Internet Out of Idaho

abeyance
articulate
camaraderie
commodity
discernible
dubious
ephemeral
fervent
impetus
mediocre
pundits
stymied
trivial
veneer

"The Evolution of the Grocery Bag"

paradigm
preclude
reviled
versatile

"Geology"

chronology
configuration
domain
dormant

"Space Probe"

extraterrestrial
sophisticated
vast
incinerated

"Elementary Particles"

annihilation
convert
emit
equivalence
properties

Invasive Plant Inventory

cumulative
dispersal
invasive
native
restoration
threshold

Name _____

Grade 6 Writing Checklist

In my writing, did I . . .

Argument	Informative/Explanatory	Narrative
☐ introduce claim(s)?	☐ introduce a topic and organize ideas, concepts, and information?	☐ establish a setting and introduce a narrator and/or characters?
☐ organize the reasons and evidence clearly?	☐ develop the topic with facts and examples?	☐ organize an event sequence that unfolds naturally and logically?
☐ support claim(s) with clear reasons and relevant evidence?	☐ use formatting, graphics, and multimedia when useful?	☐ use narrative techniques, such as dialogue and description, to develop experiences, events, and/or characters?
☐ make sure the relationships among claim(s) and reasons are clear?	☐ use transitions to clarify relationships among ideas and concepts?	☐ use transition words, phrases, and clauses?
☐ use a formal style?	☐ use precise language and specific vocabulary?	☐ use precise words, descriptive details, and sensory language?
☐ provide a concluding statement or section?	☐ provide a concluding statement or section?	☐ provide a conclusion?
☐ use correct language conventions?	☐ use correct language conventions?	☐ use correct language conventions?
☐ other: _____ _____ _____	☐ other: _____ _____ _____	☐ other: _____ _____ _____

Name _____

Grade 6 Speaking and Listening Checklist

In my speaking, did I . . .

☐	come to discussions prepared?
☐	contribute to the discussion?
☐	present claims and findings, emphasizing main ideas or themes?
☐	use appropriate eye contact, good volume, and clear pronunciation?
☐	include multimedia and other visuals when appropriate?
☐	adapt my speech to the task and situation, using formal English as appropriate?

In my listening, did I . . .

☐	follow rules for discussions?
☐	ask and respond to questions by making comments?
☐	interpret information presented in diverse media and formats?
☐	explain how information contributes to a topic?
☐	review key ideas expressed and show an understanding of different perspectives?
☐	outline a speaker's argument and distinguish claims that are/are not supported by reasons and evidence?

Other

☐	
☐	
☐	
☐	
☐	

Grade 7 Writing Checklist

In my writing, did I . . .

Argument	Informative/Explanatory	Narrative
☐ introduce claim(s) and acknowledge opposing claims?	☐ introduce a topic and organize ideas, concepts, and information?	☐ establish a setting and introduce a narrator and/or characters?
☐ organize the reasons and evidence logically?	☐ develop the topic with relevant facts and examples?	☐ organize an event sequence that unfolds naturally and logically?
☐ support claim(s) with logical reasons and relevant evidence from accurate sources?	☐ use formatting, graphics, and multimedia when useful?	☐ use narrative techniques, such as dialogue and description, to develop experiences, events, and/or characters?
☐ make sure the relationships among claim(s), reasons, and evidence are clear?	☐ use transitions to clarify relationships?	☐ use transition words, phrases, and clauses?
☐ use a formal style?	☐ use precise language and specific vocabulary?	☐ use precise words, descriptive details, and sensory language?
☐ provide a concluding statement or section?	☐ provide a concluding statement or section?	☐ provide a conclusion?
☐ use correct language conventions?	☐ use correct language conventions?	☐ use correct language conventions?
☐ other: _____ _____ _____	☐ other: _____ _____ _____	☐ other: _____ _____ _____

Name _____

Grade 7 Speaking and Listening Checklist

In my speaking, did I . . .

☐	come to discussions prepared?
☐	contribute to the discussion?
☐	present claims and findings, emphasizing main points with details, facts, and examples?
☐	use appropriate eye contact, good volume, and clear pronunciation?
☐	include multimedia and other visuals when appropriate?
☐	adapt my speech to the task and situation, using formal English as appropriate?

In my listening, did I . . .

☐	follow rules for discussions?
☐	ask and respond to questions by making comments?
☐	analyze the main ideas and details presented in diverse media and formats?
☐	explain how ideas clarify a topic, text, or issue?
☐	acknowledge new information expressed by others and, when warranted, change my own views?
☐	evaluate a speaker's argument and the reasons and evidence that support the claims?

Other

☐
☐
☐
☐
☐

Name _____

Grade 8 Writing Checklist

In my writing, did I . . .

Argument	Informative/Explanatory	Narrative
☐ introduce claim(s) and distinguish from opposing claims?	☐ introduce a topic and organize ideas, concepts, and information?	☐ establish a context and introduce a narrator and/or characters?
☐ organize the reasons and evidence logically?	☐ develop the topic with relevant, well-chosen facts and examples?	☐ organize an event sequence that unfolds naturally and logically?
☐ support claim(s) with logical reasons and relevant evidence from accurate sources?	☐ use formatting, graphics, and multimedia when useful?	☐ use narrative techniques, such as dialogue and description, to develop experiences, events, and/or characters?
☐ make sure the relationships between claim(s) and reasons/ evidence are clear?	☐ use varied transitions to clarify relationships among ideas and concepts?	☐ use a variety of transition words, phrases, and clauses?
☐ use a formal style?	☐ use precise language and specific vocabulary?	☐ use precise words, descriptive details, and sensory language?
☐ provide a concluding statement or section?	☐ provide a concluding statement or section?	☐ provide a conclusion?
☐ use correct language conventions?	☐ use correct language conventions?	☐ use correct language conventions?
☐ other: _____ _____ _____	☐ other: _____ _____ _____	☐ other: _____ _____ _____

Name _____

Grade 8 Speaking and Listening Checklist

In my speaking, did I . . .

☐	come to discussions prepared?
☐	contribute to the discussion?
☐	present claims and findings, emphasizing main points with evidence, sound reasons, and well-chosen details?
☐	use appropriate eye contact, good volume, and clear pronunciation?
☐	include multimedia and other visuals to clarify information, strengthen claims, and add interest?
☐	adapt my speech to the task and situation, using formal English as appropriate?

In my listening, did I . . .

☐	follow rules for discussions?
☐	ask questions that connect others' ideas and respond to questions by making comments?
☐	analyze the purpose of information presented in diverse media and formats?
☐	evaluate the motives behind the presentation of information?
☐	acknowledge new information expressed by others and, when warranted, defend my own views?
☐	evaluate a speaker's argument and the reasons and evidence that support the claims?

Other

☐	
☐	
☐	
☐	

Performance Rubric

Use this rubric to evaluate writing, listening, and speaking tasks.

	Advanced	Competent
DEVELOPMENT	• The introduction creates a strong impression and clearly presents a well-focused controlling idea. • Relevant details and evidence support the writer's points. • The concluding section summarizes the key points and leaves readers with something to think about.	• The introduction identifies a controlling idea but could do more to grab the reader's interest. • One or two key points could use more support. • The concluding section summarizes most of the key points but could be developed more.
ORGANIZATION	• The organization is effective for the purpose and audience; ideas progress logically. • Transitions successfully show the relationships between ideas.	• The organization is confusing in a few places. • A few more transitions are needed to clarify the relationships between ideas.
LANGUAGE	• The writing reflects a formal style. • Use of language is lively and precise. • Sentence beginnings, lengths, and structures vary and have a rhythmic flow. • Spelling, capitalization, and punctuation are correct. • Grammar and usage are correct.	• The style is informal in a few places. • Most language is precise. • Sentence beginnings, lengths, and structures vary somewhat. • Several spelling, capitalization, and punctuation mistakes occur. • Some grammatical and usage errors are repeated in a few places.

	Limited	Emerging
DEVELOPMENT	• The introduction is commonplace; it only hints at a controlling idea. • Details and evidence support some key points but are often too general. • The concluding section does not completely summarize or wrap up the main ideas.	• The introduction is missing. • The writer's points lack specific support. • The concluding section is missing.
ORGANIZATION	• The organization is logical in some places but often doesn't follow a pattern. • More transitions are needed throughout to explain the relationships between ideas.	• An organizational pattern is not apparent; ideas are presented randomly. • The transitions are ineffective or are missing.
LANGUAGE	• The style is overly casual. • Language is repetitive or too general at times. • Sentence structures barely vary, and some fragments or run-on sentences are present. • Spelling, capitalization, and punctuation are often incorrect but do not interfere with the reader's understanding of the work. • Grammar and usage are incorrect in many places, but the writer's ideas are still clear.	• The style is inappropriate for the purpose and audience. • Language is inaccurate, repetitive, and too general. • Repetitive sentence structure, fragments, and run-on sentences make the writing hard to follow. • Spelling, capitalization, and punctuation are incorrect throughout. • Many grammatical and usage errors change the meaning of the writer's ideas.

Bibliography

Adams, John. "Letter on Thomas Jefferson." *Adams on Adams*. Edited by Paul M. Zall. Lexington: University Press of Kentucky, 2004. (1776)

Alcott, Louisa May. *Little Women*. New York: Penguin, 1989. (1868)

California Invasive Plant Council. *Invasive Plant Inventory*. http://www.cal-ipc.org/ip/inventory/index.php. 2006–2010.

Carroll, Lewis. "Jabberwocky." *Through the Looking-Glass*. Cambridge, MA: Candlewick, 2005. (1872)

Churchill, Winston. "Blood, Toil, Tears and Sweat: Address to Parliament on May 13th, 1940. *Lend Me Your Ears: Great Speeches in History, 3rd Edition*. Edited by William Safire. New York: W. W. Norton, 2004. (1940)

Cisneros, Sandra. "Eleven." *Woman Hollering Creek and Other Stories*. New York: Random House, 1991.

Cooper, Susan. *The Dark Is Rising*. New York: Margaret K. McElderry Books, 1973.

Dickinson, Emily. "The Railway Train." *The Compete Poems of Emily Dickinson*. Boston: Little, Brown, 1960. (1893)

Douglass, Frederick. *Narrative of the Life of Frederick Douglass an American Slave, Written by Himself*. Boston: Anti-Slavery Office, 1845.

"Elementary Particles." *New Book of Popular Science*. New York: Scholastic, 2010.

Enzensberger, Hans Magnus. *The Number Devil: A Mathematical Adventure*. Illustrated by Rotraut Susanne Berner. Translated by Michael Henry Heim. New York: Henry Holt, 1998.

Fletcher, Lucille. *Sorry, Wrong Number*. New York: Dramatists Play Service, 1948.

Freedman, Russell. *Freedom Walkers: The Story of the Montgomery Bus Boycott*. New York: Holiday House, 2006.

Frost, Robert. "The Road Not Taken." *The Poetry of Robert Frost: The Collected Poems*. Edited by Edward Connery Lathem. New York: Henry Holt, 1979. (1915)

"Geology." *U*X*L Encyclopedia of Science*. Edited by Rob Nagel. Farmington Hills, MI: Gale Cengage Learning, 2007.

Giovanni, Nikki. "A Poem for My Librarian, Mrs. Long." *Acolytes*. New York: William Morrow, 2007.

Goodrich, Frances and Albert Hackett. *The Diary of Anne Frank*. New York: Random House, 1956.

Greenberg, Jan, and Sandra Jordan. *Vincent Van Gogh: Portrait of an Artist*. New York: Random House, 2001.

Hamilton, Virginia. "The People Could Fly." *The People Could Fly: American Black Folktales*. New York: Knopf Books for Young Readers, 1985.

Hughes, Langston. "I, Too, Sing America." *The Collected Poems of Langston Hughes*. New York: Knopf, 1994. (1925)

Isaacson, Phillip. *A Short Walk Around the Pyramids and Through the World of Art*. New York: Knopf, 1993.

Katz, John. *Geeks: How Two Lost Boys Rode the Internet Out of Idaho*. New York: Broadway Books, 2001.

L'Engle, Madeleine. *A Wrinkle in Time*. New York: Farrar, Straus and Giroux, 1962.

Longfellow, Henry Wadsworth. *Paul Revere's Ride*. New York: Puffin, 1996. (1861)

Lord, Walter. *A Night to Remember*. New York: Henry Holt, 1955.

Macaulay, David. *Cathedral: The Story of Its Construction*. Boston: Houghton Mifflin, 1973.

Mackay, Donald. *The Building of Manhattan*. New York: Harper & Row, 1987.

Monk, Linda R. *Words We Live By: Your Annotated Guide to the Constitution*. New York: Hyperion, 2003.

Murphy, Jim. *The Great Fire*. New York: Scholastic, 1995.

Neruda, Pablo. *The Book of Questions*. Translated by William O'Daly. Port Townsend, WA: Copper Canyon Press, 1991.

Partridge, Elizabeth. *This Land Was Made for You and Me: The Life and Songs of Woody Guthrie*. New York: Viking, 2002.

Paterson, Katherine. *The Tale of the Mandarin Ducks*. Illustrated by Leo and Diane Dillon. New York: Lodestar Books, 1990.

Peterson, Ivars and Nancy Henderson. *Math Trek: Adventures in the Math Zone*. San Francisco: Jossey-Bass, 2000.

Petroski, Henry. "The Evolution of the Grocery Bag." *American Scholar 72.4* (Autumn 2003).

Petry, Ann. *Harriet Tubman: Conductor on the Underground Railroad*. New York: HarperCollins, 1983.

Preamble and First Amendment to the U. S. Constitution. (1787, 1791)

Sandburg, Carl. "Chicago." *Chicago Poems*. New York: Henry Holt, 1916.

Soto, Gary. "Oranges." *Black Hair*. Pittsburgh, PA: University of Pittsburgh Press, 1985.

"Space Probe." *Astronomy & Space: From the Big Bang to the Big Crunch*. Edited by Phillis Engelbert. Farmington Hills, MI: Gale Cengage Learning, 2009.

Steinbeck, John. *Travels with Charley: In Search of America*. New York: Penguin, 1997. (1962)

Sutcliff, Rosemary. *Black Ships Before Troy: The Story of the Iliad*. New York: Delacorte Press, 1993.

Taylor, Mildred D. *Roll of Thunder, Hear My Cry*. New York: Phyllis Fogelman Books, 1976.

Twain, Mark. *The Adventures of Tom Sawyer*. New York: Modern Library, 2001. (1876)

"Twelfth Song of the Thunder." *The Mountain Chant: A Navajo Ceremony*. Hong Kong: Forgotten Books, 2008. (1887)

Whitman, Walt. "O Captain! My Captain!" *Leaves of Grass*. Oxford: Oxford University Press, 1990. (1865)

Yeats, W. B. "The Song of Wandering Aengus." *W. B. Yeats Selected Poetry*. London: Macmillan, 1962. (1899)

Yep, Laurence. *Dragonwings*. New York: HarperCollins, 1975.

Internet Resources

Use the following websites to locate additional resources for teaching the exemplar texts. Check the website for your state's department of education for specific information on the implementation of the Common Core State Standards.

http://aasl.jesandco.org/

http://www.achieve.org/achieving-common-core.

http://www.achievethecore.org/

http://www.ascd.org/common-core-state-standards/commoncore.aspx

http://www.ccsso.org/documents/2012/common_core_resources.pdf

http://www.corestandards.org/

http://www.engagingeducators.com/

http://www.ncte.org/standards/commoncore

http://www.ode.state.or.us/wma/teachlearn/commoncore/
ela-publishers-criteria.pdf

http://www.parcconline.org/

http://www.reading.org/Resources/ResourcesByTopic/
CommonCore-resourcetype/CommonCore-rt-resources.aspx

http://www.smarterbalanced.org/

https://www.teachingchannel.org/videos?categories=topics_common-core